Charles Heber Clark, America Project Making of, Arthur Burdett Frost

Elbow-Room

A Novel Without a Plot

Charles Heber Clark, America Project Making of, Arthur Burdett Frost

Elbow-Room
A Novel Without a Plot

ISBN/EAN: 9783744673617

Printed in Europe, USA, Canada, Australia, Japan

Cover: Foto ©Thomas Meinert / pixelio.de

More available books at **www.hansebooks.com**

ELBOW-ROOM

A Novel without a Plot.

BY

MAX ADELER

ELBOW-ROOM

A NOVEL WITHOUT A PLOT

BY

M A X   A D E L E R

AUTHOR OF "OUT OF THE HURLY-BURLY," ETC., ETC.

ILLUSTRATED BY ARTHUR B. FROST

PHILADELPHIA
J. M. STODDART & CO.
CHICAGO AND CINCINNATI:
A. G. NETTLETON & CO.
SAN FRANCISCO, CAL.: A. ROMAN & CO.

WESTCOTT & THOMSON,
Stereotypers and Electrotypers, Philada.

HENRY B. ASHMEAD,
Printer, Philada.

PREFACE.

IF every book that contains nothing but nonsense confessed that fact in its preface, the world would have been saved a vast amount of dreary reading. Most of such volumes, however, are believed by their authors to be full of wisdom of the solidest kind; and confession, therefore, being impossible, the reader may learn the truth only through much tribulation. The writer of this book freely admits, at the outset, that it contains only the lightest humor, and that its single purpose is to afford amusement. At the same time, he claims for it that it is wiser and far more useful than many more solemn books that have been published, with the intent to regenerate mankind, by authors who would regard such a volume as this with feelings of scorn.

This is simply an effort to tell stories of a humorous character; and although the attempt may not be so successful as it has been in the hands of others, from Boccaccio downward, it has at least one quality that some greater achievements do not possess: it is absolutely pure in thought, word and suggestion. If it is filled with nonsense, that nonsense at any rate is innocent. It is modest, cleanly and without malice or irreverence. A worthier and nobler work might have been written; a purer work could not have been.

What its other merits are he who reads it will discern. To apologize for it in any manner would be to admit that it has grave deficiencies, and such an admission the author would not make even if his conscience impelled him to do so. The book is offered to the reader with the conviction that if the man who laughs is the happiest man, it may contribute something to the sum of human felicity.

The story of the French horn, related in the twentieth chapter, will recall to the reader of the "Sparrowgrass Papers" an incident related in that most charming book of humor. Perhaps it ought to be said that the former narrative was at least suggested by the latter.

The artist who has illustrated the book, Mr. Arthur B. Frost, deserves to have it said of him that he has done his work skilfully, tastefully and with nice appreciation of the humor of the various situations.

CONTENTS.

CHAPTER I.

CHAPTER II.

CHAPTER III.

CHAPTER IV.

CHAPTER V.

CHAPTER VI.

CHAPTER VII.

CHAPTER VIII.

CHAPTER IX.

CHAPTER X.

CHAPTER XI.

CHAPTER XII.

CHAPTER XIII.

CHAPTER XIV.

CHAPTER XV.

CHAPTER XVI.

CHAPTER XVII.

CHAPTER XXVIII.

CHAPTER XXIX.

CHAPTER XXX.

CHAPTER XXXI.

ILLUSTRATIONS.

ELBOW-ROOM.

CHAPTER I.

PROLOGUE.

THE ADVANTAGES OF ELBOW-ROOM.

THE professors of sociology, in exploring the mysteries of the science of human living, have not agreed that elbow-room is one of the great needs of modern civilized society, but this may be because they have not yet reached the bottom of things and discovered the truth. In crowded communities men have chances of development in certain directions, but in others their growth is surely checked. A man who lives in a large city is apt to experience a sharpening of his wits, for attrition of minds as well as of pebbles produces polish and brilliancy; but perhaps this very process prevents the free unfolding of parts of his character. If his individuality is not partially lost amid the crowd, it is likely that, first, his imitative faculty will induce him to shape himself in accordance with another than his own pattern, and that, second, the dread of the conspicuousness which is the certain result of eccentricity will persuade him to avoid any tendency he may have to become strongly unlike his neighbors.

The house that he lives in is tightly squeezed in a row of dwellings builded upon a precisely similar plan, so that the influence brought to bear upon him by the home resembles to some extent that which operates upon his fellows. There is a pressure upon both sides of him in the house; and when he plunges into business, there is a far greater pressure there, in the shape of sharp competition, which brings him into constant collision with other men, and mayhap drives him or compels him to drive his weaker rival to the wall.

The city-man is likely to cover himself with a mantle of reserve and dissimulation. If he has a longing to wander in untrodden and devious paths, he is disposed resolutely to suppress his desire and to go in the beaten track. If Smith, in a savage state, would certainly conduct himself in a wholly original manner, in a social condition he yields to an inevitable apprehension that Jones will think queer of his behavior, and he shapes his actions in accordance with the plan that Jones, with strong impulses to unusual and individual conduct, has adopted because he is afraid he will be thought singular by Smith. And in the mean time, Robinson, burning with a desire to go wantonly in a direction wholly diverse from that of his associates, realizes that to set at defiance the theories of which Smith and Jones are apparently the earnest advocates would be to expose himself to harsh criticism, sacrifices himself to his terror of their opinion and yields to the force of their example.

In smaller and less densely-populated communities the weight of public opinion is not largely decreased, but the pressure is not so great. There is more elbow-room. A man who knows everybody about him gauges with a reasonable degree of accuracy the characters of those who are to judge him, and is able to form a pretty fair estimate of the value of their opinions. When men can do this, they are apt to feel a greater degree of freedom in following their natural impulses. If men could sound the depths of all knowledge and read with ease the secrets of the universe, they might lose much of their reverence. When they know the exact worth of the judgment of their fellow-men, they begin to regard it with comparative indifference. And so, if a dweller in a small village desires to leave the beaten track, he can summon courage to do so with greater readiness than the man of the town. If he has occasionally that proneness to make a fool of himself which seizes every man now and then, he may indulge in the perilous luxury without great carefulness of the consequences. Smith's ordinary conduct is the admiration of Jones as a regular thing; but when Smith switches off into some eccentricity for which Jones has no inclination, it is only a matter of course that Jones should indulge in his own little oddities without caring whether Smith smiles upon him or not.

It is, therefore, in such communities that search can most profitably be made for raw human nature that has had room to grow upon every side with little check or hindrance. The man who chooses to seek may find original characters, queer combinations of events, surprising revelations of individual and family experiences and an unlimited fund of amusement, especially if he is disposed, perhaps even while he submits to an overpowering conviction that all life is tragic, to summon into prominence those humorous phases of social existence which, as in the best of artificial tragedies, are permitted to appear in real life as the foil of that which is truly sorrowful. To depict events that are simply amusing may not be the highest and best function of a writer; but if he has a strong impulse to undertake such a task in the intervals of more serious work, it may be that he performs a duty which is more obvious because the common inclination of those who tell the story of human life is to present that which is sad and terrible, and to lead the reader, whose soul has bitterness enough of its own, into contemplation of the true or fictitious anguish of others.

At any rate, an attempt to show men and their actions in a purely humorous aspect is justified by the facts of human life; and if fiction is, for the most part, tragedy, there is reason why much of the remainder should be devoted to fun. To laugh is to perform as divine a function as to weep. Man, who was made only a little lower than the angels, is the only animal to whom laughter is permitted. He is the sole earthly heir of immortality, and he laughs. More than this, the process is healthful to both mind and body, for it is the man who laughs with reason and judgment who is the kindly, pure, cheerful and happy man.

It is in a village wherein there is elbow-room for the physical and intellectual man that the characters in this book may be supposed to be, to do and to suffer. It would be unfair to say that the reader can visit the spot and meet face to face all these people who appear in the incidents herein recorded, and it would be equally improper to assert that there is naught written of them but veritable history. But it might perhaps be urged that the individuals exist in less decided and grotesque forms, and that the words and deeds attributed to them are less than wholly improbable. And if any one shall consider it worth while to inquire further concerning the matter, let him discover where may be found a community which exists in such a locality as this that I will now describe.

A hamlet set upon a hillside. The top a breezy elevation crowned with foliage and commanding a view of matchless beauty. To the west, beneath, a sea of verdure rolling away in mighty billows, which here bear upon their crests a tiny wood, a diminutive dwelling, a flock of sheep or a drove of cattle, and

2

there sweep apparently almost over a shadowy town
which nestles between two of the emerald waves.
Far, far beyond the steeples which rise dimly from
the distant town a range of hills; beyond it still, a
faint film of blue, the indistinct and misty semblance
of towering mountains.

To the north a lovely plain that rises a few miles
away into a long low ridge which forms the sharp
and clear horizon. To the south and east a narrow
valley that is little more than a deep ravine, the sides
of the precipitous hills covered with forest to the
brink of the stream, which twists and turns at sharp
angles like a wounded snake, shining as burnished
silver when one catches glimpses of it through the
trees, and playing an important part in a landscape
which at brief distance seems as wild and as unconscious of the presence of man as if it were a part of
the wilderness of Oregon rather than the adjunct of
a busy town which feels continually the stir and impulse of the huge city only a dozen miles away.

He who descends from the top of the village hill
will pass pretty mansions set apart from their neighbors in leafy and flowery solitudes wherein the most
unsocial hermit might find elbow-room enough; he
will see little cottages which stand nearer to the
roadside, as if they shunned isolation and wished
to share in the life that often fills the highway in
front of them. Farther down the houses become
more companionable; they cling together in groups
with the barest possibility of retaining their indi-

viduality, until at last the thoroughfare becomes a street wherein small shops do their traffic in quite a spirited sort of a way.

Clear down at the foot of the hill, by the brink of the sweet and placid river, there are iron mills and factories and furnaces, whose chimneys in the day-time pour out huge columns of black smoke, and from which long tongues of crimson and bluish flame leap forth at night against the pitchy darkness of the sky. Here, as one whirls by in the train after night-fall, he may catch hurried glimpses of swarthy men, stripped to the waist, stirring the molten iron with their long levers or standing amid showers of sparks as the brilliant metal slips to and fro among the rollers that mould it into the forms of commerce. If upon a summer evening one shall rest amid the sweet air and the rustling trees upon the hill-top, he may hear coming up from this dusky, grimy black-ness of the mills and the railway the soughing of the blowers of the blast-furnaces, the sharp crack of the exploding gases in the white-hot iron, the shriek of the locomotive whistle and all night long the roar and rattle of the passing trains, but so mellowed by the distance that the harsh sounds seem almost mu-sical—almost as pleasant and as easily endured as the voices of nature. And in the early morning a look from the chamber window perhaps may show a locomotive whirling down the valley around the sharp curves with its white streamer flung out upon the green hillside, and seeming like a snowy ribbon cut from the huge mass of vapor which lies low upon the surface of the stream.

The name of this town among the hills is—well, it has a very charming Indian name, to reveal which might be to point with too much distinctness to the worthy people who in some sort figure in the following pages. It shall be called Millburg in those pages, and its inhabitants shall tell their stories and play their parts under the cover of that unsuggestive title; so that the curious reader of little faith shall have difficulty if he resolves to discover the whereabouts of the village and to inquire respecting the author's claim to credibility as a historian.

CHAPTER II.

R. and Mrs. Fogg have a young baby which was exceedingly restless and troublesome at night while it was cutting its teeth. Mr. Fogg, devoted and faithful father that he is, used to take a good deal more than his share of the nursing of the infant, and often, when he would turn out of bed for the fifteenth or sixteenth time and with fluttering garments and unshod feet carry the baby to and fro, soothing it with a little song, he would think how true it is, as Napoleon once said, that "the only real courage is two-o'clock-in-the-morning courage." Mr. Fogg thought he had a reasonable amount of genuine bravery, and justly, for he performed the functions of a nurse with unsurpassed patience and good humor.

One night, however, the baby was unusually wakeful and tempestuous, and after struggling with it for several hours he called Mrs. Fogg and suggested that it would be well to give the child some paregoric to relieve it from the intense pain from which it was evidently suffering. The medicine stood upon the bureau, but Mrs. Fogg had to go down stairs to the dining-room to get some sugar; and while she was fumbling about in the entry in the dark it occurred to Mr. Fogg that he had heard of persons

being relieved from pain by applications of mesmerism. He had no notion that he could exercise such power; but while musing upon the subject he rubbed the baby's eyebrows carelessly with his fingers and made several passes with his hands upon its forehead. As Mrs. Fogg began to feel her way up stairs, he was surprised and pleased to find that the baby had become quiet and had dropped off into sweet and peaceful slumber. Mrs. Fogg put the sugar away as her husband placed the child in its crib and covered it up carefully, and then they went to bed.

They were not disturbed again that night, and in the morning the baby was still fast asleep. Mrs. Fogg said she guessed the poor little darling must have gotten a tooth through, which made it feel easier. Mr. Fogg said, " Maybe it has."

But he had a faint though very dark suspicion that something was wrong.

After breakfast he went up to the bed-room to see if the baby was awake. It still remained asleep; and Mr. Fogg, when he had leaned over and listened to its breathing, shook it roughly three or four times and cleared his throat in a somewhat boisterous manner. But it did not wake, and Mr. Fogg went down stairs with a horrible dread upon him, and assuming his hat prepared to go to the office. Mrs. Fogg called to him,

" Don't slam the front door and wake the baby !"

And then Mr. Fogg did slam it with extraordinary violence; after which he walked up the street with gloom in his soul and a wretched feeling of apprehension that the baby would never waken.

" What on earth would we do if it should stay asleep for years? S'pose'n it should sleep right straight ahead for half a century, and grow to be an old man without knowing its pa and ma, and without ever learning anything or seeing anything!"

The thought maddened him. He remembered Rip Van Winkle; he recalled the Seven Sleepers of Ephesus; he thought of the afflicted woman whom he saw once at a menagerie in a trance, in which she had been for twenty years continuously, excepting when she awoke for a few moments at long intervals to ask for something to eat. Perhaps when he and Mrs. Fogg were dead the baby might be rented to a menagerie, and be carried around the country as a spectacle. The idea haunted him. It made him miserable. He tried for two or three hours to fix his mind upon his office-duties, but it was impossible. He determined to go back to the house to ascertain if the baby had returned to consciousness. When he got there, Mrs. Fogg was beginning to feel very uneasy. She said,

" Isn't it strange, Wilberforce, that the baby stays asleep? He is not awake yet. I suppose it is nervous exhaustion, poor darling! but I am a little worried about it."

Mr. Fogg felt awfully. He went up and jagged a pin into the baby's leg quietly, so that his wife could not see him. Still it lay there wrapped in slumber; and after repeating the experiment he abandoned himself to despair and went back to his office, uncertain whether to fly or to go home and confess the terrible truth to Mrs. Fogg.

In a couple of hours that lovely woman came in to see him. She was scared and breathless:

"Mr. Fogg, the baby is actually asleep yet, and I can't rouse him. I've shaken him, called to him and done *everything*, and he don't stir. What *can* be the matter with him? I'm afraid something dreadful has happened to him."

"Maybe he is sleeping up a lot ahead, so's to stay awake at night some more," said Mr. Fogg, with a feeble smile at his attempt at a joke.

"Wilberforce, you ought to be ashamed of yourself to trifle with such a matter! S'pose the baby should die while it is in that condition? I believe it *is* going to die, and I want you to go straight for the doctor."

Mr. Fogg started at once, and in half an hour he reached the house in company with Dr. Gill. The doctor examined the child carefully and said that it was a very queer case, but that, in his opinion, he must be under the influence of opium.

"Did you give him any while I was asleep last night, Mr. Fogg?" asked Mrs. Fogg, suspiciously and tearfully.

"Upon my word and honor I didn't," said Mr. Fogg, with the cold perspiration standing upon his forehead.

"Are you *sure* you didn't give him *anything?*" demanded the mother, suddenly remembering that the baby became quiet while she was down stairs upon the preceding night.

"Maria, do you think I would deceive you?" asked Mr. Fogg, in agony. "I'll take my solemn oath that I did not give it a drop of medicine of any kind."

"It is very remarkable—very," said the doctor. "I don't know that I ever encountered precisely such a case before. I think I will call in Dr. Brown and consult with him about it."

Then Mrs. Fogg began to sob; and while she fondled the baby, Mr. Fogg, feeling like a murderer, followed the doctor down stairs. When they reached the hall, Mr. Fogg drew the doctor aside and said, in a confidential whisper:

"Doctor, I am going to tell you something, but I want you to promise solemnly that you will keep it a secret."

"Very well; what is it?"

"You won't tell Mrs. Fogg?"

"No."

"Well, doctor, I—I—I—know what is the matter with that baby."

"You do! you know! Well, why didn't you— What *is* the matter with it?"

"The fact is, I mesmerized it last night."

"You did! Mesmerized it! And why don't you rouse it up again?"

"I don't know how; that's the mischief of it. I did it accidentally, you know. I was sort of fingering around the child's forehead, and all of a sudden it stopped crying and dropped off. Can't you find

me a professional mesmerizer to come and undo the
baby?"

"I don't believe I can. The only one I know of
lives in San Francisco, and he couldn't get here in
less than a week even if we should telegraph for
him."

"By that time," shrieked Mr. Fogg, "the baby'll
be dead and Maria will be insane! What, under
Heaven, are we going to do about it?"

"Let's hunt up Brown; maybe he knows."

So they went around to Dr. Brown's office and
revealed the secret to him. Brown seemed to think
that he might perhaps do something to rob the situation of its horrors, and he accompanied Mr. Fogg
and Dr. Gill to the house. When they entered, Mrs.
Fogg was rapidly becoming hysterical. Dr. Brown
placed the baby on the bed; he slapped its little
hands and rubbed its forehead and dashed cold
water in its face. In a few moments the baby opened its eyes, then it suddenly sat up and began to
cry. Mr. Fogg used to hate that noise, but now it
seemed to him sweeter than music. Mrs. Fogg was
wild with joy. She took the baby in her arms and
kissed and hugged it, and then she said,

"What do you think was the matter with him,
doctor?"

"Why, your husband says he mesmerized the
child," replied the doctor, incautiously letting the
secret drop.

Then Mrs. Fogg looked at the culprit as if she

wished to assassinate him; but she merely ejaculated,
" Monster !" and flew from the room ; and Mr. Fogg,
as he went down with the physicians, put on an
injured look and said,

" If that baby wants to holloa now, I'm going to
let him holloa, if he holloas the top of his head off."

It was this offence, according to popular rumor,
that brought things to a crisis in Mr. Fogg's family
and induced Mrs. Fogg to seek to remove the heavy
burden of woe imposed upon her by her husband.
Only a few days later Mr. and Mrs. Fogg knocked
at the door of Colonel Coffin's law office, and then
filed in, Mrs. Fogg in advance. Mr. Fogg, the reader
may care to know, was a subdued, weak-eyed and
timid person. He had the air of a victim of perpetual tyranny—of a man who had been ruthlessly and
remorselessly sat upon until his spirit was wholly
gone. And Mrs. Fogg looked as if she might have
been his despot. She opened the conversation by
addressing the lawyer :

" Colonel, I have called to engage you as my
counsel in a divorce suit against Mr. Fogg. I have
resolved to separate from him—to sunder our ties
and henceforth to live apart."

" Indeed !" replied the colonel; " I'm sorry to hear
that. What's the matter ? Has he been beating and
ill-treating you ?"

" Beating !" exclaimed Mrs. Fogg, disdainfully; "I
should think not ! I should like him to try it."

"Maria, let me—" interposed Mr. Fogg, mildly.

" Now, Wilberforce," she exclaimed, interrupting him, "you remain quiet; I will explain this matter to Colonel Coffin. You see, colonel, Mr. Fogg is eccentric beyond endurance. He goes on continually in a manner that will certainly drive me to distraction. I can stand it no longer. We *must* be cut asunder. For years, colonel, Wilberforce has been attempting to learn to play upon the flute. He has no more idea of music than a crow, but he *will* try to learn. He has been practicing upon the flute since 1862, and he has learned but a portion of but one tune— 'Nelly Bly.' He can play but four notes, ' Nelly Bly shuts—' and there he stops. He has practiced these four notes for fourteen years. He plays them upon the porch in the evening; he blows them out from the garret; he stands out in the yard and puffs them; he has frequently risen in the night and seized his flute and played ' Nel-ly Bly shuts' for hours, until I had to scream to relieve my feelings."

" Now, Maria," said Mr. Fogg, "you know that I can play as far as 'shuts her eye'—six notes in all. I learned them in the early part of June."

"Very well, now; it's of no consequence. Don't interrupt me. This is bad enough. I submitted to it because I loved him. But on Tuesday, while I was watching him through the crack of the parlor door, I saw him wink twice at my chambermaid; I saw him distinctly."

"Maria," shrieked Fogg, "this is scandalous.

You know very well that I am suffering from a nervous affection of the eye-lids."

"Wilberforce, hush! In addition to this wickedness, colonel, Mr. Fogg is becoming so absent-minded that he torments my life; he makes me utterly wretched. Four times now has he brought his umbrella to bed with him and scratched me by joggling it around with the sharp points of the ribs toward me. What on earth he means I cannot imagine. He said he thought somehow it was the baby, but that is so preposterous that I can hardly believe him."

"Why can't you? Don't you remember perfectly well that I emptied a bottle of milk into the umbrella twice? Would I have done that if I hadn't thought it was the baby?"

"There, now, Wilberforce! that's enough from you. Do let me have a chance to talk! And, colonel, the real baby he treats in the most malignant manner. A few days ago he mesmerized it secretly, and scared me so that I am ill from the effects of it yet. I thought the dear child would sleep for ever. And in addition to this, I came in on Thursday and found that he had laid the large family Bible on the darling's stomach. It was at the last gasp. I thought it would never recover."

"Maria, didn't I tell you I gave it to the child to play with to keep him quiet?"

"Mr. Fogg, will you please let me get a word in edgeways? Our older children, too, he is simply ruining. He teaches them the most pernicious and hurtful doctrines. He told Johnny the other day that Madagascar was an island in the Peruvian Ocean off the coast of Illinois, and that a walrus was a kind of a race horse used by the Caribbees. And our oldest girl told me that he instructed her that Polycarp fought the battle of Waterloo for the purpose of defeating the Saracens."

"Not the Saracens, Maria; Lucy misunderstood—"

"Wilberforce, I wish you would hush! His general treatment of me was scandalous. He was constantly taking my teeth for the purpose of k n o c k i n g around the spigot in the bath-tub at night when the baby wanted a drink, and only last week he took both sets after I had gone to bed, propped them apart, baited them with cheese, and caught two horrid mice before morning. I was so hurt by his behavior that I drank some laudanum for the purpose of committing suicide, and then Mr. Fogg borrowed a pump in at Knott's drug store and pumped me out twice in such a rude manner that I have felt hollow ever since."

"I did it from kindness, Maria."

" Don't talk of kindness to me, Wilberforce, after your conduct. And, colonel, one night last week, after I had retired, Mr. Fogg sat down in the room below and determined to see if it were true that a candle could be shot through a board from a gun. He dropped a lighted candle in his gun, and of course it exploded. It came up through the floor and made a large spot of grease upon the ceiling of my room, nearly scaring me to death and filling my legs full of bird-shot."

" Maria, I asked you to believe that I forgot about the candle being lighted. I did it in a fit of absent-mindedness."

" Do go into the other room, Wilberforce, or else hold your tongue. So, colonel, I want to get a divorce. Existence is unendurable to me. The lives of my children are in danger. I cannot remain in such slavery any longer. Can you release me ?"

Colonel Coffin said he would think it over and give her an answer in a week. His idea was to give her time to think better of it. So then she told Wilberforce to put on his hat; and when he had done so, he followed her meekly out, and they went home. It is believed in the neighborhood that she has concluded to stick to him for a while longer.

CHAPTER III.

THE village not only has a railroad running by it, but it has a canal upon which a large amount of traffic is done. There has been a good deal of agitation lately concerning the possibility of improving locomotion upon the canal, and the company offered a reward for the best device that could be suggested in that direction. A committee was appointed to examine and report upon the merits of the various plans submitted. While the subject was under discussion one boat-owner, Captain Binns, made an experiment upon his own account.

He had a pair of particularly stubborn mules to haul his boat, and it occurred to him that he might devise some scientific method of inducing the said mules to move whenever they were inclined to be baulky. Both mules had phlegmatic temperaments; and when they made up their minds to stop, they would do so and refuse to go, no matter with what vigor the boy applied the whip. Captain Binns therefore bought a tow-line made of three strands

of galvanized wire; and placing iron collars upon the
necks of the mules, he fastened the wire to them, and
then he got a very strong galvanic battery and put
it in the cabin of the boat, attaching it to the other
end of the line, forming a circuit.

The first time the mules stopped to reflect, the
captain sent a strong current through the wire. The
leading mule gave a little start of astonishment, and
then it looked around at the boy upon the tow-path

with a mournful smile that seemed to say, "Sonny, I
would like to know how you worked that?" But
the mules stood still. Then the captain turned a
stronger current on, and the mule shied a little and
looked hard at the boy, who was sitting by whit-
tling a stick. The captain sent another shock through

the line, and then the mule, convinced that that boy
was somehow responsible for the mysterious occurrence, reached over, seized the boy's jacket with his
teeth, shook him up and passed him to the hind mule,
which kicked him carefully over the bank into the
river.

The mules were about to turn the matter over in
their minds when Captain Binns sent the full force
of the current through the wire and kept it going
steadily.   Thereupon the animals became panic-
stricken.   They began to rear and plunge; they
turned around and dashed down the tow-path toward
the boat.   Then the line became taut; it jerked the
boat around suddenly with such force that the stern
of it broke through a weak place in the bank, and
before the captain could turn off his battery the
mules had dashed around the other side of the toll-
collector's cabin, and then, making a lurch to the
left, they fell over the bank themselves, the line
scraping the cabin, the collector, three children and
a colored man over with them.   By the time the line
was cut and the sufferers rescued the mules were
drowned and all the water in the canal had gone
out through the break.   It cost Captain Binns three
hundred dollars for damages; and when he had
settled the account, he concluded to wait for the report of that committee before making any new experiments.

The report of the committee upon improved locomotion was submitted to the company during the

following summer. It was a long and exceedingly entertaining document, and the following extracts from it may possess some interest :

THE REPORT.

"In reference to the plan offered by Henry Bushelson, which proposes to run the boats by means of his patent propeller, we may remark that the steam-engine with which the propeller is moved would sink the boat; and even if it would not, the propeller-blades, being longer than the depth of the canal, would dig about five hundred cubic feet of mud out of the bottom at each revolution. As a mud-dredge Bushelson's patent might be a success, but as a motive-power it is a failure; and his suggestion that the tow-path might be cut into lengths and laid side by side and sold for a farm, therefore, is not wholly practicable.

"The idea of William Bradley is that holes might be cut in the bottom of the boat, and through these the legs of the mule could be inserted, so that it could walk along the bottom, while its body is safe and dry inside. This notion is the offspring of a fruitful and ingenious intellect; and if the water could be kept from coming through the holes, it might be considered valuable but for one thing—somebody would have to invent a new kind of mule with legs about seven feet long. Mr. Bradley's mind has not yet devised any method of procuring such a mule, and unless he can induce the ordinary kind to walk upon stilts, we fear that the obstacles to success in this direction may be regarded as insurmountable.

"Mr. Peterman Bostwick urges that important results might be secured by making the canal an inclined plane, so that when a boat is placed upon it the boat will simply slide down hill by the power of the attraction of gravitation. This seems to us a beautiful method of adapting to the wants of man one of the most remarkable of the laws of Nature, and we should be inclined to give Mr. Bostwick the first prize but for the fact that we have discovered, upon investigation, that the water in the canal also would slide down hill, and that it would require about fifteen rivers the size of the Mississippi to keep up the supply. Mr. Bostwick does not mention where we are to get those rivers. He does, however, say that if it shall be deemed inadvisable to slope the canal, the boats themselves might be made in the shape of inclined planes, so that they would run down hill upon a level canal. There is something so deep, so amazing, in this proposition that your committee needs more time to consider it and brood over it.

"Mr. W. P. Robbins proposes to draw off the water from the canal, lay rails on the bottom, and then put the boats on wheels and run them with a locomotive. Your committee has been very much struck with this proposition, but has concluded, upon reflection, that it is rather too revolutionary. If canal navigation should be begun in this manner,

probably we should soon have the railroad companies
running their trains on water by means of sails, and
stage lines traveling in the air with balloons. Such
things would unsettle the foundations of society and
induce anarchy and chaos. A canal that has no
water is a licentious and incendiary canal; and it is
equally improper and equally repugnant to all con-
servative persons when, as Mr. Robbins suggests,
the boats are floated in tanks and the tanks are run
on rails.

"Your committee has given much thought and
patient examination to the plan of Mr. Thompson
McGlue. He suggests that the mules shall be clad
in submarine armor and made to walk under water
along the bottom of the canal, being fed with air
through a pump. As we have never seen a mule in
action while decorated with submarine armor, we are
unable to say with positiveness what his conduct
would be under such circumstances. But the objections to the plan are of a formidable character. The
mule would, of course, be wholly excluded from
every opportunity to view the scenery upon the route,
and we fear that this would have a tendency to discourage him. Being under water, too, he might be
tempted to stop frequently for the purpose of nibbling at the catfish encountered by him, and this
would distract his attention from his work. Somebody would have to dive whenever he got his hind
leg over the tow-line; and when the water was muddy,
he might lose his way and either pull the boat in the

wrong direction or be continually butting against the bank.

"Of the various other plans submitted, your committee have to say that A. R. Mackey's proposition to run the boat by sails, and to fill the sails with wind by means of a steam blower on the vessel; James Thompson's plan of giving the captain and crew small scows to put on their feet, so that they could stand overboard and push behind; William Black's theory that motion could be obtained by employing trained sturgeon to haul the boat ; and Martin Stotesbury's plea that propulsion could be given by placing a cannon upon the poop-deck and firing it over the stern, so that the recoil would shove the boat along,— are wonderful evidences of what the human mind can do when it exerts itself, but they are not as useful as they are marvelous."

The prize has not yet been awarded. It is thought that the canal company will have to make it larger before they secure exactly what they want.

There is nothing in common between canals and sausages, but the mention of Mr. William Bradley's name in the above report recalls another report in which it figured. Bradley is an inventor who has a very prolific mind, which, however, rarely produces anything that anybody wants. One of Mr. Bradley's inventions during the war was entitled by him "The Patent Imperishable Army Sausage." His idea was to simplify the movements of troops by

doing away with heavy provision-trains and to fur-
nish soldiers with nutritious food in a condensed form.
The sausage was made on strictly scientific principles.
It contained peas and beef, and salt and pepper, and
starch and gum-arabic, and it was stuffed in the skins
by a machine which exhausted the air, so that it
would be air-tight. Bradley said that his sausage
would keep in any climate. You might lay it on
the equator and let the tropical sun scorch it, and it
would remain as sweet and fresh as ever; and Bradley said that there was more flesh-and-muscle-pro-
ducing material in a cubic inch of the sausage than
in an entire dinner of roast turkey and other such
foolery.

So when Bradley had made up a lot of the Imperishable, he stored the bulk of them in the garret;
and putting a sample of them in his pocket, he went
down to Washington to see the Secretary of War,
to get him to introduce them to the army.

He walked into the secretary's office and pulled
out a sausage, and holding it toward him was about
to explain it to him, when the secretary suddenly
dodged behind the table. The movement struck
Bradley as being queer, and he walked around after
the secretary, still holding out a sample of the Imperishable. Then the secretary made a bolt for the
door and went out, and presently in came a couple
of clerks with shot-guns. They aimed at Bradley,
and told him to drop his weapon or they would fire.
He deposited the sausage on the table and asked

them what was the matter, and then the secretary
came in and said he mistook the sausage for a revolver. When Bradley explained his mission, the
secretary told him that nothing could be done with-

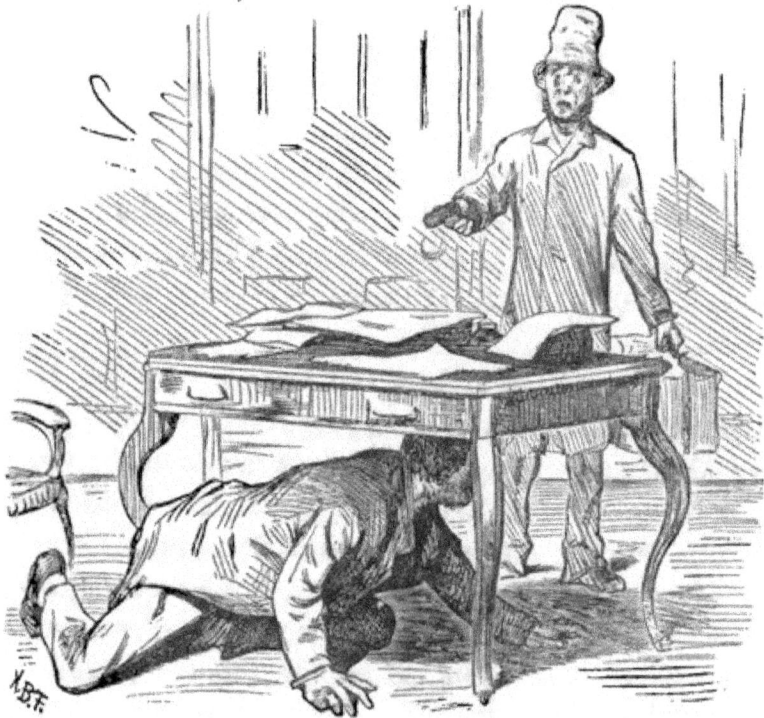

out the action of Congress, and he recommended
the inventor to go up to the Capitol and push his
sausage through there.

So Bradley was on hand next day before the session opened, and he laid a sausage on the desk of
each member. When the House assembled, there

was a large diversity of opinion respecting the meaning of the extraordinary display. Some were inclined to regard the article as an infernal machine introduced by some modern Guy Fawkes, while others leaned to the view that it was a new kind of banana developed by the Agricultural Department. After a while Bradley turned up and explained, and he spent the winter there trying to force his sausage on his beloved country. At the very end of the session a bill was smuggled through, ordering the commissary department of the army to appoint a commission to investigate Bradley's sausage, and to report to the Secretary of War.

When the commission was organized, it came on with Bradley to his home on his farm to examine his method. As the party approached the house a terrific smell greeted them, and upon entering the front door it became nearly unendurable. Mrs. Bradley said she thought there must be something dead under the washboard. But upon going into the garret the origin of the smell became obvious. About half a ton of the Patent Imperishable Sausage lay on the floor in a condition of fearful decay. Then the commissioners put their fingers to their noses and adjourned, and the chairman went to the hotel to write out his report. It was about as follows :

"After a careful examination of the Bradley Patent Imperishable Army Sausage, we find that it is eminently suitable for certain well-defined purposes.

If it should be introduced to warfare as a missile, we could calculate with precision that its projection from a gun into a besieged town would instantly induce the garrison to evacuate the place and quit; but the barbarity which would be involved in subjecting even an enemy to direct contact with the Bradley Sausage is so frightful that we shrink from recommending its use, excepting in extreme cases. The odor disseminated by the stink-pot used in war by the Chinese is fragrant and balmy compared with the perfume which belongs to this article. It might also be used profitably as a manure for poor land, and in a very cold climate, where it is absolutely certain to be frozen, it could be made serviceable as a tent-pin.

"But as an article of food it is open to several objections. Bradley's method of mixing is so defective that he has one sausage filled with peas, another with gum-arabic, another with pepper and another with beef. The beef sausages will certainly kill any man who eats a mouthful, unless they are constantly kept on ice from the hour they are made, and the gum-arabic sausages are not sufficiently nutritious to enable an army to conduct an arduous campaign. We are therefore disposed to recommend that the sausage shall not be accepted by the department, and that Bradley's friends put him in an asylum where his mind can be cared for."

When Bradley heard about the report, he was indignant; and after reflecting that republics are always ungrateful, he sent a box of the sausages to Bismarck, in order to ascertain if they could not be introduced to the German army. Three months later he was shot at one night by a mysterious person, and the belief prevails in this neighborhood that it was an assassin sent over to this country by Bismarck for the single purpose of butchering the inventor of the Imperishable Army Sausage. Since then Bradley has abandoned the project, and he is now engaged in perfecting a washing-machine which has reached such a stage that on the first trial it tore four shirts and a bolster-slip to rags.

CHAPTER IV.

THE FACTS IN REFERENCE TO MR. BUTTERWICK'S HORSE.

MR. BUTTERWICK is not a good judge of horses, but a brief while ago he thought he would like to own a good horse, and so he went to a sale at a farm over in Tulpehocken township, and for some reason that has not yet been revealed he bid upon the forlornest wreck of a horse that ever retained vitality. It was knocked down to him before he had a chance to think, and he led it home with something like a feeling of dismay. The purchase in a day or two got to be the joke of the whole village, and people poked fun at Butterwick in the most merciless manner. But he was inclined to take a philosophical view of the matter, and to present it in rather a novel and interesting light. When I spoke to him of the unkind things that were said about the horse, he said,

"Oh, I know that they say he has the heaves; but one of the things I bought him for was because he breathes so loud. That is a sign that he has a plenty of wind. You take any ordinary horse, and

you can't hear him draw a breath; his lungs are frail
and he daren't inflate 'em. But my horse fills his
up and blows 'em out again vigorously, so people
can hear for themselves how he enjoys the fresh air.
Now, I'll let you into a secret, only mind you don't
go to whispering it about: When you want to buy
a horse, go and stand off a quarter of a mile and see
if you can hear him kinder sighing. If you can,
why go for that horse; he's worth his weight in
gold. That's strictly between you and me, now
mind!

"And you know that old idiot, Potts, was trying
to joke me because the horse was sprung in the
knees, as if that was not the very thing that made
me resolve to have that horse if I ran him up to five
hundred dollars! You are a young man with no experience in the world, and I'll tell you why I like such
legs: They give the horse more leverage. Do you
see? When a horse's leg is straight, the more he
bears on it, the more likely he is to fracture the bone.
But you curve that leg a little to the front, and the
upper bone bears obliquely on the lower bone, the
pressure is distributed and the horse has plenty of
purchase. It is the well-known principle of the arch,
you know. If it's good in building a house, why isn't
it good in getting up a horse? Sprung in the knees!
Why, good gracious, man! a horse that is not sprung
is not any horse at all; he is only fit for soap-fat and
glue. Now, that's as true as my name's Butterwick.

"And as for his tail, that they talk so much about! Who'n the thunder wanted a long tail on the horse? I knew well enough it was short and had only six or seven hairs on it. But the Romans and Egyptians made their horses bob-tailed, and why? Maybe you ain't up in ancient history? Why, those old Romans knew that a horse with a fifteen-inch tail had more meat on him than a horse with a four-inch tail, and consequently required more nourishment. They knew that more muscular force is expended in brandishing a long tail than a short one, and muscular force is made by food, so they chopped off their horses' tails to make 'em eat less. They had level heads in those times. They were up in scientific knowledge. But what do these idiots around this town know about such things? Let 'em laugh. I can stand a tail that saves me a couple of bushels of oats a year. I'll bet you anything that there's millions and millions of dollars wasted—just thrown away—in this country every year furnishing nutriment to tails that are of no earthly use to the horses after they're nourished. You can depend on that. I've examined the government statistics, and they're enough to make a man cry to see how wasteful the American people are.

"And when you talk about his ribs showing so plainly through his sides, you prove that you have a very singular want of taste. Which is handsomer, a flat wall or a wall with a surface varied with columns and pilasters? Well, then, when you take a horse, no man who loves art wants to see him smooth and even from stem to stern. What you want is a varied surface—a little bit of hill and a little bit of valley; and you get it in a horse like mine. Most horses are monotonous. They tire on you. But swell out the ribs, and there you have a horse that always pleases the eye and appeals to the finer sensibilities of the mind. Besides, you are always perfectly certain that he has his full number of ribs, and that the man you buy him of is not keeping back a single, solitary bone. Your horse is all there, and you go to bed at night comfortable because you know it. That's the way I look at it; and without caring to have it mentioned around, I don't mind telling you that I know a man who came all the way from Georgia to buy my horse simply because he heard that his ribs stuck out. I got my bid in ahead of him, and he went home the worst disgusted man you ever saw.

"And about his having glanders and botts and blind staggers and a raw shoulder, I can tell you that those things never attack any but a thorough-bred horse; and for my part, I made up my mind years ago, when I was a child, that if any man ever offered me a horse that hadn't blind staggers I wouldn't take him as a gift. Now, that's as true as you're alive. Professor Owen says that so far from regarding glanders as a disease he considers it the crowning glory of a good horse, and he wants the English government to pass a law inoculating every horse on the island with it. You write to him and ask him if that ain't so."

And so Butterwick put his phenomenal horse in his stable, hired an Irishman to take care of it, and possessed his soul in peace. However, before he fairly had a chance to enjoy his purchase, he was summoned to St. Louis to look after some business matters, and he was detained there for about six weeks. During his absence Mrs. Butterwick assumed the responsibility for the management of the horse ; and as she knew as much about taking care of horses as she did about conducting the processes of the sidereal system, the result was that Mr. Butterwick's horse was the unconscious parent of infinite disaster. When Butterwick returned and had kissed his wife and talked over his journey, the following conversation ensued. Mrs. Butterwick said,

" You know our horse, dearest ?"

" Yes, sweet ; how is he getting along ?"

" Not so *very* well ; he has cost a great deal of money since you've been away."

" Indeed ?"

" Yes ; besides his regular feed and Patrick's wages as hostler, I have on hand unpaid bills to the amount of two thousand dollars on his account."

" Two thousand ! Why, Emma, you amaze me ! What on earth does it mean ?"

" I'll tell you the whole story, love. Just after you left he took a severe cold, and he coughed incessantly. You could hear him cough for miles. All the neigh-

4

bors complained of it, and Mr. Potts, next door, was
so mad that he shot at the horse four times.   Patrick
said it was whooping-cough."

"Whooping-cough, darling! Impossible! A horse
never has whooping-cough."

"Well, Patrick said so.   And as I always give
paregoric to the children when they cough, I concluded that it would be good for the horse, so I
bought a bucketful and gave it to him with sugar."

"A bucketful of paregoric, my love!   It was
enough to kill him."

"Patrick said that was a regular dose for a horse
of sedentary habits; and it didn't kill him: it put
him to sleep.   You will be surprised, dear, to learn
that the horse slept straight ahead for four weeks.
Never woke up once.   I was frightened about it, but
Patrick told me that it was a sign of a good horse.
He said that Dexter often slept six months on a
stretch, and that once they took Goldsmith Maid to
a race while she was sound asleep and she trotted a
mile in 2 : 15, I think he said, without getting awake."

"Patrick said that, did he?"

"Yes; that was at the end of the second week.
But as the horse didn't rouse up, Patrick said it
couldn't be the paregoric that kept him asleep so
long; and he came to me and asked me not to mention it, but he had suspicions that Mr. Fogg had
mesmerized him."

"I never heard of a horse being mesmerized,
dearest."

"Neither did I, but Patrick said it was a common thing with the better class of horses. And when he kept on sleeping, dear, I got frightened, and Patrick consulted the horse-doctor, who came over with a galvanic battery, which he said would wake the horse. They fixed the wires to his leg and turned on the current. It did rouse him. He got up and kicked fourteen boards out of the side of the stable and then jumped the fence into Mr. Potts' yard, where he trod on a litter of young pigs, kicked two cows to death and bit the tops off of eight apple trees. Patrick said he tried to swallow Mrs. Potts' baby, but I didn't see him do that. Patrick may have exaggerated. I don't know. It seems hardly likely, does it, that the horse would actually try to eat a child?"

"The man that sold him to me didn't mention that he was fond of babies."

"But he got over the attack. The only effect was that the paregoric or the electricity, or something, turned his hair all the wrong way, and he looks the queerest you ever saw. Oh yes; it did seem to affect his appetite, too. He appeared to be always hungry. He ate up the hay-rack and two sets of harness. And one night he broke out and nibbled off all the door-knobs on the back of the house."

"Door-knobs, Emma? Has he shown a fondness for door-knobs?"

"Yes; and he ate Louisa's hymn-book, too. She left it lying on the table on the porch. Patrick said he knew a man in Ireland whose horse would starve to death unless they fed him on Bibles. If he couldn't get Bibles, he'd take Testaments; but unless he got Scriptures of some kind, he was utterly intractable."

" I would like to have had a look at that horse, sweet."

" So we got the horse-doctor again, and he said that what the poor animal wanted was a hypodermic injection of morphia to calm his nerves. He told Patrick to get a machine for placing the morphia under the horse's skin. But Patrick said that he could do it without the machine. So one day he got the morphia, and began to bore a hole in the horse with a gimlet."

" A gimlet, Emma?"

" An ordinary gimlet. But it seemed unpleasant to the horse, and so he kicked Patrick through the partition, breaking three of his ribs. Then I got the doctor to perform the operation properly, and the horse after that appeared right well, excepting that Patrick said that he had suddenly acquired an extraordinary propensity for standing on his head."

" He is the first horse that ever wanted to do that, love."

" Patrick said not. He told me about a man he worked for in Oshkosh who had a team of mules which always stood on their heads when they were not at work. He said all the mules in Oshkosh did. So Patrick tied a heavy stone to our horse's tail to balance him and keep him straight. And this worked to a charm until I took the horse to church one Sunday, when, while a crowd stood round him looking at him, he swung his tail around and brained six boys with the stone."

" Brained them, love ?"

" Well, I didn't see them myself, but Patrick told me, when I came out of church, that they were as good as dead. And he said he remembered that that Oshkosh man used to coax his mules to stand on their legs by letting them hear music. It soothed them, he said. And so Patrick got a friend to come around and sit in the stall and calm our horse by playing on the accordion."

" Did it make him calmer ?"

" It seemed to at first; but one day Patrick undertook to bleed him for the blind staggers, and he must have cut the horse in the wrong place, for the poor brute fell over on the accordion person and died, nearly killing the musician."

" The horse is dead, then ? Where is the bill ?"

" I'll read it to you :

THE BILL.

Horse-doctor's fees..	$125 50
Paregoric for cough	80 00
Galvanic battery..	10 00
Repairing stable..	12 25
Potts' cow, pigs, apple trees and baby.........	251 00
Damage to door-knobs, etc..............	175 00
Louisa's hymn-book...	25
Gimlet and injections...	15 00
Repairing Patrick's ribs..	145 00

Music on accordion..	21 00
Damages to player...	184 00
Burying six boys..	995 00
	$2,014 00

"That is all, love, is it?"

"Yes."

Then Mr. Butterwick folded the bill up and went out into the back yard to think. Subsequently, he told me that he had concluded to repudiate the unpaid portions of the bill, and then to try to purchase a better horse. He said he had heard that Mr. Keyser, a farmer over in Lower Merion, had a horse that he wanted to sell, and he asked me to go over there with him to see about it. I agreed to do so.

When we reached the place, Mr. Keyser asked us into the parlor, and while we were sitting there we heard Mrs. Keyser in the dining-room, adjoining, busy preparing supper. Keyser would not sell his horse, but he was quite sociable, and after some conversation, he said,

"Gentlemen, in 1847 I owned a hoss that never seen his equal in this State. And that hoss once did the most extr'ordinary thing that was ever done by an animal. One day I had him out, down yer by the creek—"

Here Mrs. Keyser opened the door and exclaimed, shrilly,

"Keyser, if you want any supper, you'd better get me some kin'lin-wood pretty quick."

Then Keyser turned to us and said,

" Excuse me for a few moments, gentlemen, if you please."

A moment later we heard him splitting wood in the cellar beneath, and indulging in some very hard language with his soft pedal down, Mrs. Keyser being the object of his objurgations. After a while he came into the parlor again, took his seat, wiped the moisture from his brow, put his handkerchief in his hat, his hat on the floor, and resumed:

"As I was sayin', gentlemen, one day I had that hoss down yer by the creek; it was in '47 or '48, I most forget which. But, howsomedever, I took him down yer by the creek, and I was jest about to—"

Mrs. Keyser (opening the door suddenly). " You, Keyser! there's not a drop of water in the kitchen, and unless some's drawed there'll be no supper in this house *this* night, now mind *me !*"

Keyser (with a look of pain upon his face). " Well, well! this is too bad! too bad! Gentlemen, just wait half a minute. I'll be right back. The old woman's rarin' 'round, and she won't wait."

Then we heard Keyser at work at the well-bucket; and looking out the back window, we saw him bringing in a pail of water. On his way he encountered a dog, and in order to give his pent-up feelings adequate expression, he kicked the animal clear over the fence. Presently he came into the parlor, mopped his forehead, and began again.

Keyser. "As I was sayin', that hoss was perfeckly astonishin'. On the day of which I was speakin', I

was ridin' him down yer by the creek, clost by the
corn-field, and I was jest about to wade him in, when,
all of a suddent-like, he—"

Mrs. Keyser (at the door, and with her voice pitched
at a high key). "ARE you goin' to fetch that ham
from the smoke-house, or ARE you goin' to set there
jabberin' and go without your supper? If that
ham isn't here in short order, I'll know the reason
why. You hear me?"

Keyser (his face red and his manner excited). "*Gra-*
SHUS! If this isn't— Well, well! this just lays over
all the— Pshaw! Mr. Butterwick, if you'll hold on
for a second, I'll be with you agin. I'll be right
back."

Then we heard Keyser slam open the smoke-
house door, and presently he emerged with a ham,
which he carried in one hand, while with the other
he made a fist, which he shook threateningly at the
kitchen door, as if to menace Mrs. Keyser, who
couldn't see him.

Again he entered the parlor, smelling of smoke
and ham, and, crossing his legs, he continued.

Keyser. "Excuse these little interruptions; the old
woman's kinder sing'ler, and you've got to humor
her to live in peace with her. Well, sir, as I said, I
rode that extr'ordinary hoss down yer by the creek
on that day to which I am referrin', and after passin'
the cornfield I was goin' to wade him into the creek;
just then, all of a suddent, what should that hoss do
but—"

Mrs. Keyser (at the door again). "Keyser, you lazy vagabone! Why don't you 'tend to milkin' them cows? Not one mossel of supper do you put in your mouth this night unless you do the milkin' right off. You sha'n't touch a crust, or my name's not Emeline Keyser!"

Then Keyser leaped to his feet in a perfect frenzy of rage and hurled the chair at Mrs. Keyser; whereupon she seized the poker and came toward him with savage earnestness. Then we adjourned to the front yard suddenly; and as Butterwick and I got into the carriage to go home, Keyser, with a humble expression in his eyes, said:

"Gentlemen, I'll tell you that hoss story another time, when the old woman's calmer. Good-day."

I am going to ask him to write it out. I am anxious to know what that horse did down at the creek.

Butterwick subsequently bought another horse from a friend of his in the city, but the animal developed eccentricities of such a remarkable character that he became unpopular. Butterwick, in explaining the subject to me, said,

"I was surprised to find, when I drove him out for the first time, that he had an irresistible propensity to back. He seemed to be impressed with a conviction that nature had put his hind legs in front, and that he could see with his tail; and whenever I attempted to start him, he always proceeded backward until I whipped him savagely, and then he would go in a proper manner, but suddenly, and with the air of a

horse who had a conviction that there was a lunatic
in the carriage who didn't know what he was about.
One day, while we were coming down the street,
this theory became so strong that he suddenly
stopped and backed the carriage through the plate-
glass window of Mackey's drug-store.   After that I
always hitched him up with his head toward the carriage, and then he seemed to feel better contented,
only sometimes he became too sociable, and used to
put his head over the dasher and try to chew my
legs or to eat the lap-cover.

"Besides, the peculiar arrangement of the animal
excited unpleasant remark when I drove out; and
when I wanted to stop and would hitch him by the
tail to a post, he had a very disagreeable way of
reaching out with his hind legs and sweeping the
sidewalk whenever he saw anybody that he felt as if
he would like to kick.

"He was not much of a saddle-horse; not that he
would attempt to throw his rider, but whenever a
saddle was put on him it made his back itch, and he
would always insist upon rubbing it against the first
tree or fence or corner of a house that he came to;
and if he could bark the rider's leg, he seemed to
be better contented.   The last time I rode him was
upon the day of Mr. Johnson's wedding.   I had on
my best suit, and on the way to the festival there
was a creek to be forded.   When the horse got into
the middle of it, he took a drink, and then looked
around at the scenery.   Then he took another drink,

and gazed again at the prospect. Then he suddenly felt tired and lay down in the water. By the
time he was sufficiently rested I was ready to go
home.

"The next day he was taken sick. Patrick said it
was the epizooty, and he mixed him up some turpentine in a bucket of warm feed. That night the
horse had spasms, and kicked four of the best boards
out of the side of the stable. Jones said that horse
hadn't the epizooty, but the botts, and that the turpentine ought to have been rubbed on the outside

of him instead of going into his stomach. So we rubbed him with turpentine, and next morning he hadn't a hair on his body.

"Colonel Coffin told me that if I wanted to know what really ailed that horse he would tell me. It was glanders, and if he wasn't bled he would die. So the colonel bled him for me. We took away a tubful, and the horse thinned down so that his ribs made him look as if he had swallowed a flour-barrel.

"Then I sent for the horse-doctor, and he said there was nothing the matter with the horse but heaves, and he left some medicine 'to patch up his wind.' The result was that the horse coughed for two days as if he had gone into galloping consumption, and between two of the coughs he kicked the hired man through the partition and bit our black-and-tan terrier in half.

"I thought perhaps a little exercise might improve his health, so I drove him out one day, and he proceeded in such a peculiar manner that I was afraid he might suddenly come apart and fall to pieces. When we reached the top of White House hill, which is very steep by the side of the road, he stopped, gave a sort of shudder, coughed a couple of times, kicked a fly off his side with his hind leg, and then lay down and calmly rolled over the bank. I got out of the carriage before he fell, and I watched him pitch clear down to the valley beneath, with the vehicle dragging after him. When we got to him he was dead, and the man at the farm-house close by said he had the blind staggers.

"I sold him for eight dollars to a man who wanted to make him up into knife-handles and suspender-buttons; and since then we have walked. I hardly think I shall buy another horse. My luck doesn't seem good enough when I make ventures of that kind."

CHAPTER V.

SOME EDUCATIONAL FACTS.

T HE public-school system of the village was reorganized during a recent summer; and in consequence of a considerable enlargement of the single school-building and the great increase of the number of scholars, it was determined to engage an additional woman-teacher in the girls' department. Accordingly, the board of directors advertised for a suitable person, instructing applicants to call upon Judge Twiddler, the chairman. A day or two later, Mrs. Twiddler advertised in a city paper for a cook, and upon the same afternoon an Irish girl came to the house to obtain the place in the kitchen. The judge was sitting upon the front porch at the time reading a newspaper; and when the girl entered the gate of the yard, he mistook her for a school-mistress, and he said to her,

" Did you come about that place ?"

" Yes, sor," she answered.

" Oh, very well, then ; take a seat and I'll run over a few things in order to ascertain what your qualifications are. Bound Africa."

62

"If you please, sor, I don't know what you mean."

"I say, bound Africa."

"Bou—bou— Begorra, I don't know what ye're referrin' to."

"Very strange," said the judge. "Can you tell me if 'amphibious' is an adverb or a preposition? What is an adverb?"

"Indade, and ye bother me intirely. I never had anything to do wid such things at my last place."

"Then it must have been a curious sort of an institution," said the judge. "Probably you can tell me how to conjugate the verb 'to be,' and just mention, also, what you know about Herodotus."

"Ah, yer Honor's jokin' wid me. Be done wid yer fun, now."

"Did you ever hear of Herodotus?"

"Never once in the whole coorse of my life. Do you make it with eggs?"

"This is the most extraordinary woman I ever encountered," murmured the judge. "How she ever associated Herodotus with the idea of eggs is simply incomprehensible. Well, can you name the hemisphere in which China and Japan are situated?"

"Don't bother me wid yer fun, now. I can wash the china and the pans as well as anybody, and that's enough, now, isn't it?"

"Dumb! awful dumb! Don't know the country from the crockery. I'll try her once more. Name the limits of the Tropic of Capricorn, and tell me where Asia Minor is located."

"I have a brother that's one, sor; that's all I know about it."

"One? One what?"

"Didn't ye ask me afther the miners, sor? My brother Teddy works wid 'em."

"And this," said the judge, "is the kind of person to whom we are asked to entrust the education of youth. Woman, what *do* you know? What kind of a school have you been teaching?"

"None, sor. What should I teach school for?"

"Totally without experience, as I supposed," said the judge.

"Mrs. Ferguson had a governess teach the children when I was cookin' for her."

"Cooking! Ain't you a school-teacher? What do you mean by proposing to stop cooking in order to teach school? Why, it's preposterous."

"Begorra, I came here to get the cook's place, sor, and that's all of it."

"Oh, by George! I see now. You ain't a candidate for the grammar school, after all. You want to see Mrs. Twiddler. Maria, come down here a minute. There's a thick-headed immigrant here wants to cook for you."

And the judge picked up his paper and resumed the editorial on "The Impending Crisis."

They obtained a good teacher, however, and the course of affairs in the girls' department was smooth enough; but just after the opening of the fall session there was some trouble in the boys' department.

Mr. Barnes, the master, read in the *Educational Monthly* that boys could be taught history better than in any other way by letting each boy in the class represent some historical character, and relate the acts of that character as if he had done them himself. This struck Barnes as a mighty good idea, and he resolved to put it in practice. The school had then progressed so far in its study of the history of Rome as the Punic wars, and Mr. Barnes immediately divided the boys into two parties, one Romans and the other Carthaginians, and certain of the boys were named after the leaders upon both sides. All the boys thought it was a fine thing, and Barnes noticed that they were so anxious to get to the history lesson that they could hardly say their other lessons properly.

When the time came, Barnes ranged the Romans upon one side of the room and the Carthaginians on the other. The recitation was very spirited, each party telling about its deeds with extraordinary unction. After a while Barnes asked a Roman to describe the battle of Cannæ. Whereupon the Romans hurled their copies of Wayland's Moral Science at the enemy. Then the Carthaginians made a battering-ram out of a bench and jammed it among the Romans, who retaliated with a volley of books, slates and chewed paper-balls. Barnes concluded that the battle of Cannæ had been sufficiently illustrated, and he tried to stop it; but the warriors considered it too good a thing to let drop, and accordingly the Carthaginians dashed over to the Romans with another battering-ram and thumped a couple of them savagely.

Then the Romans turned in, and the fight became general. A Carthaginian would grasp a Roman by the hair and hustle him around over the desk in a manner that was simply frightful, and a Roman would give a fiendish whoop and knock a Carthaginian over the head with Greenleaf's Arithmetic. Hannibal got the head of Scipio Africanus under his arm, and Scipio, in his efforts to break away, stumbled, and the two generals fell and had a rough-and-tumble fight under the blackboard. Caius Gracchus prodded Hamilcar with a ruler, and the latter in his struggles to get loose fell against the stove and knocked down about thirty feet of stove-pipe. Thereupon the Romans made a grand rally, and in five minutes they chased the entire Carthaginian army out of the school-room, and Barnes along with it; and then they locked the door and began to hunt up the apples and lunch in the desks of the enemy.

After consuming the supplies they went to the windows and made disagreeable remarks to the Carthaginians, who were standing in the yard, and dared old Barnes to bring the foe once more into battle array. Then Barnes went for a policeman; and when he knocked at the door, it was opened, and all the Romans were found busy studying their lessons. When Barnes came in with the defeated troops he went for Scipio Africanus; and pulling him out of his

THE BATTLE OF CANNÆ.

seat by the ear, he thrashed that great military genius with a rattan until Scipio began to cry, whereupon Barnes dropped him and began to paddle Caius Gracchus. Then things settled down in the old way, and next morning Barnes announced that history in the future would be studied as it always had been; and he wrote a note to the *Educational Monthly* to say that in his opinion the man who suggested the new system ought to be led out and shot. The boys do not now take as much interest in Roman history as they did on that day.

The young tragedian who represented Scipio Africanus is named Smith. His family came to the village to live only a few weeks before the school opened. Scipio is a very enterprising and ingenious lad. Colonel Coffin's boy leaned over the fence one day and gave to me his impressions of Scipio, a lad about fourteen years old:

"Yes, me and him are right well acquainted now; he knows more'n I do, and he's had more experience. Bill says his father used to be a robber (Smith, by the way, is a deacon in the Presbyterian church, and a very excellent lawyer), and that he has ten million dollars in gold buried in his cellar, along with a whole lot of human bones—people he's killed. And he says his father is a conjurer, and that he makes all the earthquakes that happen anywheres in the world. The old man'll come home at night, after there's been an earthquake, all covered with perspiration and so tired he kin hardly stand. Bill says it's such hard work.

"And Bill tole me that once when a man came around there trying to sell lightning-rods his father got mad and et him—et him right up; and he takes bites out of everybody he comes acrost.

"That's what Bill tells me. That's all I know about it. And he tole me that once he used to have a dog—one of these little kind of dogs—and he was flying his kite, and just for fun he tied the kite-string onto his dog's tail. And then the wind struck her and his dog went a-scuddin' down the street with his hind legs in the air for about a mile, when the kite all of a sudden begun to go up, and in about a minute the dog was fifteen miles high and commanding a view of California and Egypt, I think Bill said. He came down, anyhow, I know, in Brazil, and Bill said he swum home all the way in the Atlantic Ocean; and when he landed, his legs were all nibbled off by sharks.

"I wish father'd buy me a dog, so's I could send him up that way. But I never have any luck. Bill said that where they used to live he went out on the roof one day to fly his kite, and he sat on top of the chimbly to give her plenty of room, and while he was sitting there thinking about nothing, the old man put a keg of powder down below in the fireplace to clean the soot out of the chimbly. And when he touched her off, Bill was blowed over agin the Baptist church steeple, and he landed on the

weather-cock with his pants torn, and they couldn't
git him down for three days, so he hung there, going
round and round with the wind, and he lived by eating the crows that came and sat on him, because
they thought he was made of sheet-iron and put up
there on purpose.

" He's had more fun than enough. He was telling me the other day about a sausage-stuffer his
brother invented. It was a kinder machine that
worked with a treadle; and Bill said the way they
did in the fall was to fix it on the hog's back, and
connect the treadle with a string, and then the hog'd
work the treadle and keep on running it up and
down until the machine cut the hog all up fine and
shoved the meat into the skins. Bill said his brother
called it ' Every Hog His Own Stuffer,' and it worked
splendid. But I do' know. 'Pears to me 'sif there
couldn't be no machine like that. But anyway, Bill
said so.

"And he told me about an uncle of his out in
Australia who was et by a big oyster once; and when
he got inside, he stayed there until he'd et the oyster.
Then he split the shell open and took half a one
for a boat, and he sailed along until he met a sea-
serpent, and he killed it and drawed off its skin, and
when he got home he sold it to an engine company
for a hose, for forty thousand dollars, to put out fires
with. Bill said that was actually so, because he
could show me a man who used to belong to the
engine company. I wish father'd let me go out to

find a sea-serpent like that; but he don't let me have a chance to distinguish myself.

"Bill was saying only yesterday that the Indians caught him once and drove eleven railroad spikes through his stomach and cut off his scalp, and it never hurt him a bit. He said he got away by the daughter of the chief sneaking him out of the wigwam and lending him a horse. Bill says she was in love with him; and when I asked him to let me see the holes where they drove in the spikes, he said he daresn't take off his clothes or he'd bleed to death. He said his own father didn't know it, because Bill was afraid it might worry the old man.

"And Bill tole me they wasn't going to get him to go to Sunday-school. He says his father has a brass idol that he keeps in the garret, and Bill says he's made up his mind to be a pagan, and to begin to go naked, and carry a tomahawk and a bow and arrow, as soon as the warm weather comes. And to prove it to me, he says his father has this town all underlaid with nitro-glycerine, and as soon as he gets ready he's going to blow the old thing out, and bust her up, let her rip, and demolish her. He said so down at the dam, and tole me not to tell anybody, but I thought they'd be no harm in mentioning it to you.

"And now I believe I must be going. I hear Bill a-whistling. Maybe he's got something else to tell me."

The Smith boy will be profitable to the youth of the community.

Barnes, the pedagogue, is a worthy man who has seen trouble. Precisely what was the nature of the afflictions which had filled his face with furrows and given him the air of one who has been overburdened with sorrows was not revealed until Mr. Keyser told the story one evening at the grocery-store. Whether his narrative is strictly true or not is uncertain. There is a bare possibility that Mr. Keyser may have exaggerated grossly a very simple fact.

"Nobody ever knew how it got in there," said Mr. Keyser, clasping his hands over his knee and spitting into the stove. "Some thought Barnes must've swallowed a tadpole while drinking out of a spring and it subsequently grew inside him, while others allowed that maybe he'd accidentally eaten frogs' eggs some time and they'd hatched out. But anyway, he had that frog down there inside of him settled and permanent and perfectly satisfied with being in out of the rain. It used to worry Barnes more'n a little, and he tried various things to git rid of it. The doctors they give him sickening stuff, and over and over agin emptied him; and then they'd hold him by the heels and shake him over a basin, and they'd bait a hook with a fly and fish down his throat hour after hour, but that frog was too intelligent. He never even gave them a nibble; and when they'd try to fetch him with an emetic, he'd dig his claws into Barnes's membranes and hold on until the storm was over.

"Not that Barnes minded the frog merely being in there if he'd only a kept quiet. But he was too vociferous—that's what Barnes said to me. A taciturn frog he wouldn't have cared about so much. But how would you like to have one down inside of you there a-whooping every now and then in the most ridiculous manner? Maybe, for instance, Barnes'd be out taking tea with a friend, and just when everybody else was quiet it'd suddenly occur to his frog to tune up, and the next minute you'd hear something go 'Blo-o-o-ood-a-noun! Blo-oo-oo-ood-a-noun!' two or three times, apparently under the table. Then the folks would ask if there was an aquarium in the house or if the man had a frog-pond in the cellar, and Barnes'd get as red as fire and jump up and go home.

"And often when he'd be setting in church, perhaps in the most solemn part of the sermon, he'd feel something give two or three quick kinder jerks under his vest, and presently that reptile would bawl right out in the meeting 'Bloo-oo-oo-ood-a-noun! Bloo-oo-oo-ood-a-nou-ou-oun!' and keep it up until the sexton would come along and run out two or three boys for profaning the sanctuary. And at last he'd fix it on poor old Barnes, and then tell him that if he wanted to practice ventriloquism he'd better wait till after church. And then the frog'd give six or seven more hollers, so that the minister would stop and look at Barnes, and Barnes'd get up and skip down the aisle and go home furious about it.

"It had a deep voice for an ordinary frog—betwixt a French horn and a bark-mill. And Mrs. Barnes told me herself that often, when John'd get comfortably fixed in bed and just dropping off into a nap, the frog'd think it was a convenient time for some music; and after hopping about a bit, it'd all at once grind out three or four awful 'Bloo-oo-ood-a-nouns' and wake Mrs. Barnes and the baby, and start things up generally all around the house. And—would you believe it?—if that frog felt, maybe, a little frisky, or p'raps had some tune running through its head, it'd keep on that way for hours. It worried Barnes like thunder.

"I dunno whether it was that that killed his wife or not; but anyhow, when she died, Barnes wanted to marry agin, and he went for a while to see Miss Flickers, who lives out yer on the river road, you know. He courted her pretty steady for a while, and we all thought there was goin' to be a consolidation. But she was telling my wife that one evening Barnes had just taken hold of her hand and told her he loved her, when all of a sudden something said, 'Bloo-oo-oo-ood-a-nou-ou-oun!'

"'What on earth's that?' asked Miss Flickers, looking sorter scared.

"'I dunno,' said Barnes; 'it sounds like somebody making a noise in the cellar.' Lied, of course, for he knew mighty well what it was.

"" 'Pears to me 'sif it was under the sofa,' says she.

"' Maybe it wasn't anything, after all,' says Barnes, when just then the frog. he feels like running up the scales again, and he yells out, ' Bloo-oo-ood-a-nou-ou-ou-oun!'

"' Upon my word,' says Miss Flickers, ' I believe you've got a frog in your pocket, Mr. Barnes; now, haven't you?'

" Then he gets down on his knees and owns up to the truth, and swears he'll do his best to git rid of the frog, and all the time he is talking the frog is singing exercises and scales and oratorios inside of him, and worse than ever, too, because Barnes drank a good deal of ice-water that day, and it made the frog hoarse—ketched cold, you know.

"But Miss Flickers, she refused him. Said she might've loved him, only she couldn't marry any man that had continual music in his interior.

"So Barnes, he was the most disgusted man you ever saw. Perfectly sick about it. And one day he was lying on the bed gaping, and that frog unexpectedly made up its mind to come up to ask Barnes to eat more carefully, maybe, and it jumped out on the counterpane. After looking about a bit it came up and tried three or four times to hop back, but he kept his mouth shut, and killed the frog with the back of a hair-brush. Ever since then he runs his drinking-water through a strainer, and he hates frogs worse than you and me hate pison. Now, that's the honest truth about Barnes; you ask him if it ain't."

Then Keyser bought some tobacco and went home.

CHAPTER VI.

THE EDITOR OF THE PATRIOT.

HE editor of the village paper, *The Patriot and Advertiser,* is Major Slott; and a very clever journalist he is. Even his bitterest adversary, the editor of *The Evening Mail,* in the town above us on the river, admits that. In the last political campaign, indeed, *The Mail* undertook to tell how it was that the major acquired such a taste for journalism. The story was that shortly after he was born the doctor ordered that the baby should be fed upon goat's milk. This was procured from a goat that was owned by an Irish woman who lived in the rear of the office of *The Weekly Startler* and fed her goat chiefly upon the exchanges which came to that journal. The consequence, according to *The Mail,* was that young Slott was fed entirely upon milk formed from digested newspapers; and he throve on it, although when the Irish woman mixed the Democratic journals carelessly with the Whig papers they disagreed after they were eaten, and the milk gave the baby colic. Old Slott intended the boy to be a minister; but as soon as he was old enough to take notice he cried for every newspaper that he happened to see, and no sooner did he learn how to write than he began to slash off editorials upon "The Need of Reform," etc. He ran away from school four times to enter a newspaper office, and finally, when the paternal Slott put him in the House of Refuge, he started a weekly in there, and called it the *House of Refuge Record;* and one day he slid over the wall and went down to the *Era* office, where he changed his name to Blott, and began his career on that paper with an article on "Our Reformatory Institutions for the Young." Then old Slott surrendered to what seemed to be a combination of manifest destiny and goat's milk, and permitted him to pursue his profession. The major, *The Mail* alleges, has the instinct so strong that if he should fall into the crater of Vesuvius his first thought on striking bottom would be to write to somebody to ask for a free pass to come out with. "But," continued *The Mail*, "you would hardly believe this story if you ever read *The Patriot*. We often suspect, when we are looking over that sheet, that the nurse used to mix the goat's milk with an unfair proportion of water."

The major has a weekly edition in which he publishes serial stories of a stirring character, and he is always looking out for good ones. Recently a tale was submitted by a certain Mr. Stack, a young man who had high ambition without much experience as a writer of fiction. After waiting a long while and hearing nothing about the story, Mr. Stack concluded to call upon the major in order to ascertain why that narrative had not attracted attention. When Stack mentioned his errand, the major reached for the manuscript; and looking very solemn, he said,

" Mr. Stack, I don't think I can accept this story. In some respects it is really wonderful; but I am afraid that if I published it, it would attract almost too much attention. People would get too wild over it. We have to be careful. For instance, here in the first chapter you mention the death of Mrs. McGinnis, the hero's mother. She dies; you inter Mrs. McGinnis in the cemetery; you give an affecting scene at the funeral; you run up a monument over her and plant honeysuckle upon her grave. You create in the reader's mind a strong impression that Mrs. McGinnis is thoroughly dead. And yet, over here in the twenty-second chapter, you make a man named Thompson fall in love with her, and she is married to him, and she goes skipping around through the rest of the story as lively as a grasshopper, and you all the time alluding to Thompson as her second husband. You see that kind of thing won't do. It excites remark. Readers complain about it."

" You don't say I did that? Well, now, do you know I was thinking all the time that it was *Mr.* McGinnis that I buried in the first chapter? I must have got them mixed up somehow."

" And then," continued the major, " when you introduce the hero, you mention that he has but one arm, having lost the other in battle. But in chapter twelve you run him through a saw-mill by an accident, and you mention that he lost an arm there, too. And yet in the nineteenth chapter you say, 'Adolph rushed up to Mary, threw his arms about her, and clasped her to his bosom;' and then you go on to relate how he sat down at the piano in the soft moonlight and played one of Beethoven's sonatas 'with sweet poetic fervor.' Now, the thing, you see, don't dovetail. Adolph couldn't possibly throw his arms around Mary if one was buried in the field of battle and the other was minced up in a saw-mill, and he couldn't clasp her to his bosom unless he threw a lasso with his teeth and hauled her in by swallowing the slack of the rope. As for the piano— well, you know as well as I do that an armless man can't play a Beethoven sonata unless he knows how to perform on the instrument with his nose, and in that case you insult the popular intelligence when you talk about 'sweet poetic fervor.' I have my fingers on the public pulse, and I know they won't stand it."

"Well, well," said Stack, "I don't know how I ever came to—"

"Let me direct your attention to another incendiary matter," interrupted the major. "In the first love-scene between Adolph and—and—let me see— what's her name?—Mary—you say that 'her liquid blue eye rested softly upon him as he poured forth the story of his love, and its azure was dimmed by

6

a flood of happy tears.' Well, sir, about twenty
pages farther on, where the villain insults her, you
observe that her black eyes flashed lightning at him
and seemed to scorch him where he stood. Now,
let me direct attention to the fact that if the girl's
eyes were blue they couldn't be black; and if you
mean to convey the impression that she had one
blue eye and one black eye, and that she only looked
softly at Adolph out of the off eye, while the near
eye roamed around, not doing anything in particular,
why, she is too phenomenal for a novel, and only
suitable for a place in the menagerie by the side of
the curiosities. And then you say that although
her eye was liquid yet it scorched the villain. People won't put up with that kind of thing. It makes
them delirious and murderous."

"Too bad!" said Stack. "I forgot what I'd said
about her eyes when I wrote that scene with the
villain."

"And here, in the twentieth chapter, you say that
Magruder was stabbed with a bowie-knife in the
hands of the Spaniard, and in the next chapter
you give an account of the *post-mortem* examination,
and make the doctors hunt for the bullet and find it
embedded in his liver. Even patient readers can't
remain calm under such circumstances. They lose
control of themselves."

"It's unfortunate," said Stack.

"Now, the way you manage the Browns in the
story is also exasperating. First you represent Mrs.

Brown as taking her twins around to church to be christened. In the middle of the book you make Mrs. Brown lament that she never had any children, and you wind up the story by bringing in Mrs. Brown with her grandson in her arms just after having caused Mr. Brown to state to the clergyman that the only child he ever had died in his fourth year. Just think of the effect of such a thing on the public mind! Why, this story would fill all the insane asylums in the country."

"Those Browns don't seem to be very definite, somehow," said Stack, thoughtfully.

"Worst of all," said major, "in chapter thirty-one you make the lovers resolve upon suicide, and you put them in a boat and drift them over Niagara Falls. Twelve chapters farther on you suddenly introduce them walking in the twilight in a leafy lane, and although afterward she goes into a nunnery and takes the black veil because he has been killed by pirates in the Spanish West Indies, in the next chapter to the last you have a scene where she goes to a surprise-party at the Presbyterian minister's and finds him there making arrangements for the wedding as if nothing had ever happened; and then, after you disclose the fact that she was a boy in disguise, and not a woman at all, you marry them to each other, and represent the boy heroine as giving her blessing to her daughter. Oh, it's awful—awful! It won't do. It really won't. You'd better go into some other kind of business, Mr. Stack."

Then Stack took his manuscript and went home to fix it up so as to make the story run together better. The *Patriot* will not publish it even if Stack reconstructs it.

Major Slott, like most other editors, is continually persecuted by bores, but recently he was the victim of a peculiarly dastardly attack from a person of this class. While he was sitting in the office of the *Patriot*, writing an editorial about "Our Grinding Monopolies," he suddenly became conscious of the presence of a fearful smell. He stopped, snuffed the air two or three times, and at last lighted a cigar to fumigate the room. Then he heard footsteps upon the stairs, and as they drew nearer the smell grew stronger. When it had reached a degree of intensity that caused the major to fear that it might break some of the furniture, there was a knock at the door. Then a man entered with a bundle under his arm, and as he did so the major thought that he had never smelt such a fiendish smell in the whole course of his life. He held his nose; and when the man saw the gesture, he said,

"I thought so; the usual effect. You hold it tight while I explain."

"What hab you god id that buddle?" asked the major.

"That, sir," said the man, "is Barker's Carbolic Disinfecting Door-mat. I am Barker, and this is the mat. I invented it, and it's a big thing."

" Is id thad thad smells so thudderig bad ?" asked the major, with his nostrils tightly shut.

" Yes, sir ; smells very strong, but it's a healthy smell. It's invigorating. It braces the system. I'll tell you—"

"Gid oud with the blabed thig!" exclaimed the major.

" I must tell you all about it first. I called to explain it to you. You see I've been investigating the causes of epidemic diseases. Some scientists think they are spread by molecules in the air ; others attribute them to gases generated in the sewers ; others hold that they are conveyed by contagion ; but I—"

"Aid you goig to tague thad idferdal thig away frob here ?" asked the major.

" But I have discovered that these diseases are spread by the agency of door-mats. Do you understand ? Door-mats ! And I'll explain to you how it's done. Here's a man who's been in a house where there's disease. He gets it on his boots. The leather is porous, and it becomes saturated. He goes to another house and wipes his boots on the mat. Now, every man who uses that mat must get some of the stuff on his boots, and he spreads it over every other door-mat that he wipes them on. Now, don't he ?"

"Why dode you tague thad sbell frob udder by dose ?"

" Well, then, my idea is to construct a door-mat

that will disinfect those boots.   I do it by saturating
the mat with carbolic acid and drying it gradually.
I have one here prepared by my process.   Shall I
unroll it ?"

"If you do, I'll blow your braids out!" shouted
the major.

"Oh, very well, then.   Now, the objection to this
beautiful invention is that it possesses a very strong
and positive odor."

"I'll bed it does," said the major.

"And as this is offensive to many persons, I give

to each purchaser a 'nose-guard,' which is to be
worn upon the nose while in a house where the carbolic mat is placed.   This nose-guard is filled with

a substance which completely neutralizes the smell, and it has only one disadvantage. Now, what is that?"

"Are you goig to quid and led me breathe, or are you goig to stay here all day log?"

"Have patience, now; I'm coming to the point. I say, what is that? It is that the neutralizing substance in the nose-guard evaporates too quickly. And how do I remedy that? I give to every man who buys a mat and a nose-guard two bottles of 'neutralizer.' What it is composed of is a secret. But the bottles are to be carried in the pocket, so as to be ready for every emergency. The disadvantage of this plan consists of the fact that the neutralizer is highly explosive, and if a man should happen to sit down on a bottle of it in his coat-tail pocket suddenly it might hist him through the roof. But see how beautiful my scheme is."

"Oh, thudder add lightnig! aid you ever goig to quid?"

"See how complete it is! By paying twenty dollars additional, every man who takes a mat has his life protected in the Hopelessly Mutual Accident Insurance Company, so that it really makes no great difference whether he is busted through the shingles or not. Now, does it?"

"Oh, dode ask me. I dode care a ced about id, adyway."

"Well, then, what I want you to do is to give me a first-rate notice in your paper, describing the in-

vention, giving the public some general notion of its
merits and recommending its adoption into general
use.   You give me a half-column puff, and I'll make
the thing square by leaving you one of the mats, with
a couple of bottles of the neutralizer and a nose-
guard.   I'll leave them now."

"Whad d'you say?"

"I say I'll just leave you a mat and the other
fixings for you to look over at your leisure."

"You biserable scoundrel, if you lay wod ob those
blasted thigs dowd here, I'll burder you od the spod!
I wod stad such foolishness."   .

"Won't you notice it, either?"

"Certaidly nod.   I woulded do id for ten thousad
dollars a lide."

"Well, then, let it alone; and I hope one of those
epidemic diseases will get you and lay you up for
life."

As Mr. Barker withdrew, Major Slott threw up
the windows, and after catching his breath, he called
down stairs to a reporter,

"Perkins, follow that man and hear what he's got
to say, and then blast him in a column of the awfulest vituperation you know how to write."

Perkins obeyed orders, and now Barker has a libel
suit pending against *The Patriot*, while the carbolic
mat has not yet been introduced to this market.

Mr. Barker was not a more agreeable visitor than
the book-canvasser who, upon the same day, circu-

lated about the village. He came into my office with a portfolio under his arm. Placing it upon the table, removing a ruined hat, and wiping his nose upon a ragged handkerchief that had been so long out of wash that it was positively gloomy, he said,

" Mister, I'm canvassing for the National Portrait Gallery; splendid work; comes in numbers, fifty cents apiece. Contains pictures of all the great American heroes from the earliest times to the present day. Everybody's subscribing for it, and I want to see if I can't take your name.

"Now, just cast your eyes over that," he said, opening his book and pointing to an engraving. "That's—lemme see—yes, that's Columbus. Perhaps you've heard sumfin about him? The publisher was telling me to-day, before I started out, that he discovered— No; was it Columbus that dis— Oh yes! Columbus, he discovered America. Was the first man here. He came over in a ship, the publisher said, and it took fire, and he stayed on deck because his father told him to, if I remember right; and when the old thing busted to pieces, he was killed. Handsome picture, ain't it? Taken from a photograph; all of 'em are; done specially for this work. His clothes are kinder odd, but they say that's the way they dressed in those days.

" Look here at this one. Now, isn't that splendid? William Penn; one of the early settlers. I was reading the other day about him; when he first arrived, he got a lot of Indians up a tree, and when

they'd shook some apples down, he set one on top
of his son's head and shot an arrow plumb through
it, and never fazed him. They say it struck them
Indians cold, he was such a terrific shooter. Fine
countenance, hasn't he? Face shaved clean; he
didn't wear a mustache, I believe, but he seems
to've let himself out on hair. Now, my view is that
every man ought to have a picture of that patriarch,
so's to see how the first settlers looked and what
kind of weskits they used to wear. See his legs,
too! Trousers a little short, maybe, as if he was
going to wade in a creek; but he's all there. Got
some kind of a paper in his hand, I see. Subscrip-
tion list, I reckon.

"Now, how does *that* strike you? There's something nice. That, I think, is—is—that is—a—a—
yes, to be sure, Washington. You recollect him, of
course. Some people call him 'Father of his Country,' George Washington. Had no middle name, I
believe. He lived about two hundred years ago,
and he was a fighter. I heard the publisher telling
a man about him crossing the Delaware River up yer
at Trenton, and seems to me, if I recollect right, I've
read about it myself. He was courting some girl
on the Jersey side, and he used to swim over at
nights to see her, when the old man was asleep.
The girl's family were down on him, I reckon. He
looks like the man to do that, now, don't he? He's
got it in his eye. If it'd been me, I'd a gone over
on the bridge, but he probably wanted to show off

before her; some men are so reckless. Now, if
you'll go in on this thing, I'll get the publisher to
write out some more stories about him, and bring
'em around to you, so's you can study up on him.
I know he did ever so many other things, but I've
forgot 'em; my memory's so thundering poor.

"Less see; who have we next? Ah, Franklin!
Benjamin Franklin. He was one of the old original
pioneers, I think. I disremember exactly what he
is celebrated for, but I believe it was flying a—oh,
yes! flying a kite, that's it. The publisher mentioned it. He was out one day flying a kite, you
know, like boys do nowadays, and while she was
flickering up in the sky, and he was giving her more
string, an apple fell off a tree and hit him on the
head, and then he discovered the attraction of gravitation, I think they call it. Smart, wasn't it? Now,
if you or me'd a been hit, it'd just a made us mad, like
as not, and set us a-cussing. But men are so different. One man's meat's another man's pison. See
what a double chin he's got. No beard on him,
either, though a goatee would have been becoming
to such a round face. He hasn't got on a sword,
and I reckon he was no soldier; fit some when he
was a boy, maybe, or went out with the home-guard,
but not a regular warrior. I ain't one myself, and I
think all the better of him for it.

"Ah, here we are! Look at that! Smith and
Pocahontas! John Smith. Isn't that just gorgeous?
See how she kneels over him and sticks out her

hands while he lays on the ground and that big
fellow with a club tries to hammer him up. Talk
about woman's love! There it is. Modocs, I believe. Anyway, some Indians out West there somewheres; and the publisher tells me that Shacknasty,
or whatever his name is, there, was going to bang old
Smith over the head with that log of wood, and this
girl here, she was sweet on Smith, it appears, and she
broke loose and jumped forward, and says to the
man with the stick, 'Why don't you let John alone?
Me and him are going to marry; and if you kill him,
I'll never speak to you again as long as I live,' or
words like them; and so the man, he give it up, and
both of them hunted up a preacher and were married, and lived happily ever afterward. Beautiful
story, ain't it? A good wife she made him, too, I
bet, if she *was* a little copper-colored. And don't
she look just lovely in that picture? But Smith
appears kinder sick. Evidently thinks his goose is
cooked; and I don't wonder, with that Modoc swoop-
ing down on him with such a discouraging club.

" And now we come to—to—ah—to Putnam—
General Putnam. He fought in the war, too; and
one day a lot of 'em caught him when he was off his
guard, and they tied him flat on his back on a horse,
and then licked the horse like the very mischief.
And what does that horse do but go pitching down
about four hundred stone steps in front of the house,
with General Putnam laying there nearly skeered to
death. Leastways, the publisher said somehow that

way, and I oncet read about it myself. But he came out safe, and I reckon sold the horse and made a pretty good thing of it. What surprises me is he didn't break his neck; but maybe it was a mule, and they're pretty sure-footed, you know. Surprising what some of these men have gone through, ain't it?

"Turn over a couple of leaves. That's General Jackson. My father shook hands with him once. He was a fighter, I know. He fit down in New Orleans. Broke up the rebel legislature, and then, when the Ku-Kluxes got after him, he fought 'em behind cotton breastworks and licked 'em till they could 't stand. They say he was terrific when he got real mad. Hit straight from the shoulder, and fetched his man every time. Andrew his first name was; and look how his hair stands up! And then here's John Adams and Daniel Boone and two or three pirates, and a whole lot more pictures, so you see it's cheap as dirt. Lemme have your name, won't yo'?"

"I believe not to-day."

"What! won't go in on William Penn and Washington and Smith, and the other heroes?"

"No."

"Well, well! Hang me if I'd a-wasted so much information on you if I'd a knowed you wouldn't subscribe. If every man was like you, it'd break up the business."

Then he wiped his nose and left. I hope he is doing better with the work than he did with me.

CHAPTER VII.

HOW MR. BUTTERWICK PURSUED HORTICULTURE.

SOON after he moved out from the city to live in the village Mr. Butterwick determined to secure the services of a good gardener who could be depended upon to produce from the acre surrounding the house the largest possible crop of fruit, vegetables and flowers. A man named Brown was recommended as an expert, and Mr. Butterwick engaged him. As Mr. Butterwick has no acquaintance with the horticultural art, he instructed Brown to use his own judgment in fixing up the place, and Brown said he would.

On the morning of the first day, while Mr. Butterwick was sitting on the front porch, he saw Brown going out of the gate with a gun upon his shoulder, and Mr. Butterwick conceived the idea that the horticultural expert intended to begin his career in his new place by taking a holiday.

In about an hour, however, Brown came sauntering up the street dragging a deceased dog by the tail. Mr. Butterwick asked him if he had accidentally shot his dog while aiming at a rabbit. But Brown simply smiled significantly and passed silently in through the gate.

Then he buried the dog beneath the grape-arbor; and when the funeral was over, Brown loaded up his gun, rubbed his muddy boots upon the grass, brought his weapon to "right shoulder shift" and sallied out again.

Mr. Butterwick asked him if he was going down to the woods after squirrels; but he put his thumb knowingly to his nose, winked at Mr. Butterwick and went mutely down the road. After a while he loomed up again upon the horizon, and this time Mr. Butterwick noticed that he was hauling after him a setter pup and a yellow dog, both dead, and yoked together with one of Brown's suspenders.

Mr. Butterwick failed to comprehend the situation exactly, but he ventured the remark that Brown must be a very poor shot to hit his own dogs every time instead of the game. Brown, however, was not open to criticism. He walked calmly down the yard, and after entombing the dogs by the grape-arbor, he put four fingers of buckshot in his gun, rearranged his suspenders, shouldered arms and struck out for the front gate with a countenance as impassive as that of a graven image.

Mr. Butterwick inquired if there was a target-shooting match over at the "King of Prussia;" but Brown didn't appear to hear him, and passed serene-ly down the street. At half-past eleven Brown came

within hail again, and presently he marched up the yard with three departed cats and a blue poodle.

Mr. Butterwick thought it was extraordinary, and he asked Brown if he was engaged in gunning for domestic animals in order to settle a bet. But Brown only coughed a couple of times, closed one eye sagaciously and began to dig a fresh grave under the arbor. When the last sad rites were over, he charged his gun as usual, rubbed his nose thoughtfully with his sleeve, took a drink at the pump and wandered away.

He had been gone about fifteen minutes, when Mr. Butterwick heard two shots in quick succession. A minute later he saw

Brown coming up the road with a considerable amount of velocity, pursued by Mr. Potts and a three-legged dog. Brown kept ahead; and when he had shot through the gate, he dashed into the house and bolted the door. Then Potts arrived with his dog, which stood by, looking as if it were very anxious to lunch upon somebody, while Potts explained to Butterwick that Brown had shot a leg off of his dog, and that he, Potts, intended to have satisfaction for the injury, if he had to go to law about it.

When Mr. Butterwick had pacified Potts and sent him away, Mr. Butterwick sought an interview with Brown:

"Brown, you have been behaving in a most preposterous manner ever since you came here. I employed you as a gardener, not as a gunner. You have nearly killed a valuable animal belonging to Mr. Potts; and I'll thank you to tell me what you mean, and right off, too."

Brown winked again, cleared his throat, pulled up his shirt-collar and said,

"I was goin' to quit soon as I ketched Potts's dog. He'd a bin splendid to bury out yer with the others. Lemme tell you how it is: The best thing to make grape-vines grow is dogs; bury 'em right down among the roots. Some people prefer grandmothers and their other relations. But gimme dogs and cats. Soon as I seen them vines of yourn I said to myself, Them vines wants a few dogs, and I concluded to put

7

in the first day rakin' in all I could find. I'm goin' out again to-morrow, down the other road."

But he didn't. Mr. Butterwick discharged him that night. He was too enthusiastic for a gardener, and Mr. Butterwick thought that life might open out to him a brighter and more beautiful vista in some other capacity.

Subsequently, Mr. Butterwick concluded to attend to his garden himself, and early in the spring he received from the Congressman of our district a choice lot of assorted seeds brought from California by the Agricultural Department. There were more than he wanted, so he gave a quantity of sugar-beet and onion seeds to Mr. Potts, and some turnip and radish seeds to Colonel Coffin; then he planted the remainder, consisting of turnip, cabbage, celery and beet seeds, in his own garden.

When the plants began to come up, he thought they looked kind of queer, but he waited until they grew larger, and then, as he felt certain something was wrong, he sent for a professional gardener to make an examination.

"Mr. Hoops," he said, "cast your eye over those turnips and tell me what you think is the matter with them."

"Turnip!" exclaimed Hoops. "Turnip! Why, bless your soul, man! that's not turnip. That's nothin' but pokeberry. You've got enough pokeberry in that bed to last a million years."

"Well, Mr. Hoops, come over here to this bed.

Now, how does that celery strike you? The munificent Federal government is spreading that celery all over this land of the free. Great, isn't it?"

"Well, well!" said Hoops; "and they shoved that off on you for celery, did they? Too bad! It's nothin' on earth but pokeberry. This is the California kind—the deadliest pokeberry that was ever invented."

"Are you sure you're not mistaken, Mr. Hoops? But you haven't seen my beets there in the adjoining bed. The seeds of those beets were sent from Honolulu by our consul there. He reports that the variety attains gigantic size."

"Really, now," said Hoops, "I don't want to hurt your feelings, but to be fair and square with you, as between man and man, those are not beets, you know. They are the Mexican pokeberry. I pledge you my word it's the awfulest variety of that plant that grows. It'll stay in this yer garden for ever. You'll never get rid of it."

"This seems a little hard, Mr. Hoops. But I'd like you to inspect my cabbages. They're all right, I know. The commissioner of agriculture got the seed from Borneo. They are the curly variety, I think. You boil them with pork, and they cut down beautifully for slaw. Look at these plants, will you? Ain't they splendid?"

"Mr. Butterwick," said Hoops, "I've got some bad news to break to you, but I hope you'll stand it like a man. These afflictions come to all of us in this life, sir. They are meant for our good. But really, sir, those are not Borneo cabbages. Cabbages! Why, thunder and lightnin'! They are merely a mixture of California and Mexican pokeberry with the ordinary kind, and a little Osage orange sprinkled through. It's awful, sir! Why, you've got about two acres of pokeberry and not a blessed bit of cabbage or turnips among them."

"Mr. Hoops, this is terrible news; and do you know I gave a lot of those seeds to Potts and Coffin?"

"I know you did; and I seen Colonel Coffin this mornin' with a shot-gun goin' round askin' people if they knew where he could find you."

"Find me! What do you mean?"

"Well, you see, sir, that there onion seed that you gave him was really the seed of the silver maple tree, and it's growed up so thick all over his garden that a cat can't crawl through it. There's about forty million shoots and suckers in that garden, and they'll have to be cut out with a handsaw. It'll take about a year to do it."

"You appall me, Hoops!"

"And that's not the worst of it. The roots are so matted and interlocked jes beneath the surface that you can't make any impression on 'em with a pickaxe. That garden of Coffin's is ruined—entirely ruined, sir. You might blast those roots with gunpowder and it would make no difference. And the suckers will grow faster than they're cut down. He'll have to sell the property, sir."

"And the commissioner of agriculture said that was onion seed. Why didn't Coffin hunt *him* with a shot-gun?"

"Yes, sir ; and Mr. Potts's got pokeberry and silver maple growin' all over his place, too, and he's as mad as— Well, you just ought to hear him snortin' around town. He'll kill somebody, I'm afeard."

Mr. Butterwick settled the difficulty with Coffin and Potts somehow, but he made up his mind to vote for another man for Congress at the next election.

Mr. Butterwick was the first man to introduce that ingenious and useful implement the lawn-mower into our section of the country. As his mower was the only one in the village, it was at once in great demand. Everybody wanted to borrow it for a few days, and Butterwick lent it with such generosity that it was out most of the time, and a good many people had to wait for it. At last there was quite a rivalry who should have it next, and the folks used to put in their claims with the owner whenever they had an opportunity.

One day Mr. Smith's wife died, and Mr. Butterwick attended the funeral. Smith was nearly wild with grief. As the remains were put into their last resting-place he cried as if his heart would break, and his friends began to get uneasy about his nervous system. Presently he took his handkerchief from his eyes for a moment to rub his nose, and as he did so he saw Butterwick looking at him. A thought seemed to strike Smith. He dashed away a couple of tears; and stepping over a heap of loose earth as they began to shovel it in, he grasped Butterwick by the hand. Butterwick gave him a sympathetic squeeze, and said,

"Sorry for you, Smith; I am indeed! A noble woman and a good wife. But bear up under it, bear up! Our loss, you know, is her gain."

"Ah! she was indeed a woman in a thousand," responded Smith; "and now to think that she has gone—gone, left us for ever! But these afflictions must not make us forget the duty we owe to the living. She has passed away from toil and suffering, but we still have much to do; and, Butterwick, I want to borrow your lawn-mower. If you can fix it for Tuesday, I think maybe the worst of my anguish will be over."

"You may have it, of course."

"Thank you; oh, thank you! Our friends are a great comfort to us in the hour of bereavement;" and then Smith gave his arm to his mother-in-law, put his handkerchief to his eyes and joined the procession of mourners.

Upon the following Sunday, Rev. Dr. Dox preached a splendid sermon over in the Free church, and just as he reached " secondly " he paused, looked around upon the congregation for a minute, and then he beckoned Deacon Moody to come up to the pulpit. He whispered something in Moody's ear, and Moody seemed surprised. The congregation was wild with curiosity to know what was the matter. Then the deacon, blushing scarlet and seeming annoyed, walked down the aisle and whispered in Butterwick's ear. Butterwick nodded, and whispered to his wife, who was perishing to know what it was. She leaned over and communicated it to Mrs. Bunnel, in the pew in front; and when the Bunnels all had it, they sent it on to the people next to them, and so before the doctor reached "thirdly" the whole congregation knew that he wanted to borrow Butterwick's lawn-mower on Monday morning early.

A day or two later, while Butterwick was crossing the creek upon a train of cars, the train ran off the track and rolled his car into the water. Butterwick got out, however, into the stream, and as he emerged, spluttering and blowing, he struck against a stranger who was treading water. The stranger apologized, and said that Butterwick might not recognize him in his dilapidated condition as Martin Thompson, but while they were together, he would like to put in a word for that lawn-mower when the parson was done with it.

At last Butterwick grew tired of lending, and refused all applicants. Then the people began to steal it, and six respectable citizens only escaped going to jail because Butterwick had consideration for their families. Finally he chained it to the pump, and then

they sawed off the pump and operated the mower
with the log as a roller. Butterwick at last put it on
top of his house, and that night fourteen ladders
were seen against the wall. They did say that Ram-
sey, the lawyer, made one effort with a hot-air balloon, and failed only because he fell out and hurt his
leg ; but this was never traced to any reliable source.

The following week a man arrived and opened an
agency for the sale of the mowers in the village, and
gradually the excitement abated. Butterwick, however, has cut his grass with a sickle ever since.

CHAPTER VIII.

THE MEETING AND ITS MISSIONARY WORK.

HE Methodist church in the village is doing now, as it has always done, a good and noble work for Christianity and the cause of public morals; but it has not escaped the trials which are permitted sometimes to afflict the Church militant. Years ago, when the congregation was first organized, it erected a small but very pretty frame meeting-house. In the course of time the people became dissatisfied with the location of the house of worship; and as they had a good offer for the site, they sold it and bought a better one in another quarter. Then they put rollers under the building, and as soon as it was off the ground the purchaser of the lot began to build a dwelling-house on the site. It was slow work pushing the church along the street, and before they got far somebody discovered that the title of the new site was not good, and so the bargain was annulled. The next day the brethren went plunging around town trying to buy another site, but nobody had one to sell; and on the following morning the supervisors got an order from the court requiring that meeting-house to be removed from the public street within twenty-four hours.

The brethren were nearly wild about it, and they begged old Brindley to let them run the concern in on his vacant lot temporarily until they could look around. But Brindley belonged to another denomination, and he said he felt that it would be wrong for him to do anything to help a church that believed false doctrines. Then they ran the meeting-house out on the turnpike beyond the town, whereupon the turnpike company notified them that its charges would be eight dollars a day for toll. So they hauled it back again; and while going down the hill it broke loose, plunged through the fence of Dr. Mackey's garden and brought up on top of his asparagus-bed. He is an Episcopalian, and he sued the meeting for damages; and the sheriff levied upon the meeting-house. The brethren paid the bill and dragged the building out again.

They wanted to put it in the court-house yard, but Judge Twiddler, who is a Presbyterian, said that after examining the statutes carefully he could find no law allowing a Methodist meeting-house to be located in that place. In despair, the brethren ran the building down to the river-shore and fitted it on a huge raft of logs, concluding to tie it to the wharf until they could buy a lot. But as the owner of the wharf handed them on the third day a bill of twenty-five dollars for wharfage, they took the building out and anchored it in the stream. That night a tug-boat, coming up the river in the dark, ran halfway through the Sunday-school room, and a Dutch brig, coming into collision with it, was drawn out with the pulpit and three of the front pews dangling from the bowsprit. The owners of both vessels sued for damages, and the United States authorities talked of confiscating the meeting-house as an obstruction to navigation. But a few days afterward the ice-gorge sent a flood down the river and broke the building loose from its anchor. It was subsequently washed ashore on Keyser's farm; and he said he was willing to let it stay there at four dollars a day rent until he was ready to plough for corn. As the cost of removing it would have been very great, the trustees ultimately sold it to Keyser for a barn, and then, securing a good lot, they built a handsome edifice of stone.

On the first Sunday that the congregation worshiped in the new church Mr. Potts attended; and in accordance with his custom, he placed his silk high hat just outside of the pew in the aisle. In a few moments Mrs. Jones entered, and as she proceeded up the aisle her abounding skirts caught Mr. Potts' hat and rolled it nearly to the pulpit. Mr. Potts pursued his hat with feelings of indignation; and when Mrs. Jones took her seat, he walked back, brushing the hat with his sleeve. A few moments later Mrs. Hopkins came into church; and as Mr. Potts had again placed his hat in the aisle, Mrs. Hopkins' skirts struck it and swept it along about twenty feet, and left it lying on the carpet in a de-

moralized condition. Mr. Potts was singing a hymn
at the time, and he didn't miss it. But a moment
later, when he looked over the end of the pew to
see if it was safe, he was furious to perceive that it
was gone. He skirmished up the aisle after it again,
red in the face, and uttering sentences which were
very much out of place in the sanctuary. However,
he put the hat down again and determined to keep
his eye on it, but just as he turned his head away for
a moment Mrs. Smiley came in, and Potts looked
around only in time to watch the hat being gathered
in under Mrs. Smiley's skirts and carried away by
them. He started in pursuit, and just as he did so
the hat must have rolled against Mrs. Smiley's ankles,
for she gave a jump and screamed right out in
church. When her husband asked her what was the
matter, she said there must be a dog under her dress,
and she gave her skirts a twist. Out rolled Mr.
Potts' hat, and Mr. Smiley, being very near-sighted,
thought it was a dog, and immediately kicked it so
savagely that it flew up into the gallery and lodged
on top of the organ. Mr. Potts, perfectly frantic with
rage, forgot where he was; and holding his clinched
fist under Smiley's nose, he shrieked, " I've half a
mind to brain you, you scoundrel !" Then he flung
down his hymn-book and rushed from the church.
He went home bareheaded, and the sexton brought
his humiliating hat around after dinner. After that
Mr. Potts expressed a purpose to go habitually to
Quaker meeting, where he could say his prayers with

his hat on his head, and where the skirts of female worshippers are smaller.

Upon a subsequent occasion Mrs. Whistler had even a greater occasion for dissatisfaction with the sanctuary.

The facts in Mrs. Whistler's case were these: Mrs. Whistler has singular absence of mind, and on the last Sunday she attended church Dr. Dox began to read from the Scriptures the account of the Deluge. Mrs. Whistler was deeply attentive; and when the doctor came to the story of how it rained for so many days and nights, she was so much absorbed in the narrative and so strongly impressed with it that she involuntarily put up her umbrella and held it over her head as she sat in the pew. It appears that Mrs. Moody, who sits in the next pew in front, frequently brings her lap-dog to church with her; and when Mrs. Whistler raised her umbrella suddenly, the action affected the sensibilities of Mrs. Moody's dog in such a manner that he began to bark furiously.

Of course the sexton came in for the purpose of removing the animal, but it dodged into a vacant pew upon the other side of the aisle and defied him, barking vociferously all the time. Then the sexton became warm and indignant, and he flung a cane at the dog, whereupon the dog flew out and bit his leg. The excitement in the church by this time, of course, was simply dreadful. Not only was

the story of the Deluge interrupted, but the unre-
generate Sunday-school scholars in the gallery actually hissed the dog at the sexton, and seemed to
enjoy the contest exceedingly.

Then Elder McGinn came after the dog with his
cane, and as he pursued the animal it dashed toward
the pulpit and ran up the steps in such a fierce manner that the doctor quickly mounted a chair and
remarked, with anger flashing through his spectacles,
that if this disgraceful scene did not soon come to an
end he should dismiss the congregation. Then the
elder crept softly up the stairs, and after a short
struggle he succeeded in grasping the dog by one
of its hind legs. Then he walked down the aisle
with it, the dog meantime yelling with supernatural
energy and the Sunday-school boys making facetious
remarks.

Mrs. Whistler turned around, with other members
of the congregation, to watch the retreating elder,
and as she did so she permitted her unconscious
umbrella to droop so that the end of one of the ribs
caught Mrs. Moody's bonnet. A moment later,
when she was straightening up the umbrella, the
bonnet was wrenched off, and hung dangling from
the umbrella. Mrs. Moody had become exceedingly
warm, at any rate, over the onslaught made upon
her dog, but when Mrs. Whistler removed her bonnet, she fairly boiled over; and turning around, white
with rage, she screamed,

"What'd you grab that bonnet for, you wretch!

Haven't you made enough fuss in this church to-day, skeering a poor innocent dog, without snatching off such bonnets as the like of you can't afford to wear, no matter how mean you live at home, you red-headed lunatic, you! You let my bonnet alone, or I'll hit you with this parasol, if it is in meeting, now mind me!"

Then Mrs. Whistler, for the first time, seemed to realize that her umbrella made her conspicuous; so she furled it and concluded to escape from an embarrassing position by going home. As she stepped into the aisle her enemy gave her a parting salute:

"Sneaking off before the collection, too! You'd better spend less for breastpins and give more to the poor heathen if you don't want to ketch it hereafter!"

Then she began to fan herself furiously, and as Mrs. Whistler emerged from the front door and things became calmer the doctor resumed the story of the Flood. But Mrs. Whistler has given up her pew and gone over to the Presbyterians, and there are rumors that Mrs. Moody is going to secede also because Elder McGinn insists that she shall leave her dog at home.

The Dorcas and missionary societies of the church are particularly active, but they were somewhat discouraged a year or two ago by certain unforeseen occurrences. The ladies of the Dorcas Society

made up a large quantity of shirts, trousers and
socks, and boxed them up and sent them to a missionary station on the west coast of Africa.   A man
named Ridley went out with the boxes and stayed
in Africa for several months.   When he returned, the
Dorcas Society, of course, was anxious to hear how
its donation was received, and Ridley one evening
met the members and told them about it in a little
speech.   He said,

"Well, you know, we got the clothes out there all
right, and after a while we distributed them among
some of the natives in the neighborhood.   We
thought maybe it would attract them to the mission, but it didn't; and after some time had elapsed
and not a native came to church with the clothes on,
I went out on an exploring expedition to find out
about it.   It seems that on the first day after the
goods were distributed one of the chiefs attempted
to dress himself in a shirt.   He didn't exactly understand it, and he pushed his legs through the
arms and gathered the tail up around his waist.   He
couldn't make it stay up, however, and they say he
went around inquiring in his native tongue what
kind of an idiot it was that constructed a garment
that wouldn't hang on, and swearing some of the
most awful heathen oaths.   At last he let it drag,
and that night he got his legs tangled in it somehow
and fell over a precipice and was killed.

"Another chief who got one on properly went
paddling around in the dark, and the people, imagin-

ing that he was a ghost, sacrificed four babies to keep off the evil spirit.

"And then, you know, those trousers you sent out? Well, they fitted one pair on an idol, and then they stuffed most of the rest with leaves and set them up as kind of new-fangled idols and began to worship them. They say that the services were very impressive. Some of the women split a few pairs in half, and after sewing up the legs used them to carry yams in; and I saw one chief with a corduroy leg on his head as a kind of helmet.

"I think, though, the socks were most popular. All the fighting-men went for them the first thing. They filled them with sand and used them as boomerangs and war-clubs. I learned that they were so

8

much pleased with the efficiency of those socks that they made a raid on a neighboring tribe on purpose to try them; and they say they knocked about eighty women and children on the head before they came home. They asked me if I wouldn't speak to you and get you to send out a few barrels more, and to make them a little stronger, so's they'd last longer; and I said I would.

"This society's doing a power of good to those heathen, and I've no doubt if you keep right along with the work you will inaugurate a general war all over the continent of Africa and give everybody an idol of his own. All they want is enough socks and trousers. I'll take them when I go out again."

Then the Dorcas passed a resolution declaring that it would, perhaps, be better to let the heathen go naked and give the clothes to the poor at home. Maybe that is the better way.

CHAPTER IX.

JUDGE TWIDDLER'S COW.

OR several months previous to last summer Judge Twiddler's family obtained milk from Mr. Biles, the most prominent milk-dealer in the village. The prevailing impression among the Twiddlers was that Mr. Biles supplied an exceedingly thin and watery fluid; and one day when the judge stepped over to pay his quarterly bill he determined to make complaint. He found Mr. Biles in the yard mending the valve of his pump; and when the judge made a jocular remark to the effect that the dairy must be in a bad way when the pump was out of order, Mr. Biles, rising with his hammer in his hand, said,

"Oh, I ain't going to deny that we water the milk. I don't mind the joking about it. But all I say is that when people say we do it from mercenary motives they slander the profession. No, sir; when I put water in the milk, I do it out of kindness for the people who drink it. I do it because I'm philanthropic—because I'm sensitive and can't bear to see folks suffer. Now, s'pos'n a cow is bilious or something, and it makes her milk unwholesome. I give it a dash or two of water, and up it comes to the usual level. Water's the only thing that'll do it. Or s'pos'n that cow eats a pison vine in the woods; am I going to let my innocent customers be killed by it for the sake of saving a little labor at the pump? No, sir; I slush in a few quarts of water, neutralize the pison, and there she is as right as a trivet.

"But you take the best milk that ever was, and it ain't fit for the human stomach as it comes from the cow. It has too much caseine in it. Prof. Huxley says that millions of poor ignorant men and women are murdered every year by loading down weak stomachs with caseine. It sucks up the gastric juice, he says, and gets daubed all around over the membranes until the pores are choked, and then the first thing you know the man suddenly curls all up and dies. He says that out yer in Asia, where the milkmen are not as conscientious as we are, there are whole cemeteries chock full of people that have died of caseine, and that before long all that country will be one vast burying-ground if they don't ameliorate the milk. When I think of the responsibility resting on me, is it singular that I look at this old pump and wonder that people don't come and silver plate it and put my statue on it? I tell you, sir, that that humble pump with the cast-iron handle is the only thing that stands betwixt you and sudden death.

"And besides that, you know how kinder flat raw milk tastes—kinder insipid and mean. Now, Prof. Huxley, he says that there is only one thing that will vivify milk and make it luxurious to the palate, and that is water. Give it a few jerks under the pump, and out it comes sparkling and delicious, like nectar. I dunno how it is, but Prof. Huxley says that it undergoes some kinder chemical change that nothing else'll bring about but a flavoring of fine old pump-water. You know the doctors all water the milk for babies. They know mighty well if they didn't those young ones'd shrink all up and sorter fade away. Nature is the best judge. What makes cows drink so much water? Instinct, sir—instinct. Something whispers to 'em that if they don't sluice in a little water that caseine'd make 'em giddy and eat 'em up. Now, what's the odds whether I put in the water or the cow does? She's only a poor brute beast, and might often drink too little; but when I go at it, I bring the mighty human intellect to bear on the subject; I am guided by reason, and I can water that milk so's it'll have the greatest possible effect.

"Now, there's chalk. I know some people have an idea that it's wrong to fix up your milk with chalk. But that's only mere blind bigotry. What is chalk? A substance provided by beneficent nature for healing the ills of the human body. A cow don't eat chalk because it's not needed by her. Poor uneducated animal! she can't grasp these higher problems, and she goes on nibbling sour-grass and other things, and filling her milk with acid, which destroys human membranes and induces colic. Then science comes to the rescue. Professor Huxley tells us that chalk cures acidity. Consequently, I get some chalk, stir it in my cans and save the membranes of my customers without charging them a cent for it—actually give it away; and yet they talk about us milkmen 'sif we were buccaneers and enemies of the race.

" But I don't care. My conscience is clear. I know mighty well that I have a high and holy mission to perform, and I'm going to perform it if they burn me at the stake. What do I care how much this pump costs me if it spreads blessings through the community? What difference does it make to a man of honor like me if chalk is six cents a pound so long as I know that without it there wouldn't be a membrane in this community? Now, look at the thing in the right light, and you'll believe me that before another century rolls around a grateful universe will worship the memory of the first milkman who ever had a pump and who doctored his milk with chalk. It will, unless justice is never to have her own."

Then Mr. Biles rigged the sucker in the pump, toned up a few cans of milk, corrected the acidity, and went into the house to receipt the judge's bill.

Mr. Biles' theory interested the judge, but the

argument did not convince him. And so the judge resolved to buy a cow and obtain pure milk, without regard for the alleged views of Professor Huxley. Accordingly, he purchased a cow of a man named Smith, who lives over at the Rising Sun. She was warranted to be fresh and a first-rate milker. When Judge Twiddler got her home, he asked his hired man, Mooney, if he knew how to milk a cow, and Mooney said of course he did. The animal, therefore, was consigned to Mooney's care. On the next day, however, Mooney came into the house to see the judge, and he said,

"Judge, that man cheated you in that cow. Why, she's the awfullest old beast that ever stood on four legs. Dry as punk; hasn't got a drop of milk in her. That's a positive fact. I've been trying to milk her for three or four hours, and can't get a drop. Might as well attempt to milk a clothes-horse. Regular fraud!"

"This is very extraordinary," exclaimed the judge.

"Yes, sir; and she's wicked. I never saw such a disposition in a cow. Why, while I was working with her she kicked like a flint-lock musket; butted and rared around. I'd rather fool with a tiger than with a cow like that."

So the judge drove over to the Rising Sun to see Smith about it; and when he complained that Smith had sold him a worthless and vicious beast, and a dry cow at that, Smith said there must be some mis-

take about it.   He agreed to go back with the judge
and investigate the matter.   When they reached the
judge's stable, Mooney was not about, but Smith
descended from the wagon, approached the cow,
and, to the astonishment of the judge, milked her
without the slightest difficulty, the cow meantime
remaining perfectly quiet, and even breaking out now
and then into what the judge thought looked like
smiles of satisfaction.   And then the judge went out
to hunt up his hired man.   He said to him,

"Mooney, what did you mean by telling me that
our cow was dry and ugly?   You said you couldn't
milk her, but Mr. Smith does so without any difficulty, and the cow remains perfectly passive."

"I'd like to see him do it," said Mooney, incredu-
lously.

Then Smith sat down and proceeded to perform
the operation again.   When he began, Mooney exclaimed,

"Why, my gracious! that isn't the way you milk
a cow, is it?"

"Of course it is," replied Smith.   "How else
would you do it?"

"Well, well! and that's the way *you* milk, is it?
I see now I didn't go about it exactly right.   Why,
you know, I never had much experience at the business; I was brought up in town, and, be George,
when I tackled her, I threw her over on her back
and tried to milk her with a clothes-pin.   I see
now I was wrong.   We live and learn, don't we?"

So Smith went home, and the cow remained, and the judge's man waxes stronger in experience with the mysteries of existence daily.

But the cow was not a perfect animal, after all. Among other things, Smith assured the judge that she had a splendid appetite. He said that she was the easiest cow with her feed that he ever saw; she would eat almost anything, and she was generally hungry.

At the end of the first week after she came, Mrs. Twiddler concluded to churn. The hired man spent the whole day at the crank, and about sunset the butter came. They got it out, and found that there was almost half a pound. Then Mrs. Twiddler began to see how economical it was to make her own butter. A half pound at the store cost thirty cents. The wages of that man for one day were one dollar, and so the butter was costing about three dollars a pound, without counting the keep of the cow. When they tried the butter, it was so poor that they couldn't eat it, and they gave it to the man to grease the wheelbarrow with. It seemed somewhat luxurious and princely to maintain a cow for the purpose of supplying grease at three dollars a pound for the wheelbarrow, but it was hard to see precisely where the profits came in. After about a fortnight the cow seemed so unhappy in the stable that the judge turned her out in the yard.

The first night she was loose she upset the grape-arbor with her horns and ate four young peach trees and a dwarf pear tree down to the roots. The next day they gave her as much hay as she would eat, and it seemed likely that her appetite was appeased. But an hour or two afterward she swallowed six croquet-balls that were lying upon the grass, and ate half a table-cloth and a pair of drawers from the clothes-line. That evening her milk seemed thin, and the judge attributed it to the indigestibility of the table-cloth.

During the night she must have got to walking in her sleep, for she climbed over the fence; and when she was discovered, she was swallowing one of Mrs. Twiddler's hoopskirts. That evening she ran dry and didn't give any milk at all. The judge thought the exercise she had taken must have been too severe, and probably the hoopskirt was not sufficiently nutritious. It was comforting, however, to reflect that she was less expensive, from the latter point of view, when she was dry than when she was fresh. Next morning she ate the spout off the watering-pot, and then put her head in the kitchen window and devoured two dinner-plates and the cream-jug. Then she went out and lay down on the strawberry-bed to think. While there something about Judge Twiddler's boy seemed to exasperate her; and when he came over into the yard after his ball, she inserted her horns into his trowsers and flung him across the fence. Then she went to the stable and ate a litter of pups and three feet of the trace-chain.

The judge felt certain that her former owner didn't deceive him when he said her appetite was good. She had hunger enough for a drove of cattle and a couple of flocks of sheep. That day the judge went after the butcher to get him to buy her. When he returned with him, she had just eaten the monkey-wrench and the screw-driver, and she was trying to put away a fence-paling. The butcher said she was a fair-enough sort of cow, but she was too thin. He said he would buy her if the judge would feed her up and fatten her; and the judge said he would try. He gave her that night food enough for four cows, and she consumed it as if she had been upon half rations for a month. When she finished, she got up, reached for the hired man's straw hat, ate it, and then, bolting out into the garden, she put away the honeysuckle vine and a coil of India-rubber hose. The man said that if it was his cow he would kill her; and the judge told him that he had perhaps better just knock her on the head in the morning.

During the night she had another attack of somnambulism, and while wandering about she ate the door-mat from the front porch, bit off all the fancywork on top of the cast-iron gate, swallowed six loose bricks that were piled up against the house, and then had a fit among the rose bushes. When the judge came down in the morning, she seemed to be breathing her last, but she had strength enough left to seize a newspaper that the judge held in his hand; and when that was down, she gave three or four kicks and rolled over and expired. It cost the judge three dollars to have the carcase removed. Since then he has bought his butter and milk and given up all kinds of live-stock.

CHAPTER X.

OUR CIVIL SERVICE.

SOME of the public officers of Millburg are interesting in their way. The civil service system of the village is based upon the principle that if there is any particular function that a given man is wholly unfitted to perform he should be chosen to perform it. The result is that the business of our very small government goes plunging along in the most surprising manner, with a promise that it will end some day in chaos and revolution—of course upon a diminutive scale.

A representative man is Mr. Bones, the solitary night-watchman of the town. One of the duties of Mr. Bones is to light the street-lamps. It is an operation which does not require any very extraordinary effort of the intellect; but during a part of the summer the mind of Mr. Bones did not seem to be equal to the strain placed upon it by this duty. It was observed that whenever there were bright moonlight nights Mr. Bones would have all the lamps burning from early in the evening until dawn, while upon the nights when there was no moon he would not light them at all, and the streets would be as dark as tar.　At last people began to complain about it, and one day one of the supervisors called to see Mr. Bones about it.　He remarked to him,

"Mr. Bones, people are finding fault because you light up on moonlight nights and don't light the lamps when it is dark.　I'd like you to manage the thing a little better."

"It struck me as being singular, too, but I can't help it.　I've got instructions to follow the almanac, and I'm going to follow it."

"Did the almanac say there'd be no moon last night?"

"Yes, it did."

"Well, the moon was shining, though, and at its full."

"I know," said Mr. Bones, "and that's what gits me.　How in the thunder the moon kin shine when the almanac says it won't beats me out.　Perhaps there's something the matter with the moon; got shoved off her course may be."

"I guess not."

"Well, it's changed off somehow, and I've got to have something regular to go by.　I'm going by what the almanac says; and if the moon's going to shuffle around kinder loose and not foller the almanac, that's its lookout.　If the almanac says no moon, then I'm bound to light the lamps if there's millions of moons shining in the sky.　Them's my orders, and I'll mind 'em."

"How d'you know the almanac is not wrong?"

" Because I know it ain't. It was always right before."

" Let's look at it."

" There it is. Look there, now. Don't it say full moon on the 20th ? and this yer's only the 9th, and yet it's full moon now."

" That's so ; and— Er—er— Less— see Er-er— Mr. Bones, do you know what year this almanac is for ?"

" Why, 1876, of course."

" No, it isn't; it's for 1866. It's ten years old."

" Oh no ! 1866 ! Well, now, it is. I declare ! 1866 ! Why, merciful Moses ! I got the wrong one off the shelf, and I've been depending on it for three months ! No wonder the lamps was wrong. Well, that beats everything."

Then Mr. Bones tore up the almanac and got one for 1876, and ever since that time the lamp-lighting department has given tolerable satisfaction.

But it is as a night-watchman that Mr. Bones shines with surpassing splendor. When he first entered the service, he was very anxious to make a good impression on Colonel Coffin, the burgess and head of the village government; and the first night upon which he went on duty Colonel Coffin was awakened about half-past twelve by a furious ring at his door-bell. He looked out of the window and perceived the watchman, who said,

" She's all right. Nobody's broke in. I've got my eye on things. You kin depend on me."

The colonel thought he was one of the most faithful watchmen he ever saw, and he returned serenely to bed. On the following night, just after twelve, there was another energetic ring at the bell; and when the burgess raised the window, the watchman said,

"Your girls ain't left the window-shutters open and the house is not afire. All right as a trivet while I'm around, you bet!"

"Louisa," said the colonel to his wife as he returned to his couch, "that is a splendid watchman, but I think he's just the least bit too enthusiastic."

A couple of nights later, when the door-bell rang at half-past one, the colonel felt somewhat angry, and he determined to stay in bed; but the person on the step below at last began to kick against the front door, when the colonel threw up the window and exclaimed,

"What do you want?"

It was the watchman, and he said,

"You know old Mrs. Biles up the street yer? Well, I've just rung Biles up, and he says her rheumatism ain't no better. Thought you might want to know, so I called. I felt kinder lonesome out here, too."

As Colonel Coffin slammed the sash down he felt mad and murderous. The next night, however, that faithful guardian applied the toe of his boot to the front door with such energy that the colonel leaped from bed, and protruding his head from the window said,

"I wish to *gracious* you'd stop kicking up this kind of fuss around here every night! What do you mean, anyhow?"

"Why, I only stopped to tell you that Butterwick has two setter pups, and that I'd get you one if you wanted it. Nothing mean about that, is there?"

The colonel uttered an ejaculatory criticism upon Butterwick and the pups as he closed the window, and a moment later he heard the watchman call up Smith, who lives next door, and remark to him,

"They tell me it's a splendid season for bananas, Mr. Smith."

When Coffin heard Smith hurling objurgations about bananas and watchmen out upon the midnight air, he knew it was immoral, but he felt his heart warm toward Smith. The next time the watchman tried to get the colonel out by ringing and kicking the colonel refused to respond, and finally the watchman banged five barrels of his revolver. Then Coffin came to the window in a rage.

"You eternal idiot," he said, "if you don't stop this racket at night, I'll have you put under bonds to keep the peace."

"Oh, all right," replied the watchman. "I had something important to tell you; but if you don't want to hear it, very well; I kin keep it to myself."

"Well, what is it? Out with it!"

"Why, I heard to-day that the kangaroo down at the Park in the city can't use one of its hind legs. Rough on the Centennial, ain't it?"

9

Then, as the colonel withdrew in a condition of awful rage, the watchman sauntered up the street to break the news to the rest of the folks.   On the next night a gang of burglars broke into Coffin's house and ransacked it from top to bottom.   Toward morning Coffin heard them; and hastily dressing himself and seizing his revolver, he proceeded down stairs.   The burglars heard him coming and fled.   Then the colonel sprang his rattle and summoned the neighbors.   When they arrived, the colonel, in the course of conversation, made some remarks about the perfect uselessness of night-watchmen.   Thereupon Mr. Potts said,

"I saw that fellow Bones only an hour ago two squares above here, at McGinnis's, routing McGinnis out to tell him that old cheese makes the best bait for catfish."

Mr. Bones was reprimanded, but he remained upon what is facetiously known as "the force."   The borough cannot afford to dispense with the services of such an original genius as he.

Our sheriff is a man of rather higher intelligence, but he also has a singular capacity for perpetrating dreadful blunders.   Over in the town of Nockamixon one of the churches last year called a clergyman named Rev. Joseph Striker.   In the same place, by a most unfortunate coincidence, resides also a prize-fighter named Joseph Striker, and rumors were afloat a few weeks ago that the latter Joseph was about to engage in a contest with a Jer-

sey pugilist for the championship. Our sheriff considered it his duty to warn Joseph against the proposed infraction of the laws, and so he determined
to call upon the professor of the art of self-defence.
Unhappily, in inquiring the way to the pugilist's
house, somebody misunderstood the sheriff, and sent
him to the residence of the Rev. Joseph Striker, of
whom he had never heard. When Mr. Striker entered the room in answer to the summons, the sheriff
said to him familiarly,

"Hello, Joe! How are you?"

Mr. Striker was amazed at this address, but he
politely said,

"Good-morning."

"Joe," said the sheriff, throwing his leg lazily over
the arm of the chair, "I came round here to see you
about that mill with Harry Dingus that they're all
talking about. I want you to understand that it
can't come off anywheres around here. You know
well enough it's against the law, and I ain't a-going
to have it."

"Mill! Mill, sir? What on earth do you mean?"
asked Mr. Striker, in astonishment. "I do not own
any mill, sir. Against the law! I do not understand you, sir."

"Now, see here, Joe," said the sheriff, biting off a
piece of tobacco and looking very wise, "that won't
go down with me. It's pretty thin, you know. I
know well enough that you've put up a thousand
dollars on that little affair, and that you've got the

whole thing fixed, with Bill Martin for referee. I
know you're going down to Pea Patch Island to have
it out, and I'm not going to allow it. I'll arrest you
as sure as a gun if you try it on, now mind me!"

"Really, sir," said Mr. Striker, "there must be
some mistake about—"

"Oh no, there isn't; your name's Joe Striker, isn't
it?" asked the sheriff.

"My name is Joseph Striker, certainly."

"I knew it," said the sheriff, spitting on the carpet; "and you see I've got this thing dead to rights.
It sha'n't come off; and I'm doing you a favor in
blocking the game, because Harry'd curl you all up
any way if I let you meet him. I know he's the best
man, and you'd just lose your money and get all
bunged up besides; so you take my advice now, and
quit. You'll be sorry if you don't."

"I do not know what you are referring to," said
Mr. Striker. "Your remarks are incomprehensible
to me, but your tone is very offensive; and if you
have any business with me, I'd thank you to state it
at once."

"Joe," said the sheriff, looking at him with a be-
nign smile, "you play it pretty well. Anybody'd
think you were innocent as a lamb. But it won't
work, Joseph—it won't work, I tell you. I've got
a duty to perform, and I'm going to do it; and I
pledge you my word, if you and Dingus don't knock
off now, I'll arrest you and send you up for ten years
as sure as death. I'm in earnest about it."

"What do you mean, sir?" asked Mr. Striker, fiercely.

"Oh, don't you go to putting on any airs about it. Don't you try any strutting before me," said the sheriff, "or I'll put you under bail this very afternoon. Let's see: how long were you in jail the last time? Two years, wasn't it? Well, you go fighting with Dingus and you'll get ten years sure."

"You are certainly crazy!" exclaimed Mr. Striker.

"I don't see what you want to stay at that business for, anyhow," said the sheriff. "Here you are, in a snug home, where you might live in peace and keep respectable. But no, you must associate with low characters, and go to stripping yourself naked and jumping into a ring to get your nose blooded and your head swelled and your body hammered to a jelly; and all for what? Why, for a championship! It's ridiculous. What good'll it do you if you're champion? Why don't you try to be honest and decent, and let prize-fighting alone?"

"This is the most extraordinary conversation I ever listened to," said Mr. Striker. "You evidently take me for a—"

"I take you for Joe Striker; and if you keep on, I'll take you to jail," said the sheriff, with emphasis. "Now, you tell me who's got those stakes and who's your trainer, and I'll put an end to the whole thing."

"You seem to imagine that I am a pugilist," said Mr. Striker. "Let me inform you, sir, that I am a clergyman."

"Joe," said the sheriff, shaking his head, "it's too bad for you to lie that way—too bad, indeed."

"But I *am* a clergyman, sir—pastor of the church of St. Sepulchre. Look! here is a letter in my pocket addressed to me."

"You don't really mean to say that you're a preacher named Joseph Striker?" exclaimed the sheriff, looking scared.

"Certainly I am. Come up stairs and I'll show you a barrelful of my sermons."

"Well, if this don't beat Nebuchadnezzar!" said the sheriff. "This is awful! Why, I mistook you for Joe Striker, the prize-fighter! I don't know how I ever— A preacher! What an ass I've made of myself! I don't know how to apologize; but if you want to kick me down the front steps, just kick away; I'll bear it like an angel."

Then the sheriff withdrew unkicked, and Mr. Striker went up stairs to finish his Sunday sermon. The sheriff talked of resigning, but he continues to hold on.

Mr. Slingsby, our assessor and tax-collector, holds on too. He is another model member of our civil service. The principal characteristic of Mr. Slingsby is enthusiasm. He has an idea that whenever a man gets anything new it ought to be taxed, and he is always on hand to perform the service. I had about fifteen feet added to one of my chimneys last spring; and when it was done, Slingsby called and assessed

it, under the head of "improved real estate," at
eighty dollars, and collected two per cent. on it. A
few days later, while I was standing by the fence,
Slingsby came up and said,

"Beautiful dog you have there."

"Yes; it's a setter."

"Indeed! A setter, hey? The tax on setters is
two dollars. I'll collect it now, while I have it on
my mind."

I settled the obligation, and the next day Slingsby
came around again. He opened the conversation
with the remark,

"Billy Jones told me down at the grocery-store
that your terrier had had pups."

"Yes."

"A large litter?"

"Four."

"Indeed! Less see: tax is two dollars; four
times two is eight—yes, eight dollars tax, please.
And hurry up, too, if you can, for they have a new
batch of kittens over at Baldwin's, and I want to
ketch old Baldwin before he goes out. By the way,
when did you put that weathercock on your stable?"

"Yesterday."

"You don't say! Well, hold on, then. Four
times two is eight, and four—on the weathercock,
you know—is twelve. Twelve dollars is the exact
amount."

"What do you mean by four dollars tax on a
weathercock? I never heard of such a thing."

"Didn't, hey? Why, she comes in under the head of 'scientific apparatus.' She's put up there to tell which way the wind blows, ain't she? Well, that's scientific intelligence, and the apparatus is liable to tax."

"Mr. Slingsby, that is the most absurd thing I ever heard of. You might just as well talk of taxing Butterwick's twins."

"Butter— You don't mean to say Butterwick has twins? Why, certainly they're taxable. They come in under the head of 'poll-tax.' Three dollars apiece. I'll go right down there. Glad you mentioned it." Then I paid him, and he left with Butterwick's twins on his memorandum-book.

A day or two afterward Mr. Slingsby called to see me, and he said,

"I've got a case that bothers me like thunder. You know Hough the tobacconist? Well, he's just bought a new wooden Indian to stand in front of his store. Now, I have a strong feeling that I ought to tax that figure, but I don't know where to place it. Would it come in as 'statuary'? Somehow that don't seem exactly the thing. I was going to assess it under the head of 'idols,' but the idiots who got up this law haven't got a word in in reference to idols. Think of that, will you? Why, we might have paganism raging all over this country, and we couldn't get a cent out of them. I'd a put that Indian under 'graven images,' only they ain't mentioned, either. I s'pose I could tax the bundle of wooden cigars in his fist as 'tobacco,' but that leaves out the rest of the figure; and he's not liable to poll-tax because he can't even vote. Now, how would it strike you if I levied on him as an 'immigrant'? He was made somewheres else than here, and he came here from there, consequently he's an immigrant. That's my view. What do you think of it?"

I advised him to try it upon that plan, and the next morning Mr. Slingsby and Mr. Hough had a fight on the pavement in front of the Indian because Mr. Slingsby tried to seize the immigrant for unpaid taxes. Slingsby was taken home and put to bed, and the business of collecting taxes was temporarily suspended. But Slingsby will be around again soon with some new and ingenious ideas that he has thought of during his illness.

CHAPTER XI.

FUNEREAL AND CONJUGAL.

MRS. BANGER has buried four husbands, and her experience of domestic life in their company was so satisfactory that she recently married a fifth, Mr. Banger. The name of her fourth was McFadden. The name of her first and third was Smyth, while that of her second, oddly enough, was Smith. Soon after her return from her last wedding-tour she was visited by Mr. Toombs, the undertaker, who called ostensibly to correct an error in his last bill. When Mrs. Banger entered the parlor, Mr. Toombs greeted her cordially and said,

"Ah! Mrs. Smy—Banger, I mean; I hope I see you well? Did you have a pleasant trip? Nice weather while you were away; a little backward, maybe, but still comfortable, and likely to make things grow. Cemetery looks beautiful now. I was out there to-day to a burying. Grass is coming up charming on your lot, and I noticed a blackberry bush growing out of Mr. Smyth's grave. He was

138

fond of 'em, I reckon. There they were lying, Smith and Smyth, and McFadden and the other Smyth, all four of them. No woman could have done fairer with those men than you did, ma'am; those mahogany coffins with silver-plated handles were good enough for the patriarchs and prophets, and the President of the United States himself daren't ask anything better than a hearse with real ostrich feathers and horses that are black as ink all over.

"I know when we laid Mr. McFadden out I said to Tim Lafferty, my foreman, that the affection you showed in having that man buried in style almost made me cry; but I never fully realized what woman's love really is till you made me line Mr. Smith's coffin with white satin and let in a French plate-glass skylight over the countenance. That worked on my feelings so that I pretty near forgot to distribute the gloves to the mourners. And Mr. Smith was worthy of it; he deserved it all. He was a man all over, no difference how you looked at him; stoutish, maybe, and took a casket that was thick through, but he was all there, and I know when you lost him it worried you like anything.

"Now, it's none of my business, Mrs. Banger; but casting my eye over those graves to-day, it struck me that I might fix 'em up a little, so's they'd be more comfortable like. I think McFadden wants a few sods over the feet, and Smith's headstone has worked a little out of plumb. He's settled some,

I s'pose. I think I'd straighten it up and put a gas-
pipe railing around Mr. Smyth. And while you're
about it, Mrs. Banger, hadn't you better buy about
ten feet beyond Mr. Smith, so's there won't be any
scrouging when you bury the next one? I like
elbow-room in a cemetery lot, and I pledge you my
word it'll be a tight squeeze to get another one in
there and leave room for you besides. It can't be
done so's to look anyways right, and I know you
don't want to take all four of 'em out and make 'em
move up, so's to let the rest of you in. Of course
it'd cut you up, and it'd cost like everything, too.

"When a person's dead and buried, it's the fair
thing to let him alone, and not to go hustling him
around. That's my view, any way; and I say that if
I was you, sooner than put Mr. Smith on top of Mc-
Fadden and Smyth on top of Smith, I'd buy in the
whole reservation and lay 'em forty feet apart.

"And how *is* Mr. Banger? Seem in pretty good
health? Do you think we are to have him with us
long? I hope so; but there's consumption in his
family, I believe. Life is mighty uncertain. We
don't know what minute we may be called. I'm a
forehanded kind of man, and while his wedding-suit
was being made I just stepped into the tailor's and
ran it over with a tape-measure, so's to get some idea
of his size. You'd hardly believe it, but I've got a
black walnut casket at the shop that'll fit him as
exact as if it had been built for him. It was the
luckiest thing. An odd size, too, and wider than we

generally make them. I laid it away up stairs for him, to be prepared in case of accident. You've been so clever with me that I feel 'sif I ought to try my best to accommodate you; and I know how women hate to bother about such things when their grief is tearing up their feelings and they are fretting about getting their mourning clothes in time for the funeral.

"And that's partly what I called to see you about, Mrs. McFa—Banger, I mean. I've got a note to pay in the morning, and the man's pushing me very hard; but I'm cleaned right out. Haven't got a cent. Now, it occurred to me that maybe you'd advance me the money on Mr. Banger's funeral if I'd offer you liberal terms. How does fifteen per cent. strike you? and if he lives for six or seven years, I'll make it twenty. Mind you, I offer the casket and the best trimmings, eight carriages, the finest hearse in the county, and ice enough for three days in the swelteringest weather in August. And I don't mind—well—yes, I'll even agree to throw in a plain tombstone. If you can do that to accommodate a friend, why, I'll— No? Don't want to speculate on it? Oh, very well; I'm sorry, because I know you'd been satisfied with the way I'd have arranged things. But no matter; I s'pose I can go round and borrow elsewhere. Good-morning; drop in some time, and I'll show you that casket."

As Toombs was going out he met Mr. Banger at the door. When he was gone, Banger said,

"My dear, who is that very odd-looking man?"

And Mrs. Banger hesitated a moment, turned very red, and answered,

"That is—that man is—a—a—he is, I believe—a —a—a—a some kind of a—an undertaker."

Then Banger looked gloomy and went up stairs to ponder. But Mrs. Banger felt that she had a duty to perform in taking care that the lot in the cemetery should not fall into such disorder as Mr. Toombs had indicated, and she resolved to call upon Mr. Mix, at his monumental marble-works, to get him to attend to the matter for her. Mr. Mix did not know her, and his ignorance of her past history turned out to be unfortunate. The following conversation occurred between them:

Mrs. Banger. "Mr. Mix, I am anxious to have my cemetery lot fixed up—to put in new tombstones and reset the railing; and I called to see if I could make some satisfactory arrangement with you."

Mix. "Certainly, madam. Tell me precisely what it is you want done."

Mrs. B. "Well, I'd like to have a new tombstone put over the grave of John—my husband, you know—and to have a nice inscription cut in it, 'Here lies John Smyth,' etc., etc. You know what I mean; the usual way, of course, and maybe some kind of a design on the stone like a broken rosebud or something."

Mix. "I understand."

Mrs. B. "Well, then, what'll you charge me for

getting up a headstone just like that, out of pretty good white marble, and with a little picture of a torch upside down or a weeping angel on it, and the name of Thomas Smith cut on it?"

Mix. " John Smyth, you mean."

Mrs. B. " No, I mean Thomas."

Mix. " But you said John before."

Mrs. B. " I know, but that was my first husband, and Thomas was my second, and I want a new headstone for each of them. Now, it seems to me, Mr. Mix, that where a person is buying more than one, that way, you ought to make some reduction in the price—throw something off. Though, of course, I want a pretty good article at all the graves. Not anything gorgeous, but neat and tasteful and calculated to please the eye. Mr. Smyth was not a man who was fond of show. Give him a thing comfortable, and he was satisfied. Now, which do you think is the prettiest, to have the name in raised letters in a straight line over the top of the stone, or just to cut the words 'Alexander P. Smyth' in a kind of a semicircle in sunken letters?"

Mix. " Did I understand you to say Alexander P.? Were you referring to John or Thomas?"

Mrs. B. " Of course not. Aleck was my third. I'm not going to neglect his grave while I'm fixing up the rest. I wish to make a complete job of it, Mr. Mix, while I am about it, and I'm willing for you to undertake it if you are reasonable in your charges. Now, what'll you ask me for the lot,

the kind I've described, plain but substantial, and
sunk about two feet I should think, at the head of
each grave? What'll you charge me for them—for
the whole four?"

   Mix. "Well, I'll put you in those three headstones—"

   Mrs. B. "*Four* headstones, Mr. Mix, not three."

   Mix. "Four, was it? No; there was John and
Thomas and Alexander P. That's all you said, I
think. Only three."

Mrs. B. "Why, I want one for Adolph too, as a matter of course, the same as the others. I thought you knew I wanted one for Adolph, one made just like John's, only with the name different. Adolph was my fourth husband. He died about three years after I buried Philip, and I'm wearing mourning for him now. Now, please give me your prices for the whole of them."

Mix. "Well, madam, I want to be as reasonable as I can, and I tell you what I'll do. You give me all your work in the future, and I'll put you in those five headstones at hardly anything above cost; say—"

Mrs. B. "*Four* headstones, not five."

Mix. "I think you mentioned five."

Mrs. B. "No; only four."

Mix. "Less see: there was John, and Thomas and Aleck, and Adolph and Philip."

Mrs. B. "Yes, but Aleck and Philip were the same one. His middle name was Philip, and I always called him by it."

Mix. "Mrs. Banger, I'll be much obliged to you if you'll tell me precisely how many husbands you have planted up in that cemetery lot. This thing's getting a little mixed."

Mrs. B. "What do you mean, sir, by saying planted? I never 'planted' anybody. It's disgraceful to use such language."

Mix. "It's a technical term, madam. We always use it, and I don't see as it's going to hurt any

10

old row of fellows named Smyth. Planted is good
enough for other men, and it's good enough for
them."

Mrs. B. " Old row of— What d'you mean, you
impudent vagabond? I wouldn't let you put a
headstone on one of my graves if you'd do it for
nothing."

Then Mrs. Banger flounced out of the shop, and
Mix called after her as she went through the door,

" Lemme know when you go for another man,
and I'll throw him in a tombstone for a wedding-
present. He'll want it soon."

Mrs. Banger subsequently procured the services
of a person in the city, and she regards Mr. Mix with
something like detestation.

But Mrs. Banger herself is not universally beloved. Colonel Coffin knows of one woman who
despises her methods and desires her complete re-
pression. A short time after the election of the
colonel to the Legislature a lady called to see him
at his law-office. When she had closed the door, she
sat down and said,

" Colonel, my name is Mooney. I am unmarried
—a single woman. I called to see you in reference
to pushing a bill through the Legislature for the
benefit of maiden ladies such as myself. Let me
direct your attention to some extraordinary facts.
Statistics tell us that in the entire population of the
world there are one-fourth more women than men.
In this country the proportion of women to men is

slightly larger. In this State there are two and one-eighth women to every man. Now, this outrageous condition of affairs—".

"Excuse me for a moment, madam," said the colonel. "Really, the Legislature can do nothing to improve the matter. It cannot regulate the proportion of the sexes by law."

"I know it," replied Miss Mooney. "That is not what I am coming at. I say that this condition of affairs is grossly unjust. If I had had the management of it, and had been compelled to arrange that there should be more women than men, I certainly should not have had any fractions. There are not only two women for every man, but an eighth of a woman besides, so that ever so many of us women would each belong to eight different men if a fair distribution were made. How do I know, for instance, that an eighth of me does not belong to you? Why, I don't know it; and I say it's awful."

"If such is the case, madam," said the colonel, "I surrender all my rights without waiting for a legislative enactment."

"Excuse me," replied Miss Mooney, "but you do not catch the drift of my remarks. Of course, while the laws against bigamy are in existence, some of those women can never be married, although for my part, when a man has two wives and an eighth of another wife, I call it polygamy. Well, now, the point I want to make is this: When more than half of us can't marry, it's only right that the other half

should have a fair chance. There are not men
enough to go round, any how, and for gracious' sake
let's make them go as far as they honestly will.
Well, then, how'll we do it? How'll we make an
equitable distribution of those men?"

"Hanged if I know, madam. The Legislature
daren't meddle with them."

"I'll tell you how to do it. Listen to me. Shut
down on the widows. You hear me! Suppress the
widows. Make it death for any widow to marry
again. That's my remedy; and there'll never be any
justice till it's the law. Just look at it! When a
woman has been married once, she's had more than
her share of the male population; she's had her own
share and the share of another woman and an eighth.
Is it right, is it honorable, for that woman to go
and marry another man, and take the share of two
more women and an eighth? I say, is it just the
thing?"

"Well, on the surface it does look a little crooked."

"Crooked is not the word. Colonel Coffin, I
know these widows. I have had my eye on them.
They've got a way of bursting into a man's feelings
and walking off with his affections that fills a modest
woman like me with gall and bitterness. You know
Mrs. Banger? No? Well, now, look at her, f'r
instance. First she married Mr. Smyth, although
what on earth he ever saw to admire about *her* I
cannot imagine. That was her allowance. Having
obtained Smyth, oughtn't she to have stood back

and given some other woman a chance—now, oughtn't she ?"

"Really, madam, I am hardly able to express an opinion."

"But no. After a while Smyth succumbed. He died. She entombed him, crying, mind you, all the time, as if, having lost Smyth, she wanted to die and join Smyth in the grave and in Paradise. But no sooner was he well settled than she began to flirt with Mr. Smith, and what does he do but yield to her blandishments and marry her? Took her, and seemed to glory in it.

"Now, you'd 've thought that she'd 've been satisfied with that, when she'd got the share of four women and a quarter. But pretty soon, as luck would have it, Smith, died and she hustled *him* into the grave. And in less than a year afterward I was amazed to hear that she was going to marry another Smyth. I was never more astonished in my life. Positively going to annex a third man, when the supply was too short anyway. Did you ever hear of such impudence? Did you, now?"

"I'll think it over and see if I can remember."

"Well, then, I thought for certain *now* that woman would knock off and give the rest of us some kind of a chance; and when Smyth was killed by cholera and interred, it never entered my head that that widow'd go after *another* man. But, bless your soul! she'd hardly got into second mourning before she began to pursue Mr. McFadden, and got him. Now,

look at it. One woman, no better'n I am, has had
the property of eight women and a half, and here I
am single and getting on in life, with the chances
growing absurdly small. No civilized country ought
to tolerate such a thing. It's worse than piracy.
You may scuttle a ship or blow her up or run her
against the rocks, and no great harm is done, because
timber's plenty and you can build another one. But
when one woman scuttles three men and then ties to
a fourth, what are you going to do about it? You
can't go out into the woods and chop down trees
and saw them up and tack them together and build
a man. Now, can you?"

"That seems to be the common impression, anyway."

"Just so. And I want you to pass a bill through
that Legislature to make it a felony for a widow to
marry again. I've drawn up a draft of a bill and I'll
leave it with you. I've made it retroactive, so that
it'll bring that woman Banger up with a short turn
and send her after Smith and the others. I don't
care to marry, myself, but I want justice. Are you
married?"

"Madam, leave the bill with me and I will
examine it."

"I say are you married?"

"I—I—married did you say? Oh yes. I've
been married for ten years."

"Very well, then; good-morning;" and Miss
Mooney withdrew.

"Thunder!" exclaimed the colonel as he shut the door. "If I'd 've been single, I believe she'd 've proposed on the spot."

It is not considered likely that the Mooney anti-widow bill will be pushed very hard in the Legislature next session.

CHAPTER XII.

A NEW MRS. TOODLES.—POTTS' ADVENTURES.

ONE evening I met Mr. Potts out upon the turnpike, taking a walk; and I joined him. As we proceeded he became rather confidential. The subject of the mania for collecting bric-a-brac came up; and after an expression of opinion from me respecting the matter, Mr. Potts told the story of his wife's fondness for that kind of thing. He said,

" My wife is the most infatuated bric-a-brac hunter I ever heard of. She's an uncommonly fine woman about most things; loves her children; makes splendid pies; don't fool with any of those fan-dangling ways women have of fixing their hair; and she's an angel for temper. But she beats Mrs. Toodles for going to auctions. She's filled my house with the wildest mess of bric-a-brac and such stuff you ever came across outside of a museum of natural curiosities. She's spent more money for wrecks that wouldn't be allowed in the cellar of a poor-house than'd keep a family in comfort for years.

" You know Scudmore, who sold out the other

day? She was there, bidding away like a million-aire. Came home with a wagon-load of things—four albata tea-pots without lids or handles; two posts of a bedstead and three slats; a couple of churns and fourteen second-hand sun-bonnets, and more mournful refuse like that. Said she didn't intend to buy, but she bid on them to run them up to help Mrs. Scudmore, and the auctioneer knocked them down quicker'n a wink. Said it was ' Lot 47,' and she had to take it all. And she said maybe she could make up the sun-bonnets into bibs for the baby and use the tea-pots for preserves. She thought she might make a pretty fair bedstead out of the posts by propping the other ends on a chair; and she said it was a lucky thing she was so fore-handed about those churns, because she might have a cow knocked down to her, and then she would be all ready for butter-making. More'n likely she'll buy some old steer and bring him home while she's rummaging around for bric-a-brac.

"When the Paxtons had their sale in January she was around there, of course, and came home after dinner with the usual dismembered furniture; and when I said to her, ' Emma, why under Heaven did you buy in the mud-dredge and the sausage-stuffer?' she said she thought the sausage-stuffer would do for a cannon for the boys on the Fourth of July, and there was no telling if Charley wouldn't want to be a civil engineer when he grew up, and perhaps he'd get a contract for deepening the channel of the river;

and then he'd rise up and bless the foresight of the mother who'd bought a mud-dredge for two dollars and saved it up for him.

"I sold that scoop on Wednesday for old iron for fifteen cents; and I'll bang the head off of Charley if he ever goes to dredging mud or playing cannon with the sausage-stuffer. I won't have my boys carrying on in that way.

"Over there at Robinson's sale I believe she'd 've bid on the whole concern if I hadn't come in while she was going it. As it was, she bought an aneroid barometer, three dozen iron skewers, a sacking-bottom and four volumes of Eliza Cook's poems. Said she thought those volumes were some kind of cookery-books, or she wouldn't have bid on them, and the barometer would be valuable to tell us which was north. *North*, mind you! She thought it indicated the points of the compass. And yet they want to let women vote! I threw in those skewers along with the mud-dredge, and she's used the sacking-bottom twice to patch Charley's pants; and that's all the good we ever got out of that auction.

"But she don't care for utility; it's simply a mania for buying things. We haven't a stove in the house, and yet what does she do at Murphy's sale but bid on sixty-two feet and three elbows of rusty stove-pipe and cart it home with four debilitated gingham umbrellas. Said the umbrellas were a bargain because, by putting in new covers and handles and a rib here and there, they would do for birthday presents for her aunts. And the stovepipe could be sent out to the farm to be put around the peach trees to keep the cows off. How in thunder she was ever going to get a stovepipe around a peach tree never crossed her mind. She is just as impractical as a baby.

"When Bailey had the auction at his insurance office, there she was, and, sure enough, that afternoon she landed in our side yard with Bailey's poll-parrot and a circular saw. It amused me. She wanted to use that saw as a dinner-gong, but it was cracked, and so she has turned it into a griddle for muffins. Bailey had taught the parrot to swear so that I was afraid it'd demoralize Charley, and I don't mind telling you in confidence that I killed it by putting bug-poison in a water-cracker.

"Now, I see there's an auction advertised for Friday at Peters'; and Peters has a pyramid of old tomato cans and bric-a-brac of that sort piled up in his back yard. Now, you see if that woman don't bid on those cans until she runs them up to a dollar apiece, and then come lugging them around to our house with some extraordinary idea about loading them up with gunpowder and selling them to the government during the next war for bombshells. If she does, that winds the thing up. I'm a good-natured man, but no woman shall bring home three hundred tomato cans to my house and retain a claim upon my affections. I'll resign first."

My feeling was that he was a little mixed in his

notions about bric-a-brac, but that he really had a grievance.

Potts told me, also, that he came home very late one night recently, and when he went up stairs his wife and children were in bed asleep. He undressed as softly as he could, and then, as he felt thirsty, he thought he would get a drink of water. Fortunately, he saw a gobletful standing on the washstand, placed there for him, evidently, by Mrs. Potts. He seized it and drank the liquid in two or three huge gulps, but just as he was draining the goblet he gagged, dropped the glass to the floor, where it was shivered to atoms, while he ejected something from his mouth. He was certain that a live animal of some kind had been in the water, and that he had nearly swallowed it. This theory was confirmed when he saw the object which he spat out go bounding over the floor. He pursued it, kicking a couple of chairs over while doing so, and at last he put his foot on it and held it. Of course Mrs. Potts was wide awake by this time and scared nearly to death, and the baby was screaming at the top of its lungs. Mrs. Potts got out of bed and turned up the gas, and said,

" Mr. Potts, what in the name of common sense is the matter ?"

" It's a mouse!" shouted Potts, in an excited manner. " It's a mouse in the goblet. I nearly swallowed it, but I spat it out, and now I've got my foot on it. Get a stick and kill it, quick !"

Mrs. Potts was at first disposed to jump on a chair and scream, for, like all women, she feared a mouse very much more than she did a tiger. But at Potts' solicitation she got the broom and prepared to demolish the mouse when Potts lifted his foot. He drew back, and she aimed a fearful blow at the object and missed it. Then, as it did not move, she took a good look at it. Then she threw down the broom, and after casting a look of scorn at Potts, she said,

"Come to bed, you old fool! that's not a mouse."

"What d'you mean?"

"Why, you simpleton, that's the baby's India-rubber bottle-top that I put in the goblet to keep it sweet. You ought to be ashamed of yourself carrying on in this manner at one o'clock in the morning."

Then Potts turned in. After this he will drink at the pump.

In the course of the conversation I remarked that I had seen some men fixing Potts' roof recently; and when I asked Potts if anything was the matter, he said,

"My roof was shingled originally; but as it leaked, I had the shingles removed and a gravel-and-felt roof put on. The first night after it was finished there was a very high wind, which blew the gravel off with such force that it broke thirty-four panes of glass in Butterwick's house, next door. The wind also tore up the felt and blew it over the edge, so that it hung down over the front of the house like a curtain. Of course it made the rooms pitch-dark, and I did not get up until one o'clock in the afternoon, but lay there wondering how it was the night seemed so long.

"Then I had a tin roof put on, and it did well enough for a while. But whenever there was a heavy rain or the wind was high, it used to rattle all night with a noise like the battle of Gettysburg. At last it began to leak, and a tinner sent a man around to find the hole. He spent a week on that roof, and he spread half a ton of solder over it, but still it leaked. And finally, when the snow came, the water trickled down the wall and ran into an eight-hundred-dollar piano, which will be closed out at a low figure to anybody who wants mahogany kindling-wood. When the tin was removed and the new slate roof was put on, the slates used to get loose and slide down on the head of the hired girl while she was hanging up the clothes. And when the man came to replace the slates, he plunged off the roof and broke four ribs and his leg, whereupon he sued me for damages. And while the case was pending in court a snow-storm came. The snow blew in under the slates, and my oldest boy spent the day with some of his friends snow-balling and sledding in the garret. Then the snow on the garret floor melted and wet the wall-paper down stairs, so that the house became frightfully damp, and we had to move over to the hotel for a fortnight.

"Then I tried the 'Patent Incombustible' roofing, because the man said it would not only keep out the rain, but it was perfectly fireproof. A week after it was on, Butterwick's stable caught fire and flung up a great many sparks. All the houses in the neighborhood, however, escaped—all except mine. My roof was in flames before the stable was done burning; and when the firemen had put it out, they got to fighting on my front stairs, with the result that the banister was broken to splinters, a two-inch stream

was played into the parlor for fifteen minutes, and
Chief Engineer Johnson bled all over our best carpet.

"I have the 'Impervious Cement Roof' on now,
and it seems to do well enough, excepting that it
isn't impervious. It lets in the water at eight different places; and whenever there is a shower, I have to
rush my family out on the roof to shelter it with
umbrellas. I fully expect it will explode some night,
or do some other deadly and infamous thing. I am
going to put the house up at auction and live in a
circus tent."

They had a big excitement over at Potts' the other
day about their cat. They heard the cat howling
and screeching somewhere around the house for two
or three days, but they couldn't find her. Potts used
to get up at night, fairly maddened with the noise,
and heave things out the back window at random,
hoping to hit her and discourage her. But she never
seemed to mind them; and although eventually he
fired off pretty nearly every movable thing in the
house excepting the piano, she continued to shriek
and scream in a manner that was simply appalling.
At last, one day, Potts made a critical examination
of the premises, and, guided by the noise, he finally
located the cat in the tin waterspout which descends
the north wall of the house. He thinks the cat must
have been skylarking on the roof some dark night
and accidentally tumbled into the spout.

Potts tried to shake her down by hammering on

the spout with a stick; but the more he pounded, the louder she yelled, and the two noises roused the entire neighborhood and attracted the attention of the police. Then he procured a clothes-prop; and ascending to the roof, he endeavored to push the animal out. But the stick was not long enough to reach her. All it was good for was to make her howl more loudly; and it did that. At last Potts concluded to take the spout down and coax the cat out. When he got it on the ground, he peeped in at the end, and he could see the animal's eyes shining like balls of fire far back in the darkness of the hole. After shaking her up for a while without inducing her to move, he made up his mind that she must be jammed in the pipe and unable to budge. He wanted to cut the pipe open, but Butterwick said it would be a pity to spoil such a good spout for a mere cat.

So Potts finally determined to blow her out with powder. He procured a small charge; and pushing it pretty well in with a stick, he "tamped" the end of the spout with clay and lighted the slow-match. Two minutes later there was an explosion, and the tamping-clay flew out and struck Butterwick with some violence in the ribs, curling him all up on the grass by the pump. When he recovered his breath, he got up and said,

"Hang your infernal cat! It's an outrage for you to be endangering the lives of people with your diabolical schemes for getting at a beast that ought to've been killed long ago."

11

Then Butterwick sullenly got over the fence and
went home, and the cat meanwhile kept up a yowl-
ing that made everybody's hair stand on end.

Potts said that he made a mistake in not placing the
butt of the spout against something solid. And so,
after putting in a couple of pounds of powder, he
turned the spout up and rested the end upon the
ground, propping it against the pump. Then he
lighted the slow-match, and the crowd scattered.
There was a loud explosion, a general distribution
of fragments of tin around the yard, and then out
from the upper end of the spout there sailed something black. It ascended; it went higher and higher
and higher, until it was a mere speck; then it came
sailing down, down, down, until it struck the earth.
It was the cat, singed off, burned to a crisp, looking
as if it had been spending the summer in Vesuvius,
but apparently still active and hearty; for as soon as
it alighted it set up a wild, unearthly screech and
darted off for the woodshed, where it continued to
howl until Potts went in and killed it with his shot-
gun. It cost him forty dollars for a new spout, but
he says he doesn't grudge the money now that he
has stopped that fiendish noise.

Potts' clock got out of order one day last winter and began to strike wrong. That was the cause
of the fearful excitement at his house on a certain
night. They were all in bed sound asleep at midnight, when the clock suddenly struck *five*. The

new hired girl, happening to wake just as it began, heard it, and bounced out of bed under the impression that morning had come. And as it is dark at 5 A. M. just at that season, she did not perceive her mistake, but went down into the kitchen and began to get breakfast.

While she was bustling about in a pretty lively manner, Potts happened to wake, and he heard the noise. He opened his room door cautiously and crept softly to the head of the stairs to listen. He could distinctly hear some one moving about the kitchen and dining-room and apparently packing up the china. Accordingly, he went back to his room and woke Mrs. Potts, and gave her orders to spring the rattle out of the front window the moment she heard his gun go off. Then Potts seized his fowling-piece; and going down to the dining-room door, where he could hear the burglars at work, he cocked the gun, aimed it, pushed the door open with the muzzle and fired. Instantly Mrs. Potts sprang the rattle, and before Potts could pick up the lacerated hired girl the front door was burst open by two policemen, who came into the dining-room.

Seeing Potts with a gun, and a bleeding woman on the floor, they imagined that murder had been committed, and one of them trotted Potts off to the station-house, while the other remained to investigate things. Just then the clock struck six. An expla-nation ensued from the girl, who only had a few bird-shot in her leg, and the policeman left to bring Potts home. He arrived at about three in the morning, just as the clock was striking eight. When the situation was unfolded to him, his first action was to jam the butt of his gun through the clock, where-upon it immediately struck two hundred and forty-three, and then Potts pitched it over the fence. He has a new clock now, and things are working better.

The Pottses celebrated their "iron wedding" one day last winter, and they invited about one hundred and twenty guests to the wedding. Of course each person felt compelled to bring a present of some kind; and each one did. When Mr. and Mrs. Smith came, they handed Potts a pair of flatirons. When Mr. and Mrs. Jones arrived, they also had a pair of flatirons. All hands laughed at the coincidence. And there was even greater merriment when the Browns arrived with two pairs of flatirons. But when Mr. and Mrs. Robinson came in with another pair of flatirons, the laughter became perfectly convulsive.

There was, however, something less amusing about it when the Thompsons arrived with four flatirons wrapped in brown paper. And Potts' face actually looked grave when the three Johnson girls were ushered into the parlor carrying a flatiron apiece. Each one of the succeeding sixty guests brought flatirons, and there was no break in the continuity until old Mr. Curry arrived from Philadelphia with a cast-iron cow-bell. Now, Potts has no earthly use for a cow-bell, and at any other time he would have treated such a present with scorn. But now he was actually grateful to Mr. Curry, and he was about to embrace him, when the Walsinghams came in with the new kind of double-pointed flatirons with wooden handles. And all the rest of the guests brought the same articles excepting Mr. Rugby, and he had with him a patent stand for holding flatirons. Potts got madder and madder every minute, and by the time the company had all arrived he was nearly insane with rage; and he went up to bed, leaving his wife to entertain the guests. In the morning they counted up the spoils, and found that they had two hundred and thirteen flat-irons, one stand and a cow-bell. And now the Pottses have cut the Smiths and Browns and John-

sons and Thompsons and the rest entirely, for they are convinced that there was a preconcerted design to play a trick upon them.

The fact, however, is that the hardware store in the place had an overstock of flatirons and sold them at an absurdly low figure, and Potts' guests unanimously went for the cheapest thing they could find, as people always do on such occasions. Potts thinks he will not celebrate his " silver wedding."

CHAPTER XIII.

THE RACES, AND SOME OTHER THINGS.

HERE was some horse-racing over at the Blank course one day last fall, and Butterwick attended to witness it. On his way home in the cars in the afternoon he encountered Rev. Dr. Dox, a clergyman who knows no more about horse-racing than a Pawnee knows about psychology. Butterwick, however, took for granted, in his usual way, that the doctor was familiar with the subject; and taking a seat beside him, he remarked loudly—for the doctor is deaf—

"I was out at the Blank course to-day to see Longfellow."

"Indeed! Was he there? Where did you say he was?"

"Why, over here at the course. I saw him and General Harney, and a lot more of 'em. He run against General Harney, and it created a big excitement, too; but he beat the general badly, and the way the crowd cheered him was wonderful. They say that a good deal of money changed hands. The fact is I had a small bet upon the general myself."

"You don't mean to say that Longfellow actually *beat* General Harney?"

"Yes, I do! Beat him the worst kind. You'd hardly 've thought it, now, would you? I was never more surprised in my life. What's queer abo.it it is that he seemed just as fresh afterward as before he commenced. Didn't faze him a bit. Why, instead of wanting to rest, he was jumping about just as lively; and when the crowd began to push around him, he kicked a boy in the back and doubled him all up—nearly killed him. Oh, he's wicked! I wouldn't trust him as far as I could see him."

"This is simply astonishing," said the doctor. "I wouldn't have believed it possible. Are you *sure* it was Longfellow, Mr. Butterwick?"

"Why, certainly, of course; I've seen him often before. And after breathing a while, he and Maggie Mitchell came out, and as soon as they stepped off he put on an extra spurt or two and led her by a neck all around the place, and she came in puffing and blowing, and nearly exhausted. I never took much stock in her, anyway."

"Led her by the neck! Why, this is the most scandalous conduct I ever heard of. Mr Butterwick, you must certainly be joking."

"I pledge you my word it's the solemn truth. I saw it myself. And after that Judge Bullerton and General Harney, they took a turn together, and that was the prettiest contest of the day. First the judge'd beat the general, and then the general'd put in a big effort and give it to the judge, and the two'd be about even for a while, and all of a sudden the general would give a kinder jerk or two and leave the judge just nowhere, and by the time the general passed the third quarter the judge keeled over against the fence and gave in. They say he broke his leg, but I don't know if that's so or not. Anyway he was used up. If he'd passed that quarter, he might have been all right."

"What was the matter with the quarter? Wasn't it good?"

"Oh yes. But you see the judge must have lost his wind or something; and I reckon when he tumbled it was something like a faint, you know."

"Served him right for engaging in such a brutal contest."

"Well, I dunno. Depends on how you look at such things. And when that was over, Longfellow entered with Mattie Evelyn. He kept shooting past her all the time, and this worried her so that she ran a little to one side, and somehow, I dunno how it happened, but his leg tripped her, and she rolled over on the ground, hurt pretty bad, I think, while Longfellow had his leg cut pretty near to the bone."

"Did any of the shots strike her?"

"I don't understand you."

"You said he kept shooting past her, and I thought maybe some of the bullets might have struck her."

"Why, I meant that he *ran* past her, of course. How in the thunder could he shoot bullets at her?"

"I thought maybe he had a gun. But I don't understand any of it. It is the most astounding thing I ever heard of, at any rate."

"Now, my dear sir, I want to ask you how Long-fellow *could* manage a gun?"

"Why, as any other man does, of course."

"Man! man! Why, merciful Moses! you didn't think I was talking about human beings all this time, did you? Why, Longfellow is a horse! They were racing—running races over at the course this afternoon; and I was trying to tell you about it."

"You don't say?" remarked the doctor, with a sigh of relief. "Well, I declare, I thought you were speaking of the poet, and I hardly knew whether to believe you or not; it seemed so strange that he should behave in that manner."

Then Mr. Butterwick went into the smoking-car to tell the joke to his friends, and the doctor sat reflecting upon the outrageous impudence of the men who name their horses after respectable people.

While he was thinking about it, another sensational occurrence attracted his attention.

A man sitting in the same car with the doctor had placed a bottle of tomato catsup neck downward in the rack above his seat. Presently a friend came in, and in a few moments the friend, who was cutting his finger-nails with a knife, introduced the subject of the races. The discussion gradually became warm, and as the excitement increased the man with the knife gesticulated violently with the hand containing the weapon while he explained his views. Meantime, the cork jolted out of the bottle overhead, and the catsup dripped down over the owner's head and coat and collar without his perceiving the fact.

Soon a nervous old lady on the back seat caught sight of the red stain, and imagining it was blood, instantly began to scream "Murder!" at the top of her voice. As the passengers, conductor and brakemen rushed up she brandished her umbrella wildly and exclaimed,

"Arrest that man there! Arrest that willin! I see him do it. I see him stab that other one with his knife until the blood spurted out. Oh, you wretch! Oh, you willinous rascal, to take human life in that scandalous manner! I see you punch him with the knife, you butcher, you! and I'll swear it agin you in court, too, you owdacious rascal!"

They took her into the rear car and soothed her, while the victim wiped the catsup off his coat. But that venerable old woman will go down to the silent grave with the conviction that she witnessed in those cars one of the most awful and sanguinary encounters that has occurred since the affair between Cain and Abel.

Dr. Dox recently was called upon to settle a bet upon a much more serious matter than a horse-race. During a religious controversy between Peter Lamb and some of his friends one of the latter asserted that Peter didn't know who was the mother-in-law of Moses, and that he couldn't ascertain. Peter offered to bet that he could find out, and the wager was accepted. After searching in vain through the Scriptures, Mr. Lamb concluded to go around and interview Deacon Jones about it. The deacon is head-man in the gas-office, and in the office there are half a dozen small windows, behind which sit clerks to receive money. Applying at one of these, Mr. Lamb said,

" Is Deacon Jones in ?"

" What's your business ?"

" Why, I want to find out the name of Moses'—"

"Don't know anything about it. Look in the directory;" and the clerk slammed the window shut.

Then Peter went to the next window and said,

"I want to see Mr. Jones a minute."

"What for?"

"I want to see if he knows Moses'—"

"Moses who?"

"Why, Moses, the Bible Moses—if he knows—"

"Patriarchs don't belong in this department. Apply across the street at the Christian Association rooms;" and then the clerk closed the window.

At the next window Mr. Lamb said,

"I want to see Deacon Jones a minute in reference to a matter about Moses."

"Want to pay his gas-bill? What's the last name?"

"Oh no. I mean the first Moses, the original one."

"Anything the matter with his meter?"

"You don't understand me. I refer to the Hebrew prophet. I want to see—"

"Well, you can't see him here. This is the gas-office. Try next door."

At the adjoining window Mr. Lamb said,

"Look here! I want to see Deacon Jones a minute about the prophet Moses, and I wish you'd tell him so."

"No, I won't," replied the clerk. "He's too busy to be bothered with anything of that kind."

"But I must see him," said Peter; "I insist on seeing him. The fact of the matter is, I've got a bet about Moses'—"

"Don't make any difference what you've got; you can't see him."

"But I will. I want you to go and tell him I'm here, and that I wish for some information respecting Moses. I'll have you discharged if you don't go."

"Don't care if you want to see him about all the children of Israel, and the Pharaohs and Nebuchadnezzars. I tell you you can't. That settles it. Turn off your gas and quit."

Then Peter resolved to give up the deacon and try Rev. Dr. Dox. When he called at the parsonage, the doctor came down into the parlor. Because of the doctor's deafness there was a little misunderstanding when Peter said,

"I called, doctor, to ascertain if you could tell me who was the mother-in-law of Moses."

"Well, really," said the doctor, "there isn't much preference. Some like one kind of roses and some like another. A very good variety of the pink rose is the Duke of Cambridge; grows large, bears early and has very fine perfume. The Hercules is also excellent, but you must manure it well and water it often."

"I didn't ask about *roses*, but *Moses*. You make a mistake," shouted Peter.

"Oh, of course! by all means. Train them up to

THE RACES, AND SOME OTHER THINGS. 175

a stake if you want to. The wind don't blow them about so and they send out more shoots."

"You misunderstand me," yelled Mr. Lamb. "I asked about Moses, not roses. I want to know who was the mother-in-law of Moses."

"Oh yes; certainly. Excuse me; I thought you were inquiring about roses. The law of Moses was the foundation of the religion of the Jews. You can find it in full in the Pentateuch. It is admirable— very admirable—for the purpose for which it was ordained. We, of course, have outlived that dispensation, but it still contains many things that are useful to us, as, for instance, the—"

"Was Moses married?" shrieked Mr. Lamb.

"Married? Oh, yes; the name of his father-in-law, you know, was Jethro, and—"

"Who was his wife?"

"Why, she was the daughter of Jethro, of course. I said Jethro was his father-in-law."

"No; Jethro's wife, I mean. I want to know to settle a bet."

"No, that wasn't her name. 'Bet' is a corruption of Elizabeth, and that name, I believe, is not found in the Old Testament. I don't remember what the name of Moses' wife was."

"I want to know what was the name of the mother-in-law of Moses, to settle a bet."

"Young man," said the old doctor, sternly, "you are trifling with a serious subject. What do you mean by wanting Moses to settle a bet?"

Then Mr. Lamb rolled up a sheet of music that lay on the piano; and putting it to the doctor's ear, he shouted,

"I made—a—bet—that—I—could—find—out— what — the — name — of Moses'— mother-in-law— was. Can—you—tell—me ?"

"The Bible don't say," responded the doctor; "and unless you can get a spiritualist to put you in communication with Moses, I guess you will lose."

Then Peter went around and handed over the stakes. Hereafter he will gamble on other than biblical games.

Mr. Lamb has an inquiring mind. He is always investigating something. He read somewhere the other day that two drops of the essential oil of tobacco placed upon the tongue of a cat would kill the animal instantly. He did not believe it, and he concluded to try the experiment to see if it was so. Old Squills, the druggist, has a cat weighing about fifteen pounds, and Mr. Lamb, taking the animal into the back room, shut the door, opened the cat's mouth, and applied the poison. One moment later a wild, unearthly "M-e-e-e-e-ow-ow-ow! was emitted by the cat, and, to Mr. Lamb's intense alarm, the animal began swishing around

the room with hair on end and tail in convulsive excitement, screeching like a fog-whistle. Mr. Lamb is
not certain, but he considers it a fair estimate to say
that the cat made the entire circuit of the room,
over chairs and under tables, seventy-four times
every minute, and he is willing to swear to seventy
times, without counting the occasional diversions
made by the brute for the purpose of snatching at
Mr. Lamb's pantaloons and hair. Just as Mr. Lamb
had about made up his mind that the cat would conclude the gymnastic exercises by eating him, the
animal dashed through the glass sash of the door
into the shop, whisked two jars of licorice root and
tooth-brushes off the counter, tore out the ipecac-
bottle and four jugs of hair-dye, smashed a bottle of
" Balm of Peru," alighted on the bonnet of a woman
who was drinking soda-water, and after a few convulsions rolled over into a soap-box and died.

Mr. Lamb is now satisfied that a cat actually can
be killed in the manner aforementioned, but he
would be better satisfied if old Squills didn't insist
upon collecting from him the price of those drugs
and the glass sash.

Last summer Peter's brother spent a few weeks
with him. He owned a " pistol cane," which he carried about with him loaded ; but when he went away,
he accidentally left it behind, and without explaining
to Peter that it was different from ordinary canes.

So, one afternoon a few days later, Peter went out

12

to Keyser's farm to
look at some stock,
and he picked up the
cane to take along with
him. When he got to
Keyser's, the latter
went to the barnyard
to show him an extra-
ordinary kind of a new
pig that he had devel-
oped by cross-breeding.

"Now that pig," said
Keyser, "just lays over
all the other pigs on the Atlantic Slope. Take him
any way you please, he's the most gorgeous pig anywheres around. Fat! Why, he's all fat! There's
no lean in him. He ain't anything but a solid mass
of lard. Put that pig near a fire, and in twenty

minutes his naked skeleton'd be standing there in a puddle of grease. That's a positive fact. Now, you just feel his shoulder."

Then Peter lifted up his cane and gave the pig a poke. He poked it two or three times, and he had just remarked, "That certainly is a splendid pig," when he gave it another poke, and then somehow the pistol in the cane went off and the pig rolled over and expired.

"What in the mischief d'you do that for?" exclaimed Keyser, amazed and indignant.

"Do it for? *I* didn't do it! This cane must've been made out of an old gun-barrel with the load left in. I never had the least idea, I pledge you my word, that there was anything the matter with it."

"That's pretty thin," said Keyser; "you had a grudge agin that pig because you couldn't scare up a pig like him, and you killed him on purpose."

"That's perfectly ridiculous."

"Oh, maybe it is. You'll just fork over two hundred dollars for that piece of pork, if you please."

"I'll see you in Egypt first."

    *   *   *   *   *

Peter whipped; but if Keyser *did* give in first, Peter went home with a bleeding nose, and the next day he was arrested for killing the pig. The case is coming up soon, and Peter's brother is on, ready to testify about that cane. Peter himself walks now with a hickory stick.

CHAPTER XIV.

RESPECTING CERTAIN SAVAGES.

HEN young Mr. Spooner, Judge Twiddler's nephew, left college, he made up his mind to enter the ministry and become a missionary. One day he met Captain Hubbs; and when he mentioned that he thought of going out as a missionary, Captain Hubbs asked him, "Where are you going?"

S. "To the Navigator Islands. I sail in October."

Capt. (shaking his head mournfully). "Pore young man! Pore young man! It is too bad—too bad indeed! Going to the Navigator Islands! Not married yet, I reckon? No? Ah! so much the better. No wife and children to make widows and orphans of. But it's sad, anyway. A promising young fellow like you! My heart bleeds for you."

S. "What d'you mean?"

Capt. "Oh, nothing. I don't want to frighten you. I know you're doing it from a sense of duty. But I've been there to the Navigator Islands, and I'm acquainted with the people's little ways, and I—well, I—I—the fact is, you see, that—well, sooner'n disguise the truth, I don't mind telling you straight

out that the last day I was there the folks et one of
my legs—sawed it off an' et it. Now you can see
how things are yourself. Those Navigators gobbled
that leg right up. It was a leg a good deal like
yours, only heavier, I reckon."

S. "You astonish me!"

Capt. "Oh, that's nothing. They did that just for
a little bit of fun. The chief told me the day before
that they never et anything but human beings. He
said his family consumed about three a day all the
year round, counting holidays and Sundays. He
was a light eater himself, he said, on account of git-
ting dyspepsia from a tough Australian that he et in
1847, but the girls and the old woman, so he said,
were very hearty eaters, and it kept him busy prowling around after human beings to satisfy 'em. The
old woman, he said, rather preferred to eat babies,
on account of her teeth being poor, but the girls
could eat the grizzliest sailor that ever went aboard
ship."

S. "This is frightful."

Capt. "And the chief said sometimes the supply was scarce, but
lately they had begun to depend
more on imported goods than on
the home products. And they
were better, anyhow, for all the
folks preferred white meat. He
said the missionary societies were
shipping them some nice lots of provender, and

the tears came in his eyes when he said how good
they were to the poor friendless savage away on a
distant island. He said he liked a missionary not
too old or too young. But let's see; what's your
age, did you say?"

S. " I am twenty-eight."

Capt. " I think he mentioned twenty-seven; but
howsomedever, he liked 'em old enough to be solid
and young enough to be tender. And he said he
liked missionaries because they never used rum or
tobacco and always kept their flavor. I know I seen
one young fellow who came out there from Boston.
He got up a camp-meeting in the woods; and while
he was giving out the hymn, one of the congregation
banged him on the head with a club, and in less than
no time he was sizzling over a fire right in front of
the pulpit. They lit the fire with his hymn-book
and kept her going with his sermons. He was a
man just about your build—a little leaner'n you,
maybe. And they like a man to be stoutish. He
eats more tender."

S. " I had no idea that such awful practices ex-
isted."

Capt. " I haven't told you half, for I don't want to
discourage you. I know you mean well, and maybe
they'll let you alone. But I remember, when I told
the chief that there was a whole lot of you chaps
studying to be missionaries, he laughed and rubbed
his hands, and ordered the old woman to plant more
horseradish and onions the following year. He was

a forehanded kind of a man for a mere pagan. He said that if they would only give his tribe time, if they would send him along the supplies regular, so's not to glut the market, they could put away the entire clergy of the United States and half the deacons without an effort. He was nibbling at a missionary-bone when he spoke, and the old woman was making a new club out of another one. They are an economical people. They utilize everything."

S. "This is the most painful intelligence that I ever received. If I felt certain about it, I would remain at home."

Capt. "Don't let me induce you to throw the thing up. I wouldn't a told you, anyway, only you kind of drew the information out of me. And as long as I've gone this far, I might as well tell you that I got a letter the other day from a man who'd just come from there, and he said the crops were short, eatable people were scarce, and not one of them savages had had a square meal for months. When he left, they were sitting on the rocks, hungry as thunder, waiting for a missionary-society ship to arrive. And now I must be going. Good-bye. I know I'll never see you again. Take a last look at me. Good-morning."

Then the captain hobbled off.

Mr. Spooner has concluded to stay at home and teach school.

Another rather more enthusiastic friend of the

savage is Mr. Dodge. He came into the office of
the *Patriot* one day and sought a desk where a reporter was writing. Seating himself and tilting the
chair until it was nicely balanced upon two legs, he
smiled a serene and philanthropic smile, and said,

"You see, I'm the friend of the poor Indian; he
regards me as his Great White Brother, and I re-
ciprocate his confidence and affection by doing what
I can to alleviate his sufferings in his present unfortunate situation. Young man, you do not know the
anguish that fills the soul of the red man as civilization makes successive inroads upon his rights. It is
too sacred for exhibition. He represses his emotion
sternly, and we philanthropists only detect it by ob-
serving that he betrays an increased longing for fire-
water and an aggravated indisposition to wash himself. Now, what do you suppose is the *last* sorrow
that has come to blast the happiness of this persecuted being? What do you think it is?"

"I don't know, and I don't care."

"I will tell you. It is the increasing tendency of
the white man to baldness. As civilization pushes
upward, the hair of the pale face recedes. Eventually, I suppose, about every other white man will be
bald. I notice that even you are gradually being
reduced to a mere fringe around the base of your
skull. Now, imagine how an Indian feels when he
considers this tendency. Is it any wonder that the
future seems dark and gloomy and hairless to him?
The scalping operation to him is a sacred rite. It is

interwoven with his most cherished traditions. When he surrenders it, he dies with a broken heart. What, then, is to be done?"

"Oh, do hush up and quit."

"There is but one thing to be done to meet this grave emergency. We cannot justly permit that grand aboriginal man who once held sway over this mighty continent to be filled with desolation and misery by the inaccessibility of the scalps of his fellow-creatures. My idea, therefore, is to bring those scalps within his reach, even when they are baldest and shiniest. But how?"

"That'll do now. Don't want to hear any more."

"Here my ingenuity comes into play. I have invented a simple little machine which I call 'The Patent Adjustable Atmospheric Scalp-lifter.' Here it is. The device consists of a disk of thin leather about six inches in diameter. In the centre is a hole through which runs a string. When the Indian desires to deal with a man with a bald head, he proceeds as follows — observe the simplicity of the operation: He wets the leather, stamps it carefully down upon the surface of the scalp, slides his knife around over the ears, gives the string a jerk, and off comes the scalp as nicely as if it had been Absalom's. In fact, you will see at once that it is an ingenious application of the 'sucker' used by boys to raise bricks and stones. I know what you are going to say—that a white man who is to be manipulated by an Indian needs succor worse than the red man. It

is an old joke, and a good one; but my desire is to
bring joy to the wigwam of the Kickapoo and to
make the heart of the Arapahoe glad."

"Oh, do dry up and go down stairs."

"You catch the idea, of course; but perhaps
you'd like to see the apparatus in operation. Wait
a moment; I'll show you how splendidly it works."

Then, as the reporter resolutely continued at his
task with his nose almost against the desk, the
friend of the disconsolate red man suddenly produced a moist sucker and clapped it firmly upon the
bald place on the reporter's head, and then, before
the indignant victim could offer resistance, the Great
White Brother, with the string in his hand, careered
around the office a couple of times, drawing the
helpless journalist after him. As he withdrew the
machine he smiled and said,

"Elegant, isn't it? Could pull a horse-car with
it. I wish you'd come to Washington with me and
lend me your head, so's I can show the Secretary of
the Interior how the thing works. You have the
best scalp for a good hold of any I've tried yet."

But the reporter was at the speaking-tube calling
for a boy to go for a policeman, and he didn't seem
to hear the suggestion. And so Mr. Dodge folded
up the machine, placed it in his carpet-bag, and went
out smiling as though he had been received with
enthusiasm and been promised a gratuitous advertisement. He passed the policeman on the stairs,
and then sailed serenely out of reach, perhaps to seek

for another and more sympathetic bald man upon whom to illustrate the value of his invention.

Reference to the Indians reminds me of the very ungenerous treatment that Mr. Bartholomew, one of our citizens, received at the hands of certain red men with whom he trafficked in the West.

A year or two ago Mr. Bartholomew was out in Colorado for a few months, and just before he started for the journey home he wrote to his wife concerning the probable time of his arrival. As a postscript to the letter he added the following message to his son, a boy about eight years old:

"Tell Charley I am going to bring with me a dear little baby-bear that I bought from an Indian."

Of course that information pleased Charley, and he directed most of his thoughts and his conversation to the subject of the bear during the next two weeks, wishing anxiously for his father to come with the little pet. On the night which been fixed by Bartholomew for his arrival he did not come, and the family were very much disappointed. Charley particularly was dreadfully sorry, because he couldn't get the bear. On the next evening, while Mrs. Bartholomew and the children were sitting in the front room with the door open into the hall, they heard somebody running through the front yard. Then the front door was suddenly burst open, and a man dashed into the hall and up stairs at a frightful speed. Mrs. Bartholomew was just about to go up after him to ascertain who it was, when a large dark animal of some kind darted in through the door and with an awful growl went bowling up stairs after the

man. It suddenly flashed upon the mind of Mrs. Bartholomew that the man was her husband, and that that was the little baby-bear. Just then the voice of Bartholomew was heard calling from the top landing:

"Ellen, for gracious sake get out of the house as quick as you can, and shut all the doors and window-shutters."

Then Mrs. Bartholomew sent the boys into Partridge's, next door, and she closed the shutters, locked all the doors and went into the yard to await further developments. When she got outside, she saw Bartholomew on the roof kneeling on the trap-door, which he kept down only by the most tremendous exertions. Then he screamed for somebody to come up and help him, and Mr. Partridge got a ladder and a hatchet and some nails, and ascended. Then they nailed down the trap-door, and Bartholomew and Partridge came down the ladder together. After he had greeted his family, Mrs. Bartholomew asked him what was the matter, and he said,

"Why, you know that little baby-bear I said I'd bring Charley? Well, I had him in a box until I got off the train up here at the dépôt, and then I thought I'd take him out and lead him around home by the chain. But the first thing he did was to fly at my leg; and when I jumped back, I ran, and he after me. He would've eaten me up in about a minute. That infernal Indian must have fooled me. He said it was a cub only two months old and it had no teeth. I believe it's a full-grown bear."

It then became a very interesting question how they should get the bear out of the house. Bartholomew thought they had better try to shoot him, and he asked a lot of the neighbors to come around to help with their shot-guns. When they would hear the bear scratching at one of the windows, they would pour in a volley at him, but after riddling every shutter on the first floor they could still hear the bear tearing around in there and growling. So Bartholomew and the others got into the cellar, and as the bear crossed the floor they would fire up through it at about the spot where they thought he was. But the bombardment only seemed to exasperate the animal, and after each shot they could hear him smashing something.

Then Partridge said maybe a couple of good dogs might whip him; and he borrowed a bulldog and a setter from Scott and pushed them through the front door. They listened, and for half an hour they could hear a most terrific contest raging; and Scott said he'd bet a million dollars that bull-dog would eat up any two bears in the Rocky Mountains. Then everything became still, and a few moments later they could hear the bear eating something and cracking bones with his teeth; and Bartholomew said that the Indian out in Colorado told him that the bear was particularly fond of dog-meat, and could relish a dog almost any time.

At last Bartholomew thought he would try strategy. He procured a huge iron hook with a sharp point to it, tied it to a rope and put three or four pounds of fresh beef on the hook. Then he went up the ladder, opened the trap-door in the roof and dropped in the bait. In a few moments he got a bite, and all hands manned the rope and pulled, when out came Scott's bull-dog, which had been hiding in the garret. Bartholomew was disgusted; but he put on fresh bait and threw in again, and in about an hour the bear took hold, and they hauled him out and knocked him on the head.

Then they entered the house. In the hall the carpet was covered with particles of dead setter, and in the parlor the carpet and the windows had been shot to pieces, while the furniture was full of bullet-holes. The bear had smashed the mirror, torn up six or seven chairs, knocked over the lamp and demolished all the crockery in the pantry. Bartholomew gritted his teeth as he surveyed the ruin, and Mrs. Bartholomew said she wished to patience he had stayed in Colorado. However, they fixed things up as well as they could, and then Mrs. Bartholomew sent into Partridge's for Charley and the youngest girl. When Charley came, he rushed up to Bartholomew and said,

"Oh, pa! where's my little baby-bear?"

Then Bartholomew gazed at him severely for a moment, looked around to see if Mrs. Bartholomew had left the room, and then gave Charley the most terrific spanking that he ever received.

The Bartholomew children have no pets at present but a Poland rooster which has moulted his tail.

CHAPTER XV.

LOVE, SUFFERING AND SUICIDE.

ETER LAMB, a young man who is employed in one of the village stores, some time ago conceived a very strong passion for a neighbor of his, Miss Julia Brown, the doctor's daughter. But the Fates seemed to be against the successful prosecution of his suit, for he managed to plunge into a series of catastrophes in the presence of the young lady, and to make himself so absurd that even his affection seemed ridiculous. One summer evening, when he was just beginning to make advances, Miss Brown came over to see Peter's sister, and the two girls sat out upon the front porch together in the darkness, talking. Peter plays a little upon the bugle, and it occurred to him that it would be a good thing to exhibit his skill to Julia. So he went into the dark parlor and felt over the top of the piano for the horn. It happened that his aunt from Penn's Grove had been there that day and had left her brass ear-trumpet lying on the piano, and Peter got hold of this without perceiving the mistake, as the two were of similar shape. He took it in his hand and went out on the porch where Miss

Brown was sitting. He asked Miss Brown if she was fond of music on the horn; and when she said she adored it, he asked her how she would like him to play " Ever of Thee;" and she said that was the only tune she cared anything for.

So Peter put the small end of the trumpet to his lips and blew. He blew and blew. Then he blew some more, and then he drew a fresh breath and blew again. The only sound that came was a hollow moan, which sounded so queerly in the darkness that Miss Brown asked him if he was not well. And when he said he was, she said that he went exactly like a second cousin of hers that had the asthma.

Then Peter remarked that somehow the horn was out of order for " Ever of Thee;" but if Miss Brown would like to hear "Sweetly I dreamed, Love," he would try to play it, and Miss Brown said that the fondest recollections clustered about the melody.

So Peter put the trumpet to his lips again and strained his lungs severely in an effort to make some music. It wouldn't come, but he made a very singular noise, which induced Miss Brown to ask if the horse in the stable back of the house had heaves. Then Peter said he thought somebody must have plugged the bugle up with something, and he asked his sister to light the gas in the entry while he cleaned it out. When she did so, the ear-trumpet became painfully conspicuous, and both the girls laughed. When Miss Brown laughed, Peter looked up at her with pain in his face, put on his hat and

13

went out into the street, where he could express his feelings in violent terms.

A few nights later the Browns had a tea-party, to which Mr. Lamb was invited. He went, determined to do his full share of entertaining the company. While supper was in progress, Mr. Lamb said in a loud voice,

"By the way, did you read that mighty good thing in the *Patriot* the other day about the woman over in Bridgeport? It was one of the most amusing things that ever came under my observation. The woman's name, you see, was Emma. Well, there were two young fellows paying attention to her, and after she'd accepted one of them the other also proposed to her and as she felt certain that the first one wasn't in earnest, she accepted the second one too. So a few days later both of 'em called at the same time, both claimed her hand, and both insisted on marrying her at once. Then, of course, she found herself face to face with a mighty unpleasant—unpleasant— Er—er—er— Less see; what's the word I want? Unpleasant— Er—er— Blamed if I haven't forgotten that word."

"Predicament," suggested Mr. Potts.

"No, that's not it. What's the name of that thing with two horns? Unpleasant— Er—er— Hang it! it's gone clear out of my mind."

"A cow," hinted Miss Mooney.

"No, not a cow."

"Maybe it's a buffalo," remarked Dr. Dox.

" No, no kind of an animal. Something else with two horns. Mighty queer I can't recall it."

" Perhaps it's a brass band," observed Butterwick.

" Or a man who's had a couple of drinks," suggested Dr. Brown.

" Of course not."

" You don't mean a fire company ?" asked Mrs. Banger.

" N—no. That's the confounded queerest thing I ever heard of, that I can't remember that word," said Mr. Lamb, getting warm and beginning to feel miserable.

" Well, give us the rest of the story without it," said Potts.

" That's the mischief of it," said Mr. Lamb. " The whole joke turns on that infernal word."

"*Two* horns did you say?" asked Dr. Dox. " Maybe it is a catfish."

" Or a snail," remarked Judge Twiddler.

" N—no ; none of those."

" Is it an elephant or a walrus ?" asked Mrs. Dox.

" I guess I'll have to give it up," said Mr. Lamb, wiping the perspiration from his brow.

" Well, that's the sickest old story I ever encountered," remarked Butterwick to Potts. Then everybody smiled, and Mr. Lamb, looking furtively at Julia, appeared to feel as if he would welcome death on the spot.

The mystery is yet unsolved; but it is believed that Peter was trying to build up the woman's name,

Emma, into a pun upon the word "dilemma." The
secret, however, is buried in his bosom.

Peter professes to be an expert in legerdemain, and
he came to Brown's prepared to perform some of his
best feats. When the company assembled in the
drawing-room after tea, he determined to redeem
the fearful blunder that he had made in the dining-
room.

Several of the magicians who perform in public do
what they call "the gold-fish trick." The juggler
stands upon the stage, throws a handkerchief over
his extended arm and produces in succession three
or four shallow glass dishes filled to the brim with
water in which live gold-fish are swimming. Of
course the dishes are concealed somehow upon the
person of the performer.

Peter had discovered how the trick was done, and
he resolved to do it now. So the folks all gathered in
one end of the parlor, and in a few moments Lamb
entered the door at the other end. He said,

"Ladies and gentlemen, you will perceive that I
have nothing about me except my ordinary clothing;
and yet I shall produce presently two dishes filled
with water and living fish. Please watch me nar-
rowly."

Then Peter flung the handkerchief over his hand
and arm, and we could see that he was working away
vigorously at something beneath it. He continued
for some moments, and still the gold-fish did not appear. Then he began to grow very red in the face,

THE GOLDFISH TRICK.

and we saw that something was the matter. Then
the perspiration began to stand on Peter's forehead,
and Mrs. Brown asked him if anything serious was
the matter. Then the company smiled, and the ma-
gician grew redder; but he kept on fumbling beneath
that handkerchief, and apparently trying to reach
around under his coat-tails. Then we heard something snap, and the next moment a quart of water
ran down the wizard's left leg and spread out over
the carpet. By this time he looked as if joy had
forsaken him for ever. But still he continued to feel
around under the handkerchief. At last another snap
was heard, and another quart of water plunged down
his right leg and formed a pool about his shoe. Then
the necromancer hurriedly said that the experiment
had failed somehow, and he darted into the dining-
room. We followed him, and found him sitting on
the sofa trying to remove his pantaloons. He exclaimed,

"Oh, gracious! Come here quick, and pull these
off! They're soaking wet, and I've got fifteen live
gold-fish inside my trousers flipping around, and
rasping the skin with their fins enough to set a man
crazy. Ouch! Hurry that shoe off, and catch that
fish there at my left knee, or I'll have to howl right
out."

Then we undressed him and picked the fish out
of his clothes, and we discovered that he had had two
dishes full of water and covered with India-rubber
tops strapped inside his trousers behind. In his

struggle to get at them he had torn the covers to
rags. We fixed him up in a pair of Dr. Brown's trousers, which were six inches too short for him, and
then he climbed over the back fence and went home.

Such misfortunes would have discouraged most
men utterly, but Peter was desperately in love ; and
a week or two later, without stopping to estimate his
chances, he proposed to his fair enchantress. She
refused him promptly, of course. He seemed almost
wild over his defeat, and his friends feared that some
evil consequences would ensue. Their apprehen-
sions were realized. Peter called upon young Potts
and asked him if he had a revolver, and Potts said
he had. Peter asked Potts to lend it to him, and
Potts did so. Then Peter informed Potts that he
had made up his mind to commit suicide. He said
that since Miss Brown had dealt so unkindly with
him he felt that life was an insupportable burden,
and he could find relief only in the tomb. He intended to go down by the river-shore and there
blow out his brains, and so end all this suffering and
grief and bid farewell to a world that had grown
dark to him. He said that he mentioned the fact to
Potts in confidence because he wanted him to perform some little offices for him when he was gone.
He entrusted to Potts a sonnet entitled "A Last
Farewell," and addressed to Julia Brown. This he
asked should be delivered to Miss Brown as soon as
his corpse was discovered. He said it might excite
a pang in her bosom and induce her to cherish his

memory. Then he gave Potts his watch as a keep-
sake, and handed him forty dollars, with which he
desired Mr. Potts to purchase a tombstone. He said
he would prefer a plain one with his simple name
cut upon it, and he wanted the funeral to be as un-
ostentatious as possible.

Potts promised to fulfill these commissions, and
he suggested that he would lend Mr. Lamb a bowie-
knife, with which he could slash himself up if the
pistol failed.

But the suicide said that he would make sure
work with the revolver, although he was much
obliged for the offer all the same. He said he would
like Potts to go around in the morning and break
the news as gently as possible to his unhappy
mother, and to tell her that his last thought was of
her. But he particularly requested that she would
not put on mourning for her erring son.

Then he said that the awful act would be performed on the beach, just below the gas-works, and
he wished Potts to come out with some kind of a
vehicle to bring the remains home. If Julia came
to the funeral, she was to have a seat in the carriage
next to the hearse; and if she wanted his heart, it
was to be given to her in alcohol. It beat only for
her. Potts was to tell his employers at the store
that he parted with them with regret, but doubtless
they would find some other person more worthy of
their confidence and esteem. He said he didn't care
where he was buried, but let it be in some lonely

place far from the turmoil and trouble of the world—
some place where the grass grows green and where
the birds come to carol in the early spring-time.

Mr. Potts asked him if he preferred a deep or a
shallow grave; but Mr. Lamb said it made very
little difference—when the spirit was gone, the mere
earthly clay was of little account. He owed seventy
cents for billiards down at the saloon, and Potts was
to pay that out of the money in his hands, and to
request the clergyman not to preach a sermon at the
cemetery. Then he shook hands with Potts and
went away to his awful doom.

The next morning Mr. Potts wrote to Julia, stopped in to tell them at the store, and nearly killed
Mrs. Lamb with the intelligence. Then he borrowed
Bradley's wagon; and taking with him the coroner,
he drove out to the beach, just below the gas-works,
to fetch home the mutilated corpse. When they
reached the spot, the body was not there, and Potts
said he was very much afraid it had been washed
away by the flood tide. So they drove up to Keyser's house, about half a mile from the shore, to ask
if any of the folks there had heard the fatal pistol-
shot or seen the body.

On going around to the wood-pile they saw Keyser
holding a terrier dog backed close up against a log.
The dog's tail was lying across the log, and another
man had the axe uplifted. A second later the axe
descended and cut the tail off close to the dog, and
while Keyser restrained the frantic animal, the other

man touched the bleeding stump with caustic. As
they let the dog go Potts was amazed to see that the
chopper was the wretched suicide. He was
amazed, but before he could ask any questions Peter stepped up to him and said,
"Hush-sh-sh! Don't say any-
thing about that matter. I
thought better of it. The
pistol looked so blamed dan-
gerous when I cocked it that I

changed my mind and came over here to Keyser's
to stay all night. I'm going to live just to spite
that Brown girl."

Then the coroner said that he didn't consider he had been treated like a gentleman, and he had half a notion to give Mr. Lamb a pounding. But they all drove home in the wagon, and just as Mrs. Lamb got done hugging Peter a letter was handed him containing the sonnet he had sent Julia. She returned it with the remark that it was the most dreadful nonsense she ever read, and that she knew he hadn't courage enough to kill himself. Then Peter went back to the store, and was surprised to find that his employers had so little emotion as to dock him for half a day's absence. What he wants now is to ascertain if he cannot compel Potts to give up that watch. Potts says he has too much respect for the memory of his unfortunate friend to part with it, but he is really sorry now that he ordered that tombstone. On the first of May, Peter's bleeding heart had been so far stanched as to enable him to begin skirmishing around the affections of a girl named Smith; and if she refuses him, he thinks that tombstone may yet come into play. But we all have our doubts about it.

CHAPTER XVI.

MR. FOGG AS A SPORTSMAN AND A SPOUSE.

GAME was so plenty about our neighborhood last fall that Mr. Fogg determined to become a sportsman. He bought a double-barrel gun, and after trying it a few times by firing it at a mark, he loaded it and placed it behind the hall door until he should want it. A few days later he made up his mind to go out and shoot a rabbit or two, so he shouldered his gun and strode off toward the open country. A mile or two from the town he saw a rabbit; and taking aim, he pulled the trigger. The gun failed to go off. Then he pulled the other trigger, and again the cap snapped. Mr. Fogg used a strong expression of disgust, and then, taking a pin, he picked the nipples of the gun, primed them with a little powder and made a fresh start. Presently he saw another rabbit. He took good aim, but both caps snapped. The rabbit did not see Mr. Fogg, so he put on more caps, and they snapped too.

Then Mr. Fogg cleaned out the nipples again, primed them and leveled the gun at a fence. The caps snapped again. Then Mr. Fogg became furi-

ous, and in his rage he expended forty-two caps trying to make the gun go off. When the forty-second
cap missed also, Mr. Fogg thought, perhaps, there
might be something the matter with the inside of
the gun, and so he sounded the barrels with his

ramrod. To his utter dismay, he discovered that
both barrels were empty. Mrs. Fogg, who is
nervous about firearms, had drawn the loads without
telling Fogg. The language used by Mr. Fogg
when he made this discovery was extremely disgraceful, and he felt sorry for it a moment afterward. As he grew cooler he loaded both barrels

and started afresh for the rabbits. He saw one in a few moments and was about to fire, when he noticed that there were no caps on the gun. He felt for one, and, to his dismay, found that he had snapped the last one off. Then he ground his teeth and walked home. On his way he saw a greater number of rabbits than he ever saw before or is likely to see again, and as he looked at them and thought of Mrs. Fogg he felt mad and murderous. He went gunning eight or ten times afterward that autumn, always with a full supply of ammunition, but he never once saw a rabbit or any other kind of game within gun-shot.

But he forgave Mrs. Fogg, and for a while their domestic peace was unruffled. One evening, however, while they were sitting together, they got to talking about their married life and their past troubles until both of them grew quite sympathetic. At last Mrs. Fogg suggested that it might help to kindle afresh the fire of love in their hearts if they would freely confess their faults to each other and promise to amend them. Mr. Fogg said it struck him as being a good idea. For his part, he was willing to make a clean breast of it, but he suggested that perhaps his wife had better begin. She thought for a moment, and this conversation ensued:

"Well, then," said Mrs. Fogg, "I am willing to acknowledge that I am the worst-tempered woman in the world."

Mr. Fogg (turning and looking at her). "Maria,

that's about the only time you ever told the square-
toed truth in your life."

Mrs. Fogg (indignantly). " Mr. Fogg, that's perfectly outrageous. You ought to be ashamed of
yourself."

F. "Well, you know it's so. You *have* got the
worst temper of any woman I ever saw—the very
worst; now haven't you?"

Mrs. F. " No, I haven't, either. I'm just as good-
tempered as you are."

F. "That's not so. You're as cross as a bear.

If you were married to a graven image, you'd quarrel with it."

Mrs. F. " That's an outrageous falsehood! There isn't any woman about this neighborhood that puts up with as much as I do without getting angry. You're a perfect brute."

F. " It's you that is the brute."

Mrs. F. " No, it isn't."

F. " Yes, it is. You're as snappish as a mad dog. It's few men that could live with you."

Mrs. F. " If you say that again, I'll scratch your eyes out."

F. " I dare you to lay your hands on me, you vixen."

Mrs. F. " You do, eh? Well, take that! and that " (cuffing him on the head).

F. " You let go of my hair, or I'll murder you."

Mrs. F. " I will; and I'll leave this house this very night; I won't live any longer with such a monster."

F. " Well, quit; get out. The sooner, the better. Good riddance to bad rubbish; and take your clothes with you."

Mrs. F. " I'm sorry I ever married you. You ain't fit to be yoked with any decent woman, you wretch you!"

F. " Well, you ain't half as sorry as I am. Goodbye. Don't come back soon."

Then Mrs. Fogg put on her bonnet and went around to her mother's, but she came back in the

14

morning. Mr. Fogg hasn't yet confessed what his principal failing is.

Mr. Fogg's life has been very troublous. He told me that he had a fit of sleeplessness one night lately, and after vainly trying to lose himself in slumber he happened to remember that he once read in an almanac that a man could put himself to sleep by imagining that he saw a lot of sheep jumping over a fence, and by counting them as they jumped. He determined to try the experiment; and closing his eyes, he fancied the sheep jumping and began to count. He had reached his one hundred and fortieth sheep, and was beginning to doze off, when Mrs. Fogg suddenly said,

" Wilberforce !"

" Oh, what ?"

" I believe that yellow hen of ours wants to set."

" Oh, don't bother me with such nonsense as that now! Do keep quiet and go to sleep."

Then Mr. Fogg started his sheep again and commenced to count. He got up to one hundred and twenty, and was feeling as if he would drop off at any moment, when, just as his one hundred and twenty-first sheep was about to take that fence, the baby began to cry.

" Hang that child!" he shouted at Mrs. Fogg. " Why don't you tend to it and put it to sleep ? Hush, you little imp, or I'll spank you !"

When Mrs. Fogg had quieted it, Mr. Fogg,

although a little nervous and excited, concluded to try it again. Turning on the imaginary mutton, he began. Only sixty-four sheep had slid over the fence, when Fogg's aunt knocked at the door and asked if he was awake. When she learned that he was, she said she believed he had forgotten to close the back shutters, and she thought she heard burglars in the yard.

Then Mr. Fogg arose in wrath and went down to see about it. He ascertained that the shutters were closed, as usual, and as he returned to bed he resolved that his aunt should leave the house for good in the morning, or he would. However, he thought he might as well give the almanac-plan another trial; and setting the sheep in motion, he began to count. This time he reached two hundred and forty, and would probably have got to sleep before the three hundredth sheep jumped, had not Mix's new dog, in the next yard, suddenly become home-sick and begun to express his feelings in a series of prolonged and exasperating howls.

Mr. Fogg was indignant. Neglecting the sheep, he leaped from bed and began to bombard Mix's new dog with boots, soap-cups and every loose object he could lay his hands on. He hit the animal at last with a plaster bust of Daniel Webster, and induced the dog to retreat to the stable and think about home in silence.

It seemed almost ridiculous to resume those sheep again, but he determined to give the almanac-man

one more chance, and soon as they began to jump
the fence he began to count, and after seeing the
eighty-second sheep safely over he was gliding
gently in the land of dreams, when Mrs. Fogg rolled
out of bed and fell on the floor with such violence
that she waked the baby and started it crying,
while Mr. Fogg's aunt came down stairs four steps
at a time to ask if they felt that earthquake.

The situation was too awful for words. Mr. Fogg
regarded it for a minute with speechless indignation,
and then, seizing a pillow, he went over to the sofa
in the back sitting-room and lay down.

He fell asleep in ten minutes without the assist-
ance of the almanac, but he dreamed all night that
he was being butted around the equator by a Cots-
wold ram, and he woke in the morning with a terrific headache and a conviction that sheep are good
enough for wool and chops, but not worth anything
as a narcotic.

Mr. Fogg has a strong tendency to exaggeration
in conversation, and he gave a striking illustration
of this in a story that he related one day when I
called at his house. Fogg was telling me about an
incident that occurred in a neighboring town a few
days before, and this is the way he related it : ·

" You see old Bradley over here is perfectly crazy
on the subject of gases and the atmosphere and such
things—absolutely wild ; and one day he was disput-
ing with Green about how high up in the air life

could be sustained, and Bradley said an animal could live about forty million miles above the earth if—"

"Not forty millions, my dear," interposed Mrs. Fogg; "only forty miles, he said."

"Forty, was it? Thank you. Well, sir, old Green, you know, said that was ridiculous; and he said he'd bet Bradley a couple of hundred thousand dollars that life couldn't be sustained half that way up, and so—"

"Wilberforce, you are wrong; he only offered to bet fifty dollars," said Mrs. Fogg.

"Well, anyhow, Bradley took him up quicker'n a wink, and they agreed to send up a cat in a balloon to decide the bet. So what does Bradley do but buy a balloon about twice as big as our barn and begin to—"

"It was only about ten feet in diameter, Mr. Adeler; Wilberforce forgets."

"—Begin to inflate her. When she was filled, it took eighty men to hold her; and—"

"Eighty men, Mr. Fogg!" said Mrs. F. "Why, you know Mr. Bradley held the balloon himself."

"He did, did he? Oh, very well; what's the odds? And when everything was ready, they brought out Bradley's tomcat and put it in the basket and tied it in, so it couldn't jump, you know. There were about one hundred thousand people looking on; and when they let go, you never heard such—"

"There was not one more than two hundred people there," said Mrs. Fogg; "I counted them myself."

"Oh, don't bother me!—I say, you never heard such a yell as the balloon went scooting up into the sky, pretty near out of sight. Bradley said she went up about one thousand miles, and—now, don't interrupt me, Maria; I know what the man said—and that cat, mind you, howling like a hundred fog-horns, so's you could a heard her from here to Peru. Well, sir, when she was up so's she looked as small as a pinhead something or other burst. I dunno know how it was, but pretty soon down came that balloon, a-hurtling toward the earth at the rate of fifty miles a minute, and old—"

"Mr. Fogg, you know that the balloon came down as gently as—"

"Oh, do hush up! Women don't know anything about such things.—And old Bradley, he had a kind of registering thermometer fixed in the basket along with that cat—some sort of a patent machine; cost thousands of dollars—and he was expecting to examine it; and Green had an idea he'd lift out a dead cat and take in the stakes. When all of a sudden, as she came pelting down, a tornado struck her— now, Maria, what in the thunder are you staring at me in that way for? It was a tornado—a regular cyclone—and it struck her and jammed her against the lightning-rod on the Baptist church-steeple; and there she stuck—stuck on that spire about eight hundred feet up in the air, and looked as if she had come there to stay."

"You may get just as mad as you like," said Mrs.

Fogg, "but I am positively certain that steeple's not an inch over ninety-five feet."

"Maria, I wish to *gracious* you'd go up stairs and look after the children.—Well, about half a minute after she struck out stepped that tomcat onto the weathercock. It made Green sick. And just then the hurricane reached the weathercock, and it began to revolve six hundred or seven hundred times a minute, the cat howling until you couldn't hear yourself speak.—Now, Maria, you've had your put; you keep quiet.—That cat stayed on the weathercock about two months—"

"Mr. Fogg, that's an awful story; it only happened last Tuesday."

"Never mind her," said Mr. Fogg, confidentially.— "And on Sunday the way that cat carried on and yowled, with its tail pointing due east, was so awful that they couldn't have church. And Sunday afternoon the preacher told Bradley if he didn't get that cat down he'd sue him for one million dollars damages. So Bradley got a gun and shot at the cat fourteen hundred times.—Now you didn't count 'em, Maria, and I did.—And he banged the top of the steeple all to splinters, and at last fetched down the cat, shot to rags; and in her stomach he found his thermometer. She'd ate it on her way up, and it stood at eleven hundred degrees, so old—"

"No thermometer ever stood at such a figure as that," exclaimed Mrs. Fogg.

"Oh, well," shouted Mr. Fogg, indignantly, "if you

think you can tell the story better than I can, why don't you tell it? You're enough to worry the life out of a man."

Then Fogg slammed the door and went out, and I left. I don't know whether Bradley got the stakes or not.

CHAPTER XVII.

HOW WE CONDUCT A POLITICAL CAMPAIGN.

THE people of Millburg feel a very intense interest in politics, and during a campaign there is always a good deal of excitement. The bitterest struggle that the town has had for a long while was that which preceded the election of a couple of years ago, when I was not a resident of the place. One incident particularly attracted a good deal of attention. Mr. Potts related the facts to me in the following language :

"You know we nominated Bill Slocum for burgess. He was the most popular man in the place; everybody liked him. And a few days after the convention adjourned Bill was standing talking to Joe Snowden about the election, and Bill happened to remark, 'I've got to win.' Mrs. Martin was going by at the time ; and as Bill was speaking very rapidly, he pronounced it like this : 'I've got t'win;' and Mrs. Martin thought he was telling Snowden that he'd got *twins.* And Mrs. Martin, just like all women about such matters, at once went through the village spreading the report that Mrs. Slocum had twins.

"So, of course, there was a fuss right off; and the

boys said that as Bill was a candidate, and a mighty good fellow anyhow you took him, it'd be nothing more than fair to congratulate him on his good luck by getting up some kind of a public demonstration from his fellow-citizens. Well, sir, you never saw such enthusiasm. The way that idea took was wonderful, and all hands agreed that we ought to have a parade. So they ran up the flags on the hotels and the town-hall, and on the two schooners down at the wharf, and Judge Twiddler adjourned the court over till the next day, and the supervisors gave the public schools a holiday and got up a turkey dinner for the convicts in the jail.

"And some of the folks drummed up the brass band, and it led off, with Major Slott following, carrying an American flag hung with roses. Then came the clergy in carriages, followed by the Masons and Odd Fellows and Knights of Pythias. And the Young Men's Christian Association turned out with the Sons of Temperance, about forty strong, in full regalia. And General Trumps pranced along on a white horse ahead of the Millburg Guards. After them came the judges on foot, followed by the City Council and the employés of the gas-works, and the members of the Bible Society and Patriotic Sons of America. Then came citizens walking two and two, afoot, while a big crowd of men and boys brought up the rear.

"The band, mind you, all this time playing the most gorgeous music—'Star-Spangled Banner,' 'Life on the Ocean Wave,' 'Beautiful Dreamer,' 'Home Again,' and all those things, with cymbals and Jenkins' colored man spreading himself on the big drum. And Bill never knew anything about it. It was a perfect surprise to him. And when the procession stopped in front of his house, they gave him three cheers, and he came rushing out on the porch to see what all the noise was about. As soon as he appeared the band struck up 'See, the Conquering Hero Comes,' and Major Slott lowered the flag, and General Trumps waved his hat, and the guard fired a salute, and everybody cheered.

" Bill bowed and made a little speech, and said how honored he was by such a demonstration, and he said he felt certain of victory, and when he was in office he would do his best to serve his fellow-citizens faithfully. Bill thought it was a political serenade ; and when he got through, General Trumps cried,

" ' Bring out the twins.'

" Bill looked puzzled for a minute, and then he says,

" ' I don't think I understand you. What d'you say ?'

" ' Bring out the twins,' said Judge Twiddler. ' Less look at 'em.'

" ' Twins !' says Bill. ' Twins ! Why, what d'ye mean, judge ?'

" ' Why, the twins. Rush 'em out. Hold 'em in the window, so's we can see 'em,' said Major Slott.

"'Gentlemen,' said Bill, 'there must be some little, some slight mistake respecting the—that is, you must have been misinformed about the—the—er—er— Why, there are no twins about this house.'

"Then they thought he was joking, and the band broke in with 'Listen to the Mocking-bird,' and Bill came down to find out the drift of Judge Twiddler's remarks. And when he really convinced them that there wasn't a twin anywhere about the place, you never saw a worse disgusted crowd in your life. Mad as fury. They said they had no idea Bill Slocum would descend to such trickery as that.

"So they broke up. The judge went back to the court-room so indignant he sentenced a prisoner for twenty years, when the law only allowed him to give ten. The supervisors, they took their spite out by docking the school-teachers half a day and cutting off the cranberry sauce from the turkey dinner at the jail. General Trumps got drunk as an owl. The City Councils held an adjourned meeting and raised the water rent on Slocum, and Jenkins' nigger burst in the head of the big drum with a brick. Mad's no word for it. They were wild with rage.

"And that killed Bill. They beat him by two hundred majority at the election, just on account of old Mrs. Martin misunderstanding him. Rough, wasn't it? But it don't seem to me like the fair thing on Bill."

Mr. Slocum was defeated, despite the fact that he wished to succeed. Mr. Walsh, it appears, was disappointed, in the same contest, in a wholly different manner. Mr. Walsh was the predecessor of our present coroner, Mr. Maginn. How Mr. Walsh was elected he informed me in these words :

" You know," said Mr. Walsh, " that I didn't want that position. When they talked of nominating me, I told them, says I, ' It's no use ; you needn't elect me ; I'm not going to serve. D'you s'pose I'm going to give up a respectable business to become a kind of State undertaker ? I'm opposed to this *postmortem* foolery, any way. When a man's blown up with gunpowder, it don't interest me to know what killed him ; so you needn't make me coroner, for I won't serve.'

" Well, do you believe that they persisted in nominating me on the Republican ticket—actually put me up as a candidate ? So I published a letter declining the nomination ; but they absolutely had the impudence to keep me on the ticket and to hold mass-meetings, at which they made speeches in my favor. I was pretty mad about it, because it showed such a disregard of my feelings ; and so I chummed in with the Democrats, and for about two months I went around to the Democratic mass-meetings and spoke against myself and in favor of the opposition candidate. I thought I had them for sure, because I knew more about my own failings than those other fellows did, and I enlarged upon them until I made myself out— Well, I heaped up the iniquity until I used to go home feeling that I was a good deal wickeder sinner than I ever thought I was before. It did me good, too: I reformed. I've been a better man ever since.

" Now, you'd a thought people would a considered me pretty fair authority about my own unfitness for the office, but hang me if the citizens of this county positively didn't go to the polls and elect me by about eight hundred majority. I was the worst disappointed of any man you ever saw. I had repeaters around at the polls, too, voting for the Democratic candidate, and I paid four of the judges to falsify the returns, so as to elect him. But it was no use; the majority was too big. And on election night the Republican executive committee came round to serenade me, and as soon as the band struck up I opened on them with a shot-gun and wounded the bass drummer in the leg. But they kept on playing; and after a while, when they stopped, they poked some congratulatory resolutions under the front door, and gave me three cheers and went home. I was never so annoyed in my life.

" Then they sent me round my certificate of election, but I refused to receive it; and those fellows seized me and held me while Harry Hammer pushed the certificate into my coat-pocket, and then they all quit. The next day a man was run over on the railroad, and they wanted me to tend to him. But I was angry, and I wouldn't. So what does the sheriff do but come here with a gang of police and carry me out there by force ? And he hunted up a jury, which brought in a verdict. Then they wanted me to take the fees, but I wouldn't touch them. I said I wasn't going to give my sanction to the proceedings. But of course it was no use. I thought I was living in

a free country, but I wasn't. The sheriff drew the money and got a mandamus from the court, and he came here one day while I was at dinner. When I said I wouldn't touch a dollar of it, he drew a pistol and said if I didn't take the money he'd blow my

brains out. So what was a man to do? I resigned
fifteen times, but somehow those resignations were
suppressed. I never heard from them. Well, sir,
at last I yielded, and for three years I kept skirmishing around, perfectly disgusted, meditating over folks
that had died suddenly.

"And do you know that on toward the end of my
term they had the face to try to nominate me again?
It's a positive fact. Those politicians wanted me to
run again; said I was the most popular coroner the
county ever had; said that everybody liked my way
of handling a dead person, it was so full of feeling
and sympathy, and a lot more like that. But what
did I do? I wasn't going to run any such risk again.
So I went up to the city, and the day before the convention met I sent word down that I was dead. Cir-
culated a report that I'd been killed by falling off a
ferry-boat. Then they hung the convention-hall in
black and passed resolutions of respect, and then
they nominated Barney Maginn.

"On the day after election I turned up, and you
never saw men look so miserable, so cut to the
heart, as those politicians. They said it was an infamous shame to deceive them in that way, and they
declared that they'd run me for sheriff at the next
election to make up for it. If they do, I'm going to
move for good. I'm going to sail for Colorado, or
some other decent place where they'll let a man
alone. I'll die in my tracks before I'll ever take another office in this county. I will, now mind me!"

CHAPTER XVIII.

THE MATUTINAL ROOSTER.

ORATIO remarks to Hamlet, "The morning cock crew loud;" and I have no doubt he did; he always does, especially if he is confined during the performance of his vocal exercises to a narrow city yard surrounded by brick walls which act as sounding-boards to carry the vibrations to the ears of a sleeper who is already restless with the summer heat and with the buzzing of early and pertinacious flies. To such a man, aroused and indignant, there comes a profound conviction that the urban rooster is far more vociferous than his rural brethren; that he can sing louder, hold on longer and begin again more quickly than the bucolic cock who has communed only with nature and known no envious longings to outshriek the morning milkman or the purveyor of catfish. And he who is thus afflicted perhaps may be justified if he regards "the cock, that trumpet of the morn," as an insufferable nuisance, whose only excuse for existence is that he is pleasant to the eye and the palate when, bursting with stuffing, he lies, brown and crisp, among the gravy, ready for the carving-knife.

But the man who is fortunate enough to dwell in the country during the ardent summer days takes a different and more kindly view of chanticleer. If he is waked early in the morning by the clarion voice of some neighboring cock, he will not repine, provided he went to bed at a reasonably early hour, for he will hear some music that is not wholly to be despised. The rooster in the neighboring barn-yard gives out the theme. His voice is a deep, but broken, bass. It is suggestive of his having roosted during the night in a draft, which has inflamed his vocal chords so that his tones have lost their sweetness. It is as if a coffee-mill had essayed to crow. The theme is taken up by a thin-voiced rooster a quarter of a mile away, and scarcely has he reached the concluding note before a baritone cock, a little more remote, repeats the cadence, only to have his song broken in upon by a nearer bird who understands exactly the part he is to play in the fugue. And so it passes on from the one to the other, growing fainter and fainter in the distance as Shanghai sings to Bantam and Chittagong to Brahmapootra, until, at last, there is silence; and then, "O hark! O hear! How thin and clear!" far, far away some rooster sends out a delicate falsetto note that might have come from a microscopic cock who is practicing ventriloquism in the cellar. Instantly the catarrhal chicken in the next yard begins the refrain again with his hoarse voice; and then again and again the fugue goes round, never tiring the listener, but always growing more musical, until the sun is fairly up, the hens awake and the scratching of the day is ready to begin.

The note of the cock has been misrepresented. Shakespeare, following usage, perhaps, has given it as "cock-a-doodle-doo," and that is the accepted interpretation of it. But this does not convey the proper impression. We should say that if human syllables can tell the story they would assume some such form as:

Ooauk-auk-auk-au-au-au-auk!

It is a song that ought to be studied and glorified in print. Think what a history it has! That identical combination of sounds which wakes and maddens the sleeping citizen of to-day was heard by Noah and his family with precisely the same cadence and accent in the ark. It was that very crow that Peter heard when he had denied his Master. It is a crow that has come down to us from Eden almost without a moment's intermission. It is a crow which has passed round the world century after century, and now passes, as the herald of the coming of the sun. It may yet be made the theme of a majestic musical composition, now that Wagner has come to teach men how to build a lyric drama upon a phrase. Perhaps the coming American national song may have this familiar crow for its inspiration and its burden. We might do worse, perhaps, than to take the rooster for our national bird, even if we reject his song as the basis of our national anthem.

We took our eagle from Rome, as France did hers; would it not have been wiser if we had taken the cock instead, as France did after the Revolution? The Romans and Greeks regarded the cock as a sacred bird. The principal thing that the average school-boy remembers about Socrates is that he killed himself immediately after ordering that a cock should be sacrificed to Æsculapius; and some have held that the reason of his suicide was the vociferousness of the cock, which he wanted to kill in revenge for the misery it had caused him while he was trying to sleep or to think.

The cock is a braver bird than the eagle. He has ever been a bold and ready warrior, and has worn a warrior's spurs from the beginning. He has one high soldierly quality: he knows when he is whipped; for who has not seen him, when defeated in a gallant contest, sneak away to a distant corner to stand, with ruffled feathers, upon a single leg, the very picture of humiliation and despair? And he is vigilant, for has he not for ages revolved upon church-steeples as the emblem of watchfulness? He has the homelier virtues. He is a kind father and a fond as well as a multitudinous husband. He knows how to protect his family from errant and disreputable roosters, and he is always willing to stand aside with unsatisfied appetite and permit them to devour a dainty he has found. He is useful and admirable in his relation to this world, and he is not without value to the next, for popular belief has credited him with the office of warning revisiting spirits to retire from the earth ; and when he crows all through the night, the Katie Kings and other ghostly persons who come from space to rap upon tables and evoke discordant twangs from guitars are deaf to the seductive entreaties of the mediums. When

> " This bird of dawning singeth all night long,
> . . . then they say no spirit dares stir abroad."

Perhaps the true method of expelling Satan from the land and of reforming the corruption which afflicts the country is to place the cock upon our standards and to offer him inducements to crow perpetually. There should be something to that effect in the political platforms. A goose saved Rome ; why should not a rooster rescue America ? Let the patriot who curses the noisy bird which crows him from his drowsy couch at an unseemly hour think of these things and allay his wrath with reflections upon the well-deserved glories of the matutinal rooster.

I have one neighbor who does not regard the crowing cock with proper enthusiasm—who is indeed inclined to look upon it with disgust; but as he has been a victim of the bird's vociferousness, perhaps his

sentiments of dislike for the proud bird may be
excused.

The agricultural society of our county held a
poultry show last fall, and Mr. Butterwick, who is a
member of the society, was invited to deliver the
address at the commencement of the fair.   Mr. Butterwick prepared what he considered a very learned
paper upon the culture of domestic fowls; and when
the time arrived, he was on the platform ready to
enlighten the audience.   The birds were arranged
around the hall in cages; and when the exhibition
had been formally opened by the chairman, the orator
came forward with his manuscript in his hand.   Just
as he began to read it a black Poland rooster close
to the stage uttered a loud and defiant crow.   There
were about two hundred roosters in the hall, and
every one of them instantly began to crow in the
most vehement manner, and the noise excited the
hens so much that they all cackled as loudly they
could.

Of course the speaker's voice could not be heard,
and he came to a dead halt, while the audience
laughed.   After waiting for ten minutes silence was
again obtained, and Butterwick began a second time.

As soon as he had uttered the words " Ladies and
gentlemen," the Poland rooster, which seemed to
have a grudge against the speaker, emitted another
preposterous crow, and all the other fowls in the
room joined in the deafening chorus.   The audience
roared, and Butterwick grew red in the face with

passion. But when the noise subsided, he went at it again, and got as far as " Ladies and gentlemen, the domestic barn-yard fowl affords a subject of the highest interest to the—" when the Poland rooster became engaged in a contest with an overgrown Shanghai chicken, and this set the hens of the combatants to cackling, and in a moment the entire collection was in another uproar. This was too much. Mr. Butterwick was beside himself with rage. He flung down his manuscript, rushed to the cage, and shaking his fist at the Poland chicken exclaimed,

" You diabolical fiend, I've half a mind to murder you !"

Then he kicked the cage to pieces with his foot, and seizing the rooster twisted its neck and flung it on the floor. Then he fled from the hall, followed by peals of laughter from the audience and more terrific clatter from the fowls. The exhibition was opened without further ceremony, and the dissertation on the domestic barn-yard fowl was ordered to be printed in the annual report of the proceedings of the society.

One day while I was talking with Mr. Keyser upon the subject of the cock he pointed to a chicken that was roosting upon an adjoining fence, and told me a story about the fowl that I must refuse to believe.

" Perhaps you never noticed that rooster," said Keyser—" very likely you wouldn't have observed

him; but I don't care in what light you look at him, the more you study him, the more talented he appears. You talk about your American iggles and birds of freedom, but that insignificant-looking chicken yonder can give any of them twenty points and pocket them at the first shot. That rooster has traits of character that'd adorn almost any walk of life.

"Most chickens are kinder stupid; but what I

like about him is that he is sympathetic, he has feeling. I know last fall that my Shanghai hen was taken sick while she was trying to hatch out some eggs, and that rooster was so compassionate that he used to go in and set on that nest for hours, trying to help her out, so that she could go off recreating after exercise. And when she died, he turned right in and took charge of things—seemed to feel that he ought to be a father to those unborn little orphans; and he straddled around over those eggs for ever so long. He never got much satisfaction out of it, though. Most of them were duck eggs, and it seemed to kinder cut him up when he looked at those birds after they hatched out. He took it to heart, and appeared to feel low-spirited and afflicted. He would go off and stand by himself—stand on one leg in a corner of the fence and let his mind brood over his troubles until you'd pity him. It disgusted him to think how the job turned out.

"Now, you wouldn't think such a chicken as that would have much courage, but he'd just as leave fight a wagon-load of tigers as not. He got a notion in his head that that rooster over there on the Baptist church-steeple was alive, and he couldn't bear to think that it was up there sailing around and putting on airs over him, and a good many times I've seen him try to fly up at it, so's to arrange a fight. When he found he couldn't make it, he'd crow at the Baptist rooster and dare it to come down, and at last, when all his efforts were useless, would you believe that rooster one day attacked the sexton as the weathercock's next friend, and drove his spurs so far into the sexton's shanks that he walked on crutches for more'n a week? I never saw a mere chicken have such fine instincts and such pluck.

"He is a splendid fighter, anyway, just as he stands. Why, he had a little fuss with Murphy's Poland rooster here some time back, and instead of going at him and taking the chances of getting whipped, that chicken actually put himself into training, ate nothing but corn, took regular exercise, went to roost early, took a cold bath every morning and got a pullet to rub him down with a corn-cob. It was wonderful; and in a week or so he was all bone and muscle, and he flickered over the fence after Murphy's rooster and sent him whizzing into the next world on the fourth round.

"I never knew such a rooster. Now, do you know I believe that chicken actually takes an interest in politics? Oh, you may laugh, but last fall during the campaign he was so excited about something that he couldn't eat, and the night they had the Republican mass-meeting here he roosted on the chandelier in the hall, and every time General Trumps made a good point that chicken would cackle and flap his wings, as much as to say, 'Them's my sentiments!' And on the day of the parade he turned out and followed the last wagon, keeping step with the music and never dropping out of line but once, when he stopped to fight a Democratic rooster belonging to old Byerly, who was on the Democratic ticket. And in the morning, after the Republicans won, he just got on the fence out here and crowed so vociferously you could've heard him across the river, particularly when I ran up the American flag and read the latest returns.

"Yes, sir. Now, I know you'll think it's ridiculous when I tell you, but it's an actual fact, that that very day my daughter was playing the 'Star-spangled Banner' on the piano, and that rooster, when he heard it, came scudding into the parlor, and after flipping up on the piano he struck out and crowed that tune just as natural as if he was an educated musician. Positive truth; and he beat time with his tail. He don't crow like any other rooster. Every morning he works off selections from Beethoven and Mozart and those people, and on Sundays he frequently lets himself out on hymn-tunes. I've known him to set on that fence for more'n an hour at a time practicing the scales, and he nearly kicked another rooster to death one day because that rooster crowed flat. I saw him do it myself. And now I really must be going. Good-morning."

I think I shall send out and kill that rooster at the first opportunity. I want Keyser to have one thing less to fib about. He has too much variety at present.

CHAPTER XIX.

AN UNRULY METER.—SCENES IN A SANCTUM.

DURING one of the cold spells of last winter the gas-meter in my cellar was frozen. I attempted to thaw it out by pouring hot water over it, but after spending an hour upon the effort I emerged from the contest with the meter with my feet and trousers wet, my hair full of dust and cobwebs and my temper at fever heat. After studying how I should get rid of the ice in the meter, I concluded to use force for the purpose, and so, seizing a hot poker, I jammed it through a vent-hole and stirred it around inside of the meter with a considerable amount of vigor. I felt the ice give way, and I heard the wheels buzz around with rather more vehemence than usual. Then I went up stairs.

I noticed for three or four days that the internal machinery of the meter seemed to be rattling around in a remarkable manner; it could be heard all over the house. But I was pleased to find that it was working again in spite of the cold weather, and I retained my serenity.

About two weeks afterward my gas-bill came. It accused me of burning during the quarter about one million five hundred thousand feet of gas, and it called on me to settle to the extent of nearly three hundred and fifty thousand dollars. I put on my hat and went down to the gas-office. I addressed one of the clerks:

" How much gas did you make at the Blank works last quarter?"

" I dunno; about a million feet, I reckon."

" Well, you have charged me in my bill for burning half a million more than you made; I want you to correct it."

" Less see the bill. Hm—m—m! this is all right. It's taken off of the meter. That's what the meter says."

" S'pose'n it does; I *couldn't* have burned more'n you made."

" Can't help that; the meter can't lie."

" Well, but how d'you account for the difference?"

" Dunno; 'tain't our business to go nosing and poking around after scientific truth. We depend on the meter. If that says you burned six million feet, why, you *must* have burned it, even if we never made a foot of gas out at the works."

" To tell you the honest truth," said I, "the meter was frozen, and I stirred it up with a poker and set it whizzing around."

" Price just the same," said the clerk. " We charge for pokers just as we do for gas."

" You are not actually going to have the audacity
to ask me to pay three hundred and fifty thousand
dollars on account of that poker ?"

" If it was seven hundred thousand dollars, I'd take
it with a calmness that would surprise you. Pay up,
or we'll turn off your gas."

"Turn it off and be hanged," I exclaimed as I
emerged from the office, tearing the bill to fragments.
Then I went home; and grasping that too lavish
poker, I approached the meter. It had registered
another million feet since the bill was made out; it
was running up a score of a hundred feet a minute;
in a month I would have owed the gas company
more than the United States Government owes its
creditors. So I beat the meter into a shapeless mass,
tossed it into the street and turned off the gas inside
the cellar.

Then I went down to the *Patriot* office to persuade
Major Slott to denounce the fraud practiced by the
company. While I was in the editorial room two or
three visitors came in. The first one behaved in a
violent and somewhat mysterious manner. He
saluted the major by throwing a chair at him. Then
he seized the editor by the hair, bumped his head
against the table three or four times and kicked him.
When this exhilarating exercise was over, the visitor
shook his fist very close to the major's nose and
said, " You idiot and outcast, if you don't put that
notice in to-morrow, I'll come round here and murder you! Do you hear me ?" Then he cuffed the

major's ears a couple of times, kicked him some more, emptied the ink-stand over his head, poured the sand from the sand-box in the same place, knocked over the table and went out. During all this time the major sat still with a sickly kind of a smile upon his face and never uttered a word. When the man left, the major picked up the table, wiped the ink and sand from his face, and turning to me said,

"Harry will have his little fun, you see."

"He is a somewhat exuberant humorist," I replied. "What was the object of the joke?"

"Well, he's going to sell his furniture at auction, and I promised to notice the fact in to-day's *Patriot*, but I forgot it, and he called to remind me of it."

"Do all of your friends refresh your memory in that vivid manner? If I'd been in your place, I'd have knocked him down."

"No, you wouldn't," said Slott—"no, you wouldn't. Harry is the sheriff, and he controls two thousand dollars' worth of official advertising. I'd sooner he'd kick me from here to Borneo and back again than to take that advertising away from the *Patriot*. What are a few bumps and a sore shin or two compared with all that fatness? No, sir; he can have all the fun he wants out of me."

The next visitor was less demonstrative. He was tall and slender and clad in the habiliments of woe. He entered the office and took a chair. Removing his hat, he wiped the moisture from his eyes, rubbed his nose thoughtfully for a moment, put his hand-kerchief in his hat, his hat upon the floor, and said,

"You didn't know Mrs. Smith?"

"I hadn't that pleasure. Who was she?"

"She was my wife. She's been sick some time. But day before yesterday she was took worse, and she kep' on sinking until evening, when she gave a kinder sudden jump a couple of times, and then her spirit flickered. Dead, you know. Passed away into another world."

"I'm very sorry."

"So am I. And I called around to see if I

couldn't get some of you. literary people to get out
some kind of a poem describing her peculiarities, so
that I can advertise her in the paper."

" I dunno ; maybe we might."

" Oh, you didn't know her, you say ?   Well, she

was a sing'lar kinder woman.   Had strong charac-
teristics.   Her nose was the crookedest in the State—
all bent around sideways.   Old Captain Binder used .
to say that it looked like the jibsail of an oyster-

sloop on the windward tack. Only his fun, you
know. But Helen never minded it. She said herself that it aimed so much around the corner that
whenever she sneezed she blew down her back hair.
There were rich depths of humor in that woman.
Now, I don't mind if you work into the poem some
picturesque allusion to the condition of her nose, so
her friends will recognize her. And you might also
spend a verse or two on her defective eye."

" What was the matter with her eye ?"

" Gone, sir—gone! Knocked out with a chip
while she was splitting kin'ling-wood when she
was a child. She fixed it up somehow with a glass
one, and it gave her the oddest expression you ever
saw. The false one would stand perfectly still while
the other one was rolling around, so that 'bout half
the time you couldn't tell whether she was studying
astronomy or watching the hired girl pare potatoes.
And she lay there at night with the indisposed eye
wide open glaring at me, while the other was tight
shut, so that sometimes I'd get the horrors and
kick her and shake her to make her get up and fix
it. Once I got some mucilage and glued the lid
down myself, but she didn't like it when she woke
in the morning. Had to soak her eye in warm
water, you know, to get it open.

" Now, I reckon you could run in some language
about her eccentricities of vision, couldn't you ?
Don't care what it is, so that I have the main facts."

" Was she peculiar in other respects ?"

"Well, yes. One leg was gone—run over by a wagon when she was little. But she wore a patent leg that did her pretty well. Bothered her sometimes, but most generally gave her a good deal of comfort. She was fond of machinery. She was very grateful for her privileges. Although sometimes it worried her, too. The springs'd work wrong now and then, and maybe in church her leg'd give a spurt and begin to kick and hammer away at the board in front of the pew until it sounded like a boiler-factory. Then I'd carry her out, and most likely it'd kick at me all the way down the aisle and end up by dancing her around the vestibule, until the sexton would rebuke her for waltzing in church. Seems to me there's material for poetry in that, isn't there? She was a self-willed woman. Often, when she wanted to go to a sewing-bee or to gad about somewhere, maybe, I'd stuff that leg up the chimney or hide it in the wood-pile. And when I wouldn't tell her where it was, do you know what she'd do?"

"What?"

"Why, she'd lash an umbrella to her stump and drift off down the street 'sif that umbrella was born there. You couldn't get ahead of her. She was ingenious.

"So I thought I'd mention a few facts to you, and you can just throw them together and make them rhyme, and I'll call 'round and pay you for them. What day? Tuesday? Very well; I'll run in on Tuesday and see how you've fixed her up."

Then Mr. Smith smoothed up his hat with his handkerchief, wiped the accumulated sorrow from his eyes, placed his hat upon his head, and sailed serenely out and down the stairs toward his desolated hearthstone.

The last caller was an artist. He took a chair and said,

"My name is Brewer; I am the painter of the allegorical picture of 'The Triumph of Truth' on exhibition down at Yelverton's. I called, major, to make some complaint about the criticism of the work which appeared in your paper. Your critic seems to have misunderstood somewhat the drift of the picture. For instance, he says— Let me quote the paragraph:

" 'In the background to the left stands St. Augustine with one foot on a wooden Indian which is lying upon the ground. Why the artist decorated St. Augustine with a high hat and put his trousers inside his boots, and why he filled the saint's belt with navy revolvers and tomahawks, has not been revealed. It strikes us as being ridiculous to the very last degree.'

"Now, this seems to me to be a little too harsh. That figure does *not* represent St. Augustine. It is meant for an allegorical picture of Brute Force, and it has its foot upon Intellect—*Intellect*, mind you! and *not* a cigar-store Indian. It is a likeness of Captain Kidd, and I set it back to represent the fact that Brute Force belonged to the Dark Ages. How

on earth that man of yours ever got an idea that it
was St. Augustine beats me."

"It is singular," said the major.

"And now let me direct your attention to another
paragraph. He says,

"'We were astonished to notice that while Noah's
ark goes sailing in the remote distance, there is
close to it a cotton-factory, the chimney of which is
pouring out white smoke that covers the whole of
the sky in the picture, while the ark seems to be
trying to sail down that chimney. Now, they didn't
have cotton-factories in those days; the thing don't
hang. The artist must have been drunk.'

"Now, this insinuation pains me. How would
you like it if you painted a picture of the tower of
Babel, and somebody should come along and insist
that it was the chimney of a cotton-factory, and that
the clouds with which the sky is covered were smoke?
Cotton-factory! Your man certainly cannot be familiar with the Scriptures; and when he talks about
the ark sailing down that chimney, he forgets that
the reason why it is standing on one end is that the
water is so rough as to make it pitch. You know
the Bible says that arks did pitch 'without and
within.' Now, don't it?"

"I think maybe it does," said the major.

"But that's not the worst. I can stand that; but
what do you think of a man that goes to criticising
a work of art, and says— Now just listen to this:

"'On the right is a boy who has his clothes off,

246   *ELBOW-ROOM.*

and has apparently been in swimming, and has been rescued by a big yellow dog just as he was about to drown. What this has to do with the Triumph of Truth we don't know, but we do know that the dog is twice as large as the boy, and that he has the boy's head in his mouth, while the boy's hands are tied behind his back. Now, for a boy to go in swimming with his hands tied, and for a dog to swallow his head so as to drag him out, appears to us the awfulest foolishness on earth.'

"You will probably be surprised to learn that your critic is here referring to a very beautiful study of a Christian martyr who has been thrown among the wild beasts of the arena, and who is engaged in being eaten by a lion. The animal is not a yellow dog; that human being has not been in swimming; and the reason that he is smaller than the lion is that I had to make him so in order to get his head into the lion's mouth. Would you have me represent the lion as large as an elephant? Would you have me paste a label on the Christian martyr to inform the public that 'This is not a boy who has been treading water with his hands tied'? Now, look at the matter calmly. Is the *Patriot* encouraging art when it goes on in this manner? Blame me if I think it is."

"It certainly doesn't seem so."

"Well, then, what do you say to this? What do you think of a critic who remarks,

"'But the most extraordinary thing in the picture

is the group in the foreground. An old lady with
an iron coal-scuttle on her head is handing some
black pills to a ballet-dancer dressed in pink tights,
while another woman in a badly-fitting chemise
stands by them brushing off the flies with the branch
of a tree, with a canary-bird resting upon her shoulder and trying to sing at some small boys who are
seen in the other corner of the field. What this
means we haven't the remotest idea; but we do know
that the ballet-dancers' legs have the knee-pans at
the back of the joint, and that the canary-bird looks
more as if he wanted to eat the coal-scuttle than as
if he desired to sing.'

"This is too bad. Do you know what that beautiful group really represents? That old lady, as
your idiot calls her, is Minerva, the goddess of War,
handing cannon balls to the goddess of Love
as a token there shall be no more war. And the
figure in what he considers the chemise is the genius
of Liberty holding out an olive branch with one
hand, while upon her shoulder rests an American
eagle screaming defiance at the enemies of his country, who are seen fleeing in the distance. Canary
bird! small boys! ballet-girl! The man is crazy,
sir; stark, staring mad. And now I want you to
write up an explanation for me. This kind of thing
exposes me to derision. I can't stand it, and, by
George! I won't! I'll sue you for libel."

Then the major promised to make amends, and
Mr. Brewer withdrew in a calmer mood.

CHAPTER XX

HIGH ART.

N itinerant theatrical company gave two or three performances in Millburg last winter, and in a very creditable fashion, too. One of the plays produced was Shakespere's "King John," with the "eminent tragedian Mr. Hammer" in the character of the *King*. It is likely that but for an unfortunate misunderstanding the entertainment would have been wholly delightful. There is a good deal of flourishing of trumpets in the drama, and the manager, not having a trumpeter of his own, engaged a German musician named Schenck to supply the music. Schenck doesn't understand the English language very well, and the manager put him behind the scenes on the left of the stage, while the manager stood in the wing at the right of the stage. Then Schenck was instructed to toot his trumpet when the manager signaled with his hand. Everything went along smoothly enough until *King John* (Mr. Hammer) came to the passage, "Ah, me! this tyrant fever burns me up!" Just as *King John* was about to utter this the manager brushed a fly off of his nose, and Schenck, mistaking the movement for the appointed signal, blew out a frightful blare upon his bugle. The *King* was furious and the manager made wild gestures for Schenck to stop, but that estimable German musician imagined that the manager wanted him to play louder, and every time a fresh motion was made Schenck emitted a more terrific blast. The result was something like the following :

King John. "Ah, me! this tyrant—"

Schenck (with his cheeks distended and his eyes beaming through his spectacles). "Ta-tarty; ta-ta-tarty, rat-tat tarty-tarty-tarty, ta-ta-ta, tanarty-arty, te-tarty."

King John. "Fever burns—"

Schenck. "Rat-tat-tarty, poopen-arty, oopen-arty, ta-tarty-arty-oopen-arty; ta-ta ; ta-ta-ta-tarty poopen-arty, poopen a-a-a-arty-arty."

King John. "Ah, me! this—"

Schenck (ejecting a hurricane from his lungs). "Hoopen-oopen-oopen-arty, ta-tarty; tat-tat-ta-tarty-ti-ta-tarty; poopen-ta-poopen-ta-poopen-ta-a-a-a-tarty-whoop ta-ta."

King John (quickly). "Tyrant fever burns me up."

Schenck (with perspiration standing out on his forehead). "To-ta ta-ta. Ta-ta ta-ta tatten-atten-atten arty te-tarty poopen oopen-oo-oo-oo-oo-oopen te-tarty ta-ta-ar-ar-ar-te tarty-to-ta-a-a-a-*a*-A-A-*A !*"

King John (to the audience). "Ladies and gentlemen—"

Schenck. "Ta-ta, ta-ta, ta-ta, poopen-oopen, poopen-oopen, te-ta, tarty oo-hoo oo-hoo-te tarty arty, appenarty."

King John. "There is a German idiot behind the scenes here who is—

Schenck. "Whoopen-arty te-tarty-arty-arty-ta-ta-a-a-a tat-tarty."

King John. "Blowing infamously upon a horn, and—"

Schenck. "Poopen-arty."

King John. "If you will excuse me—"

Schenck. "Pen-arty-arty."

King John. "I will go behind the scenes and check him in his wild career."

Schenck. "Poopen-arty ta-tarty-arty poopen-a-a-a-arty tat-tat-ta-tarty."

Then *King John* disappeared and a scuffle was heard, with some violent expressions in the German language. Ten minutes later a gentleman from the Fatherland might have been seen standing on the pavement in front of the theatre with a bugle under his arm and a handkerchief to his bleeding nose, wondering what on earth was the matter. In the mean time the *King* had returned to the stage, and the performance concluded without any music. After this the manager will employ home talent when he wants airs on the bugle.

I have been studying the horn to some extent myself. Nothing is more delightful than to have sweet

music at home in the evenings. It lightens the bur-
dens of care, it soothes the ruffled feelings, it exercises a refining influence upon the children, it calms
the passions and elevates the soul. A few months
ago I thought that it might please my family if I
learned to play upon the French horn. It is a beautiful
instrument, and after hearing a man perform on it at
a concert I resolved to have one. I bought a splendid one in the city, and concluded not to mention
the fact to any one until I had learned to play a tune.
Then I thought I would serenade Mrs. A. some
evening and surprise her. Accordingly, I determined to practice in the garret. When I first tried
the horn I expected to blow only a few gentle notes
until I learned how to handle it; but when I put the
mouth-piece to my lips, no sound was evoked. Then
I blew harder. Still the horn remained silent. Then
I drew a full breath and sent a whirlwind tearing
through the horn; but no music came. I blew at it
for half an hour, and then I ran a wire through the
instrument to ascertain if anything blocked it up. It
was clear. Then I blew softly and fiercely, quickly
and slowly. I opened all the stops. I puffed and
strained and worked until I feared an attack of apo-
plexy. Then I gave it up and went down stairs; and
Mrs. A. asked me what made me look so red in the
face. For four days I labored with that horn, and
got my lips so puckered up and swollen that I went
about looking as if I was perpetually trying to whistle. Finally, I took the instrument back to the store

and told the man that the horn was defective.
What I wanted was a horn with insides to it; this
one had no more music to it than a terra-cotta drain-
pipe.   The man took it in his hand, put it to his lips
and played "Sweet Spirit, Hear my Prayer," as easily
as if he were singing.   He said that what I needed
was to fix my mouth properly, and he showed me
how.

After working for three more afternoons in the
garret the horn at last made a sound.   But it was
not a cheering noise; it reminded me forcibly of the
groans uttered by Butterwick's horse when it was
dying last November.   The harder I blew, the more
mournful became the noise, and that was the only
note I could get.   When I went down to supper,
Mrs. A. asked me if I heard that awful groaning.
She said she guessed it came from Twiddler's cow,
for she heard Mrs. Twiddler say yesterday that the
cow was sick.

For four weeks I could get nothing out of that
horn but blood-curdling groans; and, meantime, the
people over the way moved to another house because
our neighborhood was haunted, and three of our
hired girls resigned successively for the same reason.

Finally, a man whom I consulted told me that
" No One to Love" was an easy tune for beginners;
and I made an effort to learn it.

After three weeks of arduous practice, during
which Mrs. A. several times suggested that it was
brutal that Twiddler didn't kill that suffering cow

and put it out of its misery, I conquered the first three notes; but there I stuck. I could play "No One to—" and that was all. I performed "No One to—" over eight thousand times; and as it seemed

unlikely that I would ever learn the whole tune, I determined to try the effect of part of it on Mrs. A. About ten o'clock one night I crept out to the front of the house and struck up. First, "No One to—"

about fifteen or twenty times, then a few of those
groans, then more of the tune, and so forth.   Then
Butterwick set his dog on me, and I suddenly went
into the house.   Mrs. A. had the children in the
back room, and she was standing behind the door
with my revolver in her hand.   When I entered, she
exclaimed,

"Oh, I'm so glad you've come home! Somebody's
been murdering a man in our yard.   He uttered the
most awful shrieks and cries I ever heard.   I was
dreadfully afraid the murderers would come into the
house.   It's perfectly fearful, isn't it?"

Then I took the revolver away from her—it was
not loaded, and she had no idea that it would have
to be cocked—and went to bed without mentioning
the horn.   I thought perhaps it would be better not
to.   I sold it the next day; and now if I want music
I shall buy a good hand-organ.   I know I can play
on that.

As music and sculpture are the first of the arts, I
may properly refer in this chapter to some facts rela-
tive to the condition of the latter in the community
in which I live.   Some time ago there was an auction out at the place of Mr. Jackson, and a very
handsome marble statue of William Penn was
knocked down to Mr. Whitaker.   He had the
statue carted over to the marble-yard, where he
sought an interview with Mr. Mix, the owner.   He
told Mix that he wanted that statue "fixed up some-

how so that 'twould represent one of the heathen gods." He had an idea that Mix might chip the clothes off of Penn and put a lyre in his hand, " so that he might pass muster as Apollo or Hercules."

But Mix said he thought the difficulty would be in wrestling with William's hat. It was a marble hat, with a rim almost big enough for a race-course; and Mix said that although he didn't profess to know much about heathen mythology as a general thing, still it struck him that Hercules in a broad-brimmed hat would attract attention by his singularity, and might be open to criticism.

Mr. Whitaker said that what he really wanted with that statue, when he bought it, was to turn it into Venus, and he thought perhaps the hat might be chiseled up into some kind of a halo around her head.

But Mix said that he didn't exactly see how he could do that when the rim was so curly at the sides. A halo that was curly was just no halo at all. But, anyway, how was he going to manage about Penn's waistcoat? It reached almost to his knees, and to attempt to get out a bare-legged Venus with a halo on her head and four cubic feet of waistcoat around her middle would ruin his business. It would make the whole human race smile.

Then Whitaker said Neptune was a god he always liked, and perhaps Mix could fix the tails of Penn's coat somehow so that it would look as if the figure was riding on a dolphin; then the hat might be made to represent seaweed, and a fish-spear could be put in the statue's hand.

Mix, however, urged that a white marble hat of those dimensions, when cut into seaweed, would be more apt to look as if Neptune was coming home with a load of hay upon his head; and he said that although art had made gigantic strides during the past century, and evidently had a brilliant future before it, it had not yet discovered a method by which a swallow-tail coat with flaps to the pockets could be turned into anything that would look like a dolphin.

Then Mr. Whitaker wanted to know if Pan wasn't the god that had horns and split hoofs, with a shaggy look to his legs; for if he was, he would be willing to have the statue made into Pan, if it could be done without too much expense.

And Mr. Mix said that while nothing would please him more than to produce such a figure of Pan, and while William Penn's square-toed shoes, probably, might be made into cloven hoofs without a very strenuous effort, still he hardly felt as if he could fix up those knee-breeches to resemble shaggy legs; and as for trying to turn that hat into a pair of horns, Mr. Whitaker might as well talk of emptying the Atlantic Ocean through a stomach-pump.

Thereupon, Mr. Whitaker remarked that he had concluded, on the whole, that it would be better to split the patriarch up the middle and take the two halves to make a couple of little Cupids, which he could hang in his parlor with a string, so that they would appear to be sporting in air. Perhaps the flap of that hat might be sliced up into wings and glued on the shoulders of the Cupids.

But Mr. Mix said that while nobody would put himself out more to oblige a friend than he would, still he must say, if his honest opinion was asked, that to attempt to make a Cupid out of one leg and half the body of William Penn would be childish, because, if they used the half one way, there would be a very small Cupid with one very long leg; and if they used it the other way, he would have to cut Cupid's head out of the calf of William's leg, and there wasn't room enough, let alone the fact that the knee-joint would give the god of Love the appearance of having a broken back. And as for wings, if the man had been born who could chisel wings out of the flap of a hat, all he wanted was to meet that man, so that he could gaze on him and study him. Finally Whitaker suggested that Mix should make the statue into an angel and sell it for an ornament to a tombstone.

But Mix said that if he should insult the dead by putting up in the cemetery an angel with a stubby nose and a double-chin, that would let him out as a manufacturer of sepulchres.

And so Whitaker sold him the statue for ten dollars, and Mix sawed it up into slabs for marble-top tables. High art doesn't seem to flourish to any large extent in this place.

17

CHAPTER XXI.

*CERTAIN DENTAL EXPERIENCES.—AN UNFORTU-
NATE OFFICIAL.*

R. POTTS has suffered a good deal from the toothache, and one day he went around to the office of Dr. Slugg, the dentist, to have the offending tooth pulled. The doctor has a very large practice; and in order to economize his strength, he invented a machine for pulling teeth. He constructed a series of cranks and levers fixed to a movable stand and operating a pair of forceps by means of a leather belt, which was connected with the shafting of a machine-shop in the street back of the house. The doctor experimented with it several times on nails firmly inserted in a board, and it worked splendidly. The first patient he tried it on was Mr. Potts. When the forceps had been clasped upon Potts' tooth, Dr. Slugg geared the machine and opened the valve. It was never known with any degree of exactness whether the doctor pulled the valve too far open or whether the engine was working at that moment under extraordinary pressure. But in the twinkling of an eye Mr. Potts was twisted out of the

258

chair and the movable stand began to execute the
most surprising manœuvres around the room. It
would jerk Mr. Potts high into the air and souse
him down in an appalling manner, with one leg
among Slugg's gouges and other instruments of tor-

ture, and with the other in the spittoon. Then it
would rear him up against the chandelier three or
four times, and shy across and drive Potts' head
through the oil portrait of Slugg's father over the
mantel-piece. After bumping him against Slugg's
ancestor it would swirl Potts around among the

crockery on the wash-stand and dance him up and
down in an exciting manner over the stove, until
finally the molar " gave," and as Potts landed with
his foot through the pier-glass and his elbow on a
pink poodle worked in a green rug, the machine
dashed violently against Dr. Slugg and tried to seize
his leg with the forceps.   When they carried Potts
home, he discovered that Slugg had pulled the wrong
tooth; and Dr. Slugg never sent to collect his bill.
He canceled his contract with the man who owned
the planing-mill, and began to pull teeth in the old
way, by hand.   I have an impression that Slugg's
patent can be bought at a sacrifice.

Mr. Potts, a day or two later, resolved to take the
aching tooth out himself.   He had heard that a tooth
could be removed suddenly and without much pain
by tying a string around it, fixing the string to a
bullet and firing the bullet from a gun.   So he got
some string and fastened it to the tooth and to a
ball, rammed the latter into his gun, and aimed the
gun out of the window.   Then he began to feel nervous about it, and he cocked and uncocked the gun
about twenty times, as his mind changed in regard
to the operation.   The last time the gun was cocked
he resolved *not* to take the tooth out in that way,
and he began to let the hammer down preparatory
to cutting the string.   Just then the hammer slipped,
and the next minute Mr. Potts' tooth was flying
through the air at the rate of fifty miles a minute,
and he was rolling over on the floor howling and

spitting blood. After Mrs. Potts had picked him up and given him water with which to wash out his mouth he went down to the front window. While he was sitting there thinking that maybe it was all for the best, he saw some men coming by carrying a body on a shutter. He asked what was the matter, and they told him that Bill Dingus had been murdered by somebody.

Mr. Potts thought he would put on his hat and go down to the coroner's office and see what the tragedy was. When he got there, Mr. Dingus had revived somewhat, and he told his story to the coroner. He was trimming a tree in Butterwick's garden, when he suddenly heard the explosion of a gun, and the next minute a bullet struck him in the thigh and he fell to the ground. He said he couldn't imagine who did it. Then the doctor examined the wound and found a string hanging from it, and a large bullet suspended upon the string. When he pulled the string it would not move any, and he said it must be tied to some other missile still in the flesh. He said it was the most extraordinary case on record. The medical books reported nothing of the kind.

Then the doctor gave Mr. Dingus chloroform and proceeded to cut into him with a knife to find the other end of the string, and while he was at work Mr. Potts began to feel sick at his stomach and to experience a desire to go home. At last the doctor cut deep enough ; and giving the string a jerk, out came a molar tooth that looked as if it might have been aching. Then the doctor said the case was more extraordinary than he had thought it was. He said that tooth couldn't have been fired from a gun, because it would have been broken to pieces; it couldn't have been swallowed by Dingus and then broken through and buried itself in his thigh, for then how could the string and ball be accounted for?

"The occurrence is totally unaccountable upon any reasonable theory," said the doctor, "and I do not know what to believe, unless we are to conceive that the tooth and the ball were really meteoric stones that have assumed these remarkable shapes and been shot down upon the earth with such force as to penetrate Mr. Dingus' leg, and this is so very improbable that we can hardly accept it unless it is impossible to find any other. Hallo! What's the matter with you, Potts? Your mouth and shirt are all stained with blood!"

"Oh, nothing," said Potts, forgetting himself. "I just lost a tooth, and—"

"You lost a— Who pulled it?" asked the doctor.

"Gentlemen," said Potts, "the fact is I shot it out with my gun."

Then they put Potts under bail for attempted assassination, and Dingus said that as soon as he got well he would bang Mr. Potts with a club. When the crowd had gone, the coroner said to Potts,

"You're a mean sort of a man, now, ain't you?"

"Well, Mr. Maginn," replied Potts, "I really

didn't know Mr. Dingus was there; and the gun went off accidentally, any way."

"Oh, it isn't that," said the coroner — "it isn't that. I don't mind your shooting him, but why in the thunder didn't you kill him while you were at it, and give me a chance? You want to see me starve, don't you? I wish you'd a buried the tooth in his lung and the ball in his liver, and then I'd a had my regular fees. But as it is, I have all the bother and get nothing. I'd starve to death if all men were like you."

And Potts went away with a dim impression that he had injured Maginn rather more than Mr. Dingus.

Coroner Maginn's condition, however, is one of chronic discontent. Upon the occasion of a recent encounter with him I said to him,

"Business seems to be dull to-day, Mr. Maginn."

"Dull! Well, that's just no name for it. This is the deadest town I ever— Well, exceptin' Jim Busby's tumblin' off the market-house last month, there hasn't been a decent accident in this place since last summer. How'm I goin' to live, I want to know? In other countries people keep things movin'. There are murders and coal-oil explosions and roofs fallin' in—'most always somethin' lively to afford a coroner a chance. But here! Why, I don't get 'nough fees in a year to keep a poll-parrot in water-crackers. I don't—now, that's the honest truth."

"That does seem discouraging."

"And then the worst of it is a man's friends won't stand by him. There's Doolan, the coroner in the next county. He found a drowned man up in the river just beyond the county line. I ought to have had the first shy at the body by rights, for I know well enough he fell in from this county and then skeeted up with the tide. But no; Doolan would hold the inquest; and do you believe that man actually wouldn't float the remains down the river so's I could sit on 'em after he'd got through? Actually took 'em out and buried 'em, although I offered to go halves with him on my fees if he would pass the body down this way. That's a positive fact. He refused. Now, what do you think of a man like that? He hasn't got enough soul in him to be worth preachin' to. That's my opinion."

"It wasn't generous."

"No, sir. Why, there's Stanton come home from Peru with six mummies that he dug out of some sepulchre in that country. They look exackly like dried beef. Now, my view is that I ought to sit on those things. They're human beings; nobody 'round here knows what they died of. The law has a right to know. Stanton hasn't got a doctor's certificate about 'em, and I'm sworn to look after all dead people that can't account for bein' dead, or that are suspicioned of dyin' by foul play. I could have made fifty dollars out of those deceased Peruvians, and I ought to've done it. But no! Just as I was about to begin, the supervisors, they shut down on it; they

said the county didn't care nothin' about people
that had been dead for six hundred years, and they
wouldn't pay me a cent. Just as if *six thousand*
years was anything in the eye of the law, when
maybe a man's been stabbed, or something, and
when I'm under oath to tend to him! But it's just
my luck. Everything appears to be agin me,
'specially if there's money in it."

"You do seem rather unfortunate."

"Now, there's some countries where they frequently have earthquakes which rattle down the
houses and mash people, and volcanoes which
burst out and set hundreds of 'em afire, and hurri-
canes which blow 'em into Hereafter. A coroner
can have some comfort in such a place as that. He
can live honest and respectable. Just think of settin'
on four or five hundred bodies killed with an earthquake! It makes my mouth water. But nothin' of
that sort ever happens in this jackass kind of a land.
Things go along just 'sif they were asleep. We've
got six saw-mills 'round this town, but nobody ever
gets tangled in the machinery and sawed in half.
We've got a gunpowder-factory out beyond the
turnpike, but will that ever go up? It wouldn't
if you was to toss a red-hot stove in among the
powder—leastways, not while I'm coroner. There's
a river down there, but nobody ever drowns in it
where I can have a hitch at him; and if there's a
freshet, everybody at once gets out of reach. If
there's a fire, all the inmates get away safe, and no

fireman ever falls off a ladder or stands where a wall might flatten him out. No, sir; I don't have a fair show. There was that riot out at the foundry. In any other place three or four men would have been killed, and there'd a been fatness for the coroner; but of course, bein' in my county, nothin' occurred exceptin' Sam Dixon got kicked in the ribs and had part of his ear bitten off. A man can't make an honest livin' under sech circumstances as them; he can't, really."

"It does appear difficult."

"I did think maybe I might get the supervisors to let me go out to the cemetery and set on the folks that are buried there, so's I could overhaul 'em and kinder revise the verdicts that've been rendered on 'em. I'd a done it for half price; but those fellows have got such queer ideas of economy that they wouldn't listen to it; said the town couldn't go to any fresh expense while it was buildin' water-works. And I wanted to put the new school-house out yer by the railroad or down by the river, so's some of the children'd now and then get run over or fall in; but the parents were 'posed to it for selfish reasons, and so I got shoved out of that chance. Yes, sir, it's rough on me; and I tell you that if there are not more sudden deaths in this county the law's got to give me a salary, or I'm goin' to perish by starvation. Not that I'd mind that much for myself, but it cuts me up to think that as soon as I stepped out the next coroner'd begin right off to earn a livin' out of me."

Then I said "Good-morning" and left, while Mr. Maginn selected a fresh stick to whittle. Mr. Maginn, however, had one good chance recently to collect fees.

The country around the town of Millburg is of limestone formation. The town stands, as has already been mentioned, on a high hill, at the foot of which there is a wonderful spring, and the belief has always been that the hill is full of great caves and fissures, through which the water makes its way to feed the spring. A year or two ago they organized a cemetery company at Millburg, and they located the graveyard upon the hill a short distance back of the town. After they had deposited several bodies in the ground, one day somebody discovered a coffin floating in the river. It was hauled out, and it turned out to be the remains of Mr. Piggott, who was buried in the cemetery the day before. The coroner held an inquest, and they reinterred the corpse.

On the following morning, however, Mr. Piggott was discovered bumping up against the wharf at the gas-works in the river. People began to be scared, and there was some talk to the effect that he had been murdered and couldn't rest quietly in his grave. But the coroner was not scared. He empaneled a jury, held another inquest, collected his fees and buried the body. Two days afterward some boys, while in swimming, found a burial-casket floating under the bushes down by the saw-mill. They called for help, and upon examining the interior of

the casket they discovered the irrepressible Mr. Piggott again. This was too much. Even the ministers
began to believe in ghosts, and hardly a man in
town dared to go out of the house that night alone.
But the coroner controlled his emotions sufficiently
to sit on the body, make the usual charges and bury
Mr. Piggott in a fresh place in his lot.

The next morning, while Peter Lámb was drinking out of the big spring, he saw something push
slowly out of the mud at the bottom of the pool.
He turned as white as a sheet as he watched it; and
in a few minutes he saw that it was a coffin. It
floated out, down the creek into the river, and then
Peter ran to tell the coroner. That official had a
jury waiting, and he proceeded to the coffin. It was
old Mr. Piggott, as usual; and they went through
the customary routine with him, and were about to
bury him, when his family came forward and said
they would prefer to inter him in another place, being
convinced now there must be a subterranean channel
leading from the cemetery to the spring. The coroner couldn't object; but after the Piggotts were gone
he said to the jury that people who would take the
bread out of the mouth of a poor man in that way
would be certain to come to want themselves some
day. He said he could easily have paid off the mortgage on his house and let his little girl take lessons
on the melodeon besides, if they'd just allowed Piggott to wobble around the way he wanted to.

There was no more trouble up at the cemetery

after that until they buried old Joe Middles, who used to have the fish-house over the river at Deacon's. They entombed the old man on Thursday night. On Friday morning one of the Keysers was walking down on the river-bank, and he saw a man who looked very much like Mr. Middles sitting up

in a canoe out in the stream fishing. He watched the man as he caught two or three fish, and was just about to conclude that it was some unknown brother of Mr. Middles, when the fisherman looked up and said,

" Hello, Harry."

" Who are you ?" asked Keyser.

" Who am I?   Why, Joe Middles, of course.
Who'd you think I was?" remarked the fisherman.

" You ain't Joe Middles, for he's dead.   I went to
his funeral yesterday."

" Funeral !" exclaimed the fisherman as he stepped
ashore.   " Well, now, by George ! maybe that ex-
plains the thing.   I've been bothering myself the
worst kind to understand something.   You know
that I remember being at home in bed, and then I
went to sleep somehow ; and when I woke up, it was
dark as pitch.   I gave a kick to stretch myself, and
knocked the lid off of this thing here—a canoe I
thought it was ; and then I set up and found myself
out here in the river.   I took the lid to split into
paddles, and I saw on it a plate with the words ' Joseph Middles, aged sixty-four ;' and I couldn't imagine how in thunder that ever got on that lid.
Howsomdever, I pulled over to the shanty and got
some lines and bait and floated out again, thinking
while I was here I might as well get a mess of fish
before I got home.   And so it's a coffin, after all,
and they buried me yesterday.   Well, that beats the
very old Harry, now, don't it?   I'm going to row
right over to the house.   How it'll skeer the old
woman to see me coming in safe and sound !"

Then the resurrected Mr. Middles paddled off.
The cemetery company failed the following month,
from inability to sell the lots.

CHAPTER XXII.

JUSTICE, AND A LITTLE INJUSTICE.

THE administration of justice in this county is chiefly in the hands of Judge Twiddler; and while his methods generally are excellent, he sometimes makes unpleasant mistakes. Mr. Mix was the victim of one such blunder upon a recent occasion. Mr. Mix is bald; and in order to induce his hair to grow again, he is using a very excellent article of "hair vigor" upon his scalp. Some time ago he was summoned as a juryman upon a case in the court, and upon the day of the trial, just before the hour at which the court met, he remembered that he had not applied the vigor to his head that morning. He had only a few minutes to spare, but he flew up stairs and into the dark closet where he kept the bottle; and pouring some fluid upon a sponge, he rubbed his head energetically. By some mishap Mr. Mix got hold of the wrong bottle, and the substance with which he inundated his scalp was not vigor, but the black varnish with which Mrs. Mix decorated her shoes. However, Mix didn't perceive the mistake, but darted down stairs, put on his hat and walked off to the court-

room. It was a very cold morning, and by the time
Mix reached his destination the varnish was as stiff
as a stone. He felt a little uncomfortable about the
head, and he endeavored to remove his hat to discover the cause of the difficulty, but to his dismay
it was immovable. It was glued fast to the skin, and
his efforts to take it off gave him frightful pain.

Just then he heard his name called by the crier,
and he had to go into court to answer. He was wild
with apprehension of coming trouble; but he took
his seat in the jury-box and determined to explain
the situation to the court at the earliest possible
moment. As he sat there with a guilty feeling in
his soul it seemed to him that his hat kept getting
bigger and bigger, until it appeared to him to be
as large as a shot-tower. Then he was conscious
that the lawyers were staring at him. Then the
clerk looked hard at him and screamed, "Hats off
in court!" and Mix grew crimson. "Hats off!"
yelled the clerk again, and Mix was about to reply
when the judge came in, and as his eye rested on
Mix he said,

"Persons in the court-room must remove their
hats."

"May it please Your Honor, I kept my hat on because—"

"Well, sir, you must take it off now."

"But I say I keep it on because I—"

"We don't want any arguments upon the subject,
sir. Take your hat off instantly!" said the judge.

"But you don't let me—"

"Remove that hat this moment, sir! Are you going to bandy words with me, sir? Uncover your head at once!"

"Judge, if you will only give me a chance to—"

"This is intolerable! Do you mean to insult the court, sir? Do you mean to profane this sacred temple of justice with untimely levity? Take your hat off, sir, or I will fine you for contempt. Do you hear me?"

"Well, it's very hard that I can't say a word by way of ex—"

"This is too much," said the judge, warmly—"this is just a little too much. Perhaps you'd like to come up on the bench here and run the court and sentence a few convicts? Mr. Clerk, fine that man fifty dollars. Now, sir, remove your hat."

"Judge, this is rough on me. I—"

"Won't do it yet?" said the judge, furiously. "Why, you impudent scoundrel, I've a notion to—Mr. Clerk, fine him one hundred dollars more, and, Mr. Jones, you go and take that hat off by force."

Then the tipstaff approached Mix, who was by this time half crazy with wrath, and hit the hat with his stick. It did not move. Then he struck it again and caved in the crown, but it still remained on Mix's head. Then he picked up a volume of Brown *On Evidence*, and mashed the crown in flat. Then Mix sprang at him; and shaking his fist under the nose of Jones, he shrieked,

18

"You miserable scullion, I've half a notion to kill you! If that jackass on the bench had any sense, he could see that the hat is glued fast. I can't take it off if I wanted to, and I wouldn't take it off now if I could."

Then the judge removed the fines and excused him, and Mix went home. He slept in his hat for a week; and even when it came off, the top of his head looked as black as if mortification had set in.

But if the judge is too particular, our sheriff is hardly careful enough. The manner in which he permits our jail to be conducted always seemed to me interesting and original.

One day I wanted to hire a man to wheel half a dozen loads of rubbish out of my garden, and after looking around a while I found a seedy chap sitting on the end of a wharf fishing. When I asked him if he would attend to the job, he replied thus:

"I really can't. I'm sorry; but the fact is I'm in jail for six months for larceny—sentenced last December. I don't mind it much, only they don't act honest with me up at the jail. The first week I was there Mrs. Murphy—she's the keeper's wife—wanted to clean up, and so she turned me out, and I had to hang round homeless for more'n a week. Then, just as I was getting settled agin comfortably, the provisions ran short, and Murphy tried to borrow money of me to feed the convicts; and as I had none to lend, out I had to go agin. In about two weeks I started in fresh and got everything snug and cheerful, when Murphy's aunt stepped out. Then what does that ass do but put me out agin and lock up the jail and put crape on the door, while he went off to the funeral.

"So, of course, I had to browse around, huntin' up meals where I could get them, sometimes nibblin' somethin' at the tavern and other times takin' tea with a friend. Well, sir, hardly was that old woman buried, and me once more in the cell with the home

like feelin' beginnin' to creep over me, but Murphy,
he says he and his wife's got to go up to the city to
get a hired girl; and when I refused to quit, Murphy
grabbed me by the collar and pushed me into the
street, and said he'd sick his dog on me if I came
around there makin' a fuss.

"I hung about a few days; and when I went to the
jail, the boy said Murphy hadn't got back and I'd
have to call agin. Next time I applied the boy hol-
lered from the window that he was 'engaged' and
couldn't see me. Murphy was still rummagin' for
that hired girl. I went there eight times, and there
was always some jackass of an excuse for crowdin'
me out, and I don't know if I'll ever get in agin.
Night afore last I busted a window with a brick and
tried to crawl in through the hole, but the boy fired
a gun at me, and said if I'd just wait till Mr. Murphy
came back he'd have me arrested for burglary.

"Now, I think I've been treated mighty bad. I've
got a right in that jail, and it's pretty mean in a man
like Murphy to shove me off in weather like this;
and I'm bound to live six months in the prison some
time or other, whether he likes it or not. I don't
mind puttin' myself to some trouble to oblige a
friend, but I hate like thunder to be imposed on.

"'Pears to me it's no way to run a penal institution
any way. There's Botts; he's in jail for perjury for
nine years, and Murphy's actually turned that convict
out so often and made him run 'round after his meals
that Botts has lost heart, and has gone to canvassin'

for a life insurance company—gone to perambulatin'
all over the country tryin' to do a little somethin' to
keep clothes on his back, when he ought to be layin'
serenely in that jail. But I ain't goin' to do that
If the law keeps me in custody, it's got to support
me; and that's what Simpson says, too. Ketch him
workin' for his livin'. He's in for four years for assault and battery; and when they turn him out of
the jail, he puts up at a hotel and has the bills sent
in to Murphy.

" Murphy don't have consideration for the prisoners,
any way. You know he raises fowls in the jail-yard;
and just after Christmas he had a big lot of turkeys
left on his hands, and do you believe that man actually kept feedin' us on those turkeys for more than
a month? Positively refused to allow us anything
else until they was gone. I had half a notion to quit
for good. I was disgusted. And Simpson said if
that is the way they were goin' to treat convicts,
why, civilization is a failure. All through Lent, too,
wouldn't allow us an oyster; kept stuffin' us with
beef and such trash, although Botts said he'd never
been used to such wickedness, for his parents were
very particular. Wouldn't even give us fish-balls
twice a week. But what does Murphy care? He's
perfectly enthusiastic when he can tread on a man's
feelin's and stamp all the moral sensibility out of
him.

"And Mrs. Murphy, she's not much better. All the
warm days she's home she hustles that baby of hers

onto me. Makes me take the little sucklin' out in his carriage for an airin', and then gets mad if he falls out while I'm conversin' for a few minutes with a friend. I'd a slid him into the river long ago, only I know well enough they'd sentence me for life, and then I'd maybe have to stand Murphy's persecution for about forty years ; and that'd kill me. It would indeed. He's so inconsiderate.

" He used to give me the key of the jail to keep while he'd go over to Barnes' to fight roosters or to play poker, and one day I lost it. He raised an awful fuss, and even Botts was down on me because they couldn't keep the boys out, and they used to come in and tickle Botts with straws while he was sleepin' in his cell. I believe they expect Murphy back day after to-morrow, but I know mighty well I'm not goin' to have much satisfaction when he does come. He'll find some excuse for shufflin' me out 'bout as soon as I get stowed away in my old quarters. If he does, I've got a notion to lock him out some night and run the jail myself for a while, so's I kin have some peace. There's such a thing as carryin' abuses a little too far. Excuse me for a minute. I think I have a bite."

Then I left to hunt for another man. I feel that the Society for the Alleviation of the Sufferings of Prisoners has a great work to perform in our town.

CHAPTER XXIII.

THE TRAMP WITH GENIUS AND WITHOUT IT.

THE tramp is as familiar a figure in the village and the surrounding country as he is in other populous rural neighborhoods. The ruffian tramp, of course, is the most constant of the class, but now and then appears one of the fraternity who displays something like genius in his attempts to impose himself upon people as a being of a higher order than an idle, worthless vagabond. A fellow of this description came into the editorial room of the *Patriot* one day while I was sitting there, and announced in a loud voice that he was a professor of pisciculture and an aspirant for a position upon the State Fish Commission. As the statement did not attract the attention of anybody, he seated himself in a chair, placed his feet upon the table, and aiming with surprising accuracy at a spittoon, said his name was Powell. Still nobody paid any attention to him, but the fact did not seem to depress his spirits, for he talked straight ahead fluently and with some vehemence:

"What are they doing for the fishery interest, any way, these commissioners? What do they know

about fishing? More'n likely when they go out
they hold the hook in their hands and let the pole
float in the water. Why, one of 'em was talking
with me the other day, and says he, 'Powell, I
want the Legislature to make an appropriation for
the cultivation of canned lobsters in the Susquehanna.' 'How are you going to do it?' says I.
'Why,' says he, 'my plan is to cross the original
lobster with some good variety of tin can, breed
'em in and in, and then feed the animal on solder
and green labels.'

"Perfect ass, of course; but I let him run along,
and pretty soon he says, 'I've just bought half a
barrel of salt mackerel, which I'm going to put in
the Schuylkill. My idea,' says he, 'is to breed a
mackerel that'll be all ready soaked when you catch
him. The ocean mackerel always tastes too much
of the salt. What the people want is a fish that is
fresher.' And so, you know, that immortal idiot is
actually going to dump those mackerel overboard
in the hope that they'll swim about and make themselves at home. Well, if the governor *will* appoint
such chuckle-head commissioners, what else can you
expect?

"However, I said nothing. I wasn't going to set
him up in business with my brains and experience,
and so, directly, he says to me, 'Powell, I'm now
engaged in transplanting some desiccated codfish
into the Schuylkill; but it scatters too much when it
gets into the water. Now, how would it do to breed

the ordinary codfish with a sausage-chopper or a
mince-meat machine? Do you think a desiccated
codfish would rise to a fly, or wouldn't you have to
fish for him with a colander?' And so he kept reel-
ing out a jackassery like that until directly he said,
'I'll tell you, professor, what this country needs is a
fresh-water oyster. Now, it has occurred to me that
maybe the best variety to plant would be the ordinary fried oyster. It seems to be popular, and it
has the advantage of growing without a shell. One
of the other commissioners,' so this terrific block-
head said, 'insisted on trying the experiment with
the oyster that produces tripe, so's to enable the
people to catch tripe and oysters when they go a-
fishing. But for my part,' says he, 'I want either the
fried oyster or the kind that grow in pie crust, like
they have 'em at the restaurants.' Actually said
that.

"Well, he driveled along for a while, talking the
awfulest bosh ; and pretty soon he asked me if I
was fond of mock-turtle soup. Said that the commission had discovered the feasibility of adding the
mock-turtle to the food-animals of our rivers. He
allowed that he had understood that they could be
cultivated best by spawning calves' heads on force-
meat balls, and that they were in season for the table
during the same months of the year that gravy is.
And he said that a strenuous effort ought to be
made to have our rivers swarming with this delicious
fish.

"And then he talked a whole lot of delirious slush of that kind, and about improving the tadpole crop, and so on, until I— Wh-wh-what d'you say? Want me to take my legs off that table and quit? You don't want to hear any more news about the fisheries? Oh, all right; there's plenty of other papers that'll be glad to get the intelligence. Next time you want my views about pisciculture you'll have to send for me."

Then the professor aimed again at the spittoon, missed it, rubbed the ragged crown of his forlorn hat with his shining elbow, buttoned up his coat over a shirt-bosom which last saw the washerwoman during the presidency of General Harrison, and sauntered out and down stairs. The impression that he left was that he would be more available to the Fish Commission as bait than in any other capacity.

Upon another occasion a more forlorn and dismal vagabond, a cripple, too, sauntered into Brown's grocery-store, where a crowd was sitting around the stove discussing politics. Taking position upon a nail-keg, he remarked,

"Mr. Brown, you don't want to buy a first-rate wooden leg, do you? I've got one that I've been wearing for two or three years, and I want to sell it. I'm hard up for money; and although I'm attached to that leg, I'm willing to part with it so's I kin get the necessaries of life. Legs are all well enough; they are handy to have around the house, and all that; but a man must attend to his stomach if he has to walk about on the small of his back. Now, I'm going to make you an offer. That leg is Fairchild's patent; steel springs, India-rubber joints, elastic toes and everything, and it's in better order now than it was when I bought it. It'd be a comfort to any man. It's the most luxurious leg I ever came across. If bliss ever kin be reached by a man this side of the tomb, it belongs to the person that gets that leg on and feels the consciousness creeping over his soul that it is his. Consequently, I say that when I offer it to you I'm doing a personal favor; and I think I see you jump at the chance and want to clinch the bargain before I mention—you'll hardly believe it, I know—that I'll actually knock that leg down to you at four hundred dollars. Four hundred, did I say? I meant six hundred; but let it stand. I never back out when I make an offer; but it's just throwing that leg away—it is, indeed."

" But I don't want an artificial leg," said Brown.

"The beautiful thing about the limb," said the stranger, pulling up his trousers and displaying the article, " is that it is reliable. You kin depend on it. It's always there. Some legs that I've seen were treacherous — most always some of the springs bursting out, or the joints working backward, or the toes turning down and ketching in things. Regular frauds. But it's almost pathetic the way this leg goes on year in and year out like an old faithful friend, never knowing an ache or a pain, no rheumatism, nor any such foolishness as that, but always good-natured and ready to go out of its way to oblige you. A man feels like a man when he gets such a thing under him. Talk about your kings and emperors and millionaires, and all that sort of nonsense! Which of 'em's got a leg like that? Which of 'em kin unscrew his knee-pan and look at the gum thingamajigs in his calf? Which of 'em kin leave his leg down stairs in the entry on the hat-rack and go to bed with only one cold foot? Why, it's enough to make one of them monarchs sick to think of such a convenience. But they can't help it. There's only one man kin buy that leg, and that's you. I want you to have it so bad that I'll deed it to you for fifty dollars down. Awful, isn't it? Just throwing it away; but take it, take it, if it does make my heart bleed to see it go out of the family."

"Really, I have no use for such a thing," said Mr. Brown.

"You can't think," urged the stranger, "what a benediction a leg like that is in a family. When you don't want to walk with it, it comes into play for the children to ride horsey on; or you kin take it off and stir the fire with it in a way that would depress the spirits of a man with a real leg. It makes the most efficient potato-masher you ever saw. Work it from the second joint and let the knee swing loose; you kin tack carpets perfectly splendid with the heel; and when a cat sees it coming at him from the winder, he just adjourns *sine die* and goes down off the fence screaming. Now, you're probably afeard of dogs.

When you see one approaching, you always change your base. I don't blame you; I used to be that way before I lost my home-made leg. But you fix yourself with this artificial extremity, and then what do you care for dogs? If a million of 'em come at you, what's the odds? You merely stand still and smile, and throw out your spare leg, and let 'em chaw, let 'em fool with that as much as they're a mind to, and howl and carry on, for you don't care. An' that's the reason why I say that when I reflect on how imposing you'd be as the owner of such a leg I feel like saying that if you insist on offering only a dollar and a half for it, why, take it; it's yours. I'm not the kinder man to stand on trifles. I'll take it off and wrap it up in paper for you; shall I?"

"I'm sorry," said Brown, "but the fact is I have no use for it. I've got two good legs already. If I ever lose one, why, maybe then I'll—"

"I don't think you exactly catch my idea on the subject," said the stranger. "Now, any man kin have a meat-and-muscle leg; they're as common as dirt. It's disgusting how monotonous people are about such things. But I take you for a man who wants to be original. You have style about you. You go it alone, as it were. Now, if I had your peculiarities, do you know what I'd do? I'd get a leg snatched off some way, so's I could walk around on this one. Or if you hate to go to the expense of amputation, why not get your pantaloons altered and mount this beautiful work of art just as you stand?

A centipede, a mere ridicklous insect, has half a
bushel of legs, and why can't a man, the grandest
creature on earth, own three? You go around this
community on three legs, and your fortune's made.
People will go wild over you as the three-legged
grocer; the nation will glory in you; Europe will
hear of you; you will be heard of from pole to pole.
It'll build up your business. People'll flock from
everywheres to see you, and you'll make your sugar
and cheese and things fairly hum. Look at it as an
advertisement! Look at it any way you please,
and there's money in it—there's glory, there's immortality. I think I see you now moving around
over this floor with your old legs working as usual,
and this one going clickety-click along with 'em,
making music for you all the time and attracting attention in a way to fill a man's heart with rapture.
Now, look at it that way; and if it strikes you, I
tell you what I'll do: I'll actually swap that imperishable leg off to you for two pounds of water-
crackers and a tin cup full of Jamaica rum. Is it
a go?"

Then Brown weighed out the crackers, gave him
an awful drink of rum, and told him if he would take
them as a present and quit he would confer a favor.
And he did. After emptying the crackers in his
pockets and smacking his lips over the rum, he went
to the door, and as he opened it he said,

"Good-bye. But if you ever really do want a leg,
Old Reliable is ready for you; it's yours. I consider

that you've got a mortgage on it, and you kin fore-close at any time. I dedicate this leg to you. My will shall mention it; and if you don't need it when I die, I'm going to have it put in the savings' bank to draw interest until you check it out. I'll bid you good-evening."

The tramp that has a dog to sell is a little more common than such children of genius as the professor and the owner of the patent leg. But I had with one of them a queer experience which may be worth relating.

One day recently a rough-looking vagabond called at my house, accompanied by a forlorn mongrel dog. I came out upon the porch to see him, and he said,

"I say, pardner, I understood that you wanted to buy a watch-dog, and I brought one around for you. You never seen such a dog for watching as this one. You tell that dog to watch a thing, and bet your life he'll sit down and watch it until he goes stone blind. Now, I'll tell you what I'll let you have—"

I cut his remarks short at this point with the information that I didn't want a dog, and that if I had wanted a dog nothing on earth could induce me to accept that particular dog. So he left and went down the street. He must have made a mistake and come in again through the back gate, thinking it was another place, for in a few minutes the cook said there was a man in the kitchen who wanted to see me; and when I went down, there was the same man with the same dog. He didn't recognize me, and as soon as I entered he remarked,

"I say, old pard, somebody was saying that you wanted to buy a watch-dog. Now, here's a watch-dog that'd rather watch than eat any time. Give that dog something to fasten his eye on—don't care what it is: anything from a plug hat to a skating-rink—and there his eye stays like it was chained with a trace-chain. Now, I'll tell you what I'll do with—"

I suddenly informed him in a peremptory tone that nothing would induce me to purchase a dog at that moment, and then I pushed him out and shut the door. When he was gone, I went across the street to see Butterwick about top-dressing my grass-plot. He was out, and I sat down on the porch chair to wait for him. A second later the proprietor of the dog came shuffling through the gate with the dog at his heels. When he reached the porch, he said, not recognizing me,

"I say, pardner, the man across the street there told me you wanted a good watch-dog, and I came right over with this splendid animal. Look at him! Never saw such an eye as that in a dog, now, did you? Well, now, when this dog fixes that eye on anything, it remains. There it stays. Earthquakes, or fires, or torchlight processions, or bones, or nothing, can induce him to move. Therefore, what I say is that I offer you that dog for—"

Then I got up in silence and walked deliberately out into the street, and left the man standing there.

As I reached the sidewalk I saw Butterwick going
into Col. Coffin's office. I went over after him,
while the man with the dog went in the opposite
direction. Butterwick was in the back office; and as
19

the front room was empty, I sat down in a chair until he got through with Coffin and came out. In a few minutes there was a rap at the door. I said,

" Come in !"

The door slowly opened, and a dog crept in. Then the man appeared. He didn't seem to know me. He said,

" I say, old pardy—I dunno your right name—I'm trying to sell a watch-dog; that one there; and I thought maybe you might be hungry to get a valuable animal who can watch the head off of any other dog in this yer county, so I concluded to call and throw him away for the ridic'lous sum of—"

" I wouldn't have him at any price."

" What! don't want him ? Don't want a dog with an eye like a two-inch auger, that'll sit and watch a thing for forty years if you'll tell him to ? Don't want a dog like that ?"

" Certainly I don't."

" Well, this *is* singular. There don't appear to be a demand for watch-dogs in this place, now, does there ? You're the fourth man I've tackled about him. You really don't want him ?"

" Of course not."

" Don't want any kind of a dog—not even a litter of good pups or a poodle ?"

" No, sir."

" Well, maybe you could lend me five dollars on that dog. I'll pay you back to-morrow."

" Can't do it."

"Will you take him as a gift, and give me a chaw of terbacker?"

"I don't chew."

"Very strange," he muttered, thoughtfully. "There's no encouragement for a man in this world. Sure you won't take him?"

"Yes, certain."

"Then, you miserable whelp, git out of here, or I'll kick the breath out of you. Come, now, git!" And he gave the dog a kick that sent him into the middle of the street, and then withdrew himself.

The trade in dogs certainly is not active in Millburg.

CHAPTER XXIV.

THE DOG OF MR. BUTTERWICK'S, AND OTHER DOGS.

NE day I met Mr. Butterwick in the street leading his dog with a chain. He said that it was a very valuable dog and he was anxious to get it safely home, but he had to catch a train, and I would confer a personal favor upon him if I would take the dog to my house and keep it until he returned from the city. The undertaking was not a pleasant one, but I disliked to disoblige Butterwick, and so I consented. Butterwick gave me his end of the chain and left in a hurried manner. I got the dog home with the greatest difficulty, and turned it into the cellar. About an hour later I received a telegram from Butterwick saying that he had been compelled to go down to the lower part of Jersey, and that he wouldn't be home for a week or two. That was on the 12th of June, and after that time only two persons entered the cellar. The hired girl went down once after the cold beef, and came up disheveled and bleeding, with a number of appalling dog-bites in her legs, and I descended immediately afterward for the purpose of pacifying

the infuriated animal. He did not feel disposed
to become calm, however, and I deem it probable
that if I had not
suddenly clamber-
ed into the coal-
bin, where I re-
mained until he
fell asleep in a
d i s t a n t corner
about four hours
later, I should cer-
tainly have been
t o r n to pieces.
We thought we
would have to try
to get along with-

out using the cellar until Butterwick could come up
and take away his dog. But Butterwick wrote to

say that he couldn't come, and the dog, after eating everything in the cellar and barking all through every night, finally bolted up stairs into the kitchen on the 2d of July, and established himself in the back yard. After that we used the front door exclusively while we were waiting for Butterwick to come up. The dog had fits regularly, and he always got on the geranium-bed when he felt them coming on; and consequently, we did not enjoy our flowers as much as we hoped to. The cherries were ripe during the reign of Butterwick's dog, but they rotted on the trees, all but a few, which were picked by Smith's boy, who subsequently went over the fence in a sensational manner without stopping to ascertain what Butterwick's dog was going to do with the mouthful of drawers and corduroy trousers that he had removed from Smith's boy's leg. As Butterwick did not come up, the dog enjoyed himself roaming about the yard a while; but one day, finding the back window in the parlor open, he jumped in and assumed control of that apartment and the hall. I tried to dislodge him with a clothes-prop, but I only succeeded in knocking two costly vases off of the mantel-piece, and the dog became so excited and threatening that I shut the door hurriedly and went up stairs four steps at a time.

There was nothing to interest him especially in the parlor, and I cannot imagine why he wanted to stay there. But he did; and as Butterwick didn't come up, we couldn't dislodge him. On Thursday he smashed the mirror during an attempt to get up a fight with another dog that he thought he saw in there, and he clawed the sofa to rags. On Saturday he had a fit in the hall, and spoiled about eight square yards of Brussels carpet utterly. When he recovered, he went back into the parlor. At last I borrowed Coffin's dog and sent him in to fight Butterwick's dog out. It was an exhilarating contest. They fought on the chairs and sofas; they upset a table and smashed all the ornaments on it; they scattered blood and hair in blotches all over the carpet; they got entangled in one of the lace curtains and dragged it and the frame down with a crash; they scratched and bit and tore and frothed and yelled; and at last Coffin's dog gave in, put his tail between his legs and retreated, while Butterwick's dog got on a sixty-dollar Turkish rug, so that he could bleed comfortably.

It didn't seem to occur to him to go home, and still Butterwick didn't come up. The next day I loaded a shot-gun and determind to kill him at any sacrifice. I aimed carefully at him, but at the critical moment he dodged, and two handfuls of bird-shot went into the piano and tore it up badly. Then I tossed some poisoned meat at him, but he ate all around the poison, and seemed to feel better after the meal than he had done for years. Finally, Butterwick came home, and he called to get his dog. He entered the parlor bravely and attempted to seize the animal, when it bit him. I was never so glad in my

life. Then Butterwick got mad; and seizing the dog
by the tail, he smashed him through my French
glass window into the street. Then I was not so
very glad. Then the dog went mad and a policeman
killed him. The next time I am asked to take a
strange dog home I will kill him to begin with.

When I explained to Colonel Coffin the unpleasant
nature of my experience with Mr. Butterwick's dog,
the colonel said that he had had a good deal to do
lately, in a legal way, with dogs; and he gave me
the facts respecting two interesting cases. The first
was Tompkins' case.

A man called at the colonel's law-office one day
and said,

" Colonel, my name is Tompkins. I called to see
you about a dog difficulty that bewilders me, and I
thought maybe you might throw some light on it—
might give me the law points, so's I'd know whether
it was worth while suing or not.

" Well, colonel, you see me and Potts went into
partnership on a dog; we bought him. He was a
setter; and me and Potts went shares on him, so's to
take him out a-hunting. It was never exactly settled
which half of him I owned and which half belonged
to Potts; but I formed an idea in my own mind that
the hind end was Tompkins' and the front end Potts'.
Consequence was that when the dog barked I always
said, ' There goes Potts' half exercising himself;' and
when the dog's tail wagged, I always considered that
my end was being agitated. And, of course, when

one of my hind legs scratched one of Potts' ears or
one of his shoulders, I was perfectly satisfied—first,
because that sort of thing was good for the whole
dog; and, second, because the thing would get about
even when Potts' head would reach around and bite
a flea off my hind legs or snap at a fly.

"Well, things went along smooth enough for a
while, until one day that dog began to get into the
habit of running around after his tail. He was the
foolishest dog about that I ever saw. Used to chase
his tail round and round until he'd get so giddy he
couldn't bark. And you know I was scared lest it
might hurt the dog's health; and as Potts didn't seem
to be willing to keep his end from circulating in pursuit of my end, I made up my mind to chop the dog's
tail off, so's to make him reform and behave. So last
Saturday I caused the dog to back up agin a log, and
then I suddenly dropped the axe on his tail pretty
close up, and the next minute he was running around
that yard howling like a boat-load of wild-cats. Just
then Potts came up, and he let on to be mad because
I'd cut off that tail. One word brought on another;
and pretty soon Potts set that dog on me—my own
half too, mind you—and the dog bit me in the leg.
See that! look at that leg! About half a pound
gone; et up by that dog.

"Now, what I want to see you about is this: Can't
I recover damages for assault and battery from Potts?
What I chopped off belonged to me, recollect. I
owned an undivided half of that setter pup, from the

tip of his tail clear up to his third rib, and I had a right to cut away as much of it as I'd a mind to; while Potts, being sole owner of the dog's head, is responsible when he bites anybody, or when he barks at nights."

"I don't know," replied the colonel, musingly. "There haven't been any decisions on cases exactly like this. But what does Mr. Potts say upon the subject?"

"Why, Potts' view is that I divided the dog the wrong way. When he wants to map out his half he draws a line from the middle of the nose right along the spine and clear to the end of the tail. That gives me one hind leg and one fore leg and makes him joint proprietor in the tail. And he says that if I wanted to cut off my half of the tail I might have done it, and he wouldn't 've cared, but what made him mad was that I wasted his property without consulting him. But that theory seems to me a little strained; and if it's legal, why, I'm going to close out my half of the dog at a sacrifice sooner than hold any interest in him on those principles. Now, what do you think about it?"

"Well," said the colonel, "I can hardly decide so important a question off-hand; but at the first glance my opinion is that you own the whole dog, and that Potts also owns the whole dog. So when he bites you, a suit won't lie against Potts, and the only thing you can do to obtain justice is to make the dog bite Potts also. As for the tail, when it is separated from the dog it is no longer the dog's tail, and it is not worth fighting about."

"Can't sue Potts, you say?"

"I think not."

"Can't get damages for the piece that's been bit out of me?"

"I hardly think you can."

"Well, well, and yet they talk about American civilization, and temples of justice, and such things! All right. Let it go. I can stand it; but don't anybody ever undertake to tell me that the law protects human beings in their rights. Good-morning."

"Wait a moment, Mr. Tompkins; you've forgotten my fee."

"F-f-f-fee! Why, you don't charge anything when I don't sue, do you?"

"Certainly, for my advice. My fee is ten dollars."

"Ten dollars! Ten dollars! Why, colonel, that's just what I paid for my half of that dog. I haven't got fifty cents to my name. But I'll tell you what I'll do: I'll make over all my rights in that setter pup to you, and you kin go round and fight it out with Potts. If that dog bites me again, I'll sue you and Potts as sure as my name's Tompkins."

The other case was of a somewhat more serious character. Upon a subsequent occasion a man hobbled into the office upon crutches. Proceeding to a chair and making a cushion of some newspapers, he sat down very gingerly, placed a bandaged leg upon another chair, and said,

"Col. Coffin, my name is Briggs. I want to get your opinion about a little point of law. Now, colonel, s'posin' you lived up the 'pike here a half a mile, next door to a man named Johnson. And s'posin' you and Johnson was to get into an argument about the human intellect, and you was to say to Johnson that a splendid illustration of the superiority of the human intellect was to be found in the power of the human eye to restrain the ferocity of a wild animal. And s'posin' Johnson was to remark that that was all bosh, because nobody *could* hold a wild animal with the human eye, and you should declare that you could hold the savagest beast that was ever born if you could once fix your gaze on him.

"Well, then, s'posin' Johnson was to say he'd bet a hundred dollars he could bring a tame animal that you couldn't hold with your eye, and you was to take him up on it, and Johnson was to ask you to come down to his place to settle the bet. You'd go, we'll say, and Johnson'd wander round to the back of the house and pretty soon come front again with a dog bigger'n any four decent dogs ought to be. And then s'posin' Johnson'd let go of that dog and set him on you, and he'd come at you like a sixteen-inch shell out of a howitzer, and you'd get scary about it and try to hold the dog with your eye, and couldn't. And s'posin' you'd suddenly conclude that maybe your kind of an eye wasn't calculated to hold that kind of a dog, and you'd conclude to run for a plum tree in order to have a chance to collect your thoughts, and to try to reflect what sort of an eye would be best calculated to mollify that sort of a dog. You ketch my idea, of course?

"Very well, then; s'posin you'd take your eye off of that dog, Johnson, mind you, all the time hissing him on and laughing, and you'd turn and rush for the tree, and begin to swarm up as fast as you could. Well, sir, s'posin' just as you got three feet from the ground Johnson's dog would grab you by the leg and hold on like a vise, shaking you until you nearly lost your hold. And s'posin' Johnson was to stand there and holloa, ' Fix your eye on him, Briggs! Why don't you manifest the power of the human intellect?' and so on, howling out ironical remarks like those; and s'posin' he kept that dog on that leg until he made you swear to pay the bet, and then at last had to pry the dog off with a hot poker, bringing away at the same time some of your flesh in the dog's mouth, so that you had to be carried home on a stretcher, and to hire several doctors to keep you from dying with lockjaw.

"S'posin' this, what I want to know is, couldn't you sue Johnson for damages and make him pay heavily for what that dog did? That's what I want to get at."

The colonel thought for a minute and then said,

"Well, Mr. Briggs, I don't think I could. If I

agreed to let Johnson set the dog at me, I should be a party to the transaction and I could not recover."

"Do you mean to say that the law won't make that infernal scoundrel Johnson suffer for letting his dog eat me up?"

"I think not, if you state the case properly."

"It won't, hey?" exclaimed Mr. Briggs, hysterically. "Oh, very well, very well! I s'pose if that dog had chewed me all up and spit me out it'd 've been all the same to this constitutional republic. But hang me if I don't have satisfaction. I'll kill Johnson, poison his dog, and emigrate to some country where the rights of citizens are protected. If I don't, you may bust me open!"

Then Mr. Briggs got on his crutches and hobbled out. He is still a citizen, and will vote at the next election.

CHAPTER XXV.

THAT the editor of every daily paper is persecuted by poetasters is an unquestionable fact; and it is probable that some of the worst of the sufferers would be justified in taking extreme measures to protect themselves from such outrages. But that Major Slott of *The Patriot* ever proposed to murder a poet in self-defence I doubt. The editor of a rival sheet in our county declares, however, that the major actually thirsts for blood; and in proof of the assertion he has printed the following narrative, which, he says, he obtained from Mr. Grady, the policeman:

"One day recently the major sent for a policeman; and when Mr. Grady, of the force, arrived, the major shut the door of his sanctum and asked him to take a seat.

"'Mr. Grady,' he said, 'your profession necessarily brings you into contact with the criminal classes and familiarizes you with them. This is why I have sent for you. My business is of a confidential nature, and I trust to your honor to regard it as a sacred trust confided in you. Mr. Grady, I wish to

203

ascertain if among your acquaintances of the criminal sort you know of any one who is a professional
assassin—who rents himself out to any one who
wants to destroy a fellow-creature? Do you know
of such a person?'

" ' I dunno as I do,' said Mr. Grady, thoughtfully
rubbing his chin. 'There's not much demand for
murderers now.'

" ' Well,' said the editor, 'I wish you'd look around
and see if you can light on such a man, and get him
to do a little job for me. I want a butcher who will
slay a person whom I will designate. I don't care
how he does it. He may stab him, or drown him,
or bang him with a shot-gun. It makes no difference
to me; I will pay him all the same. Now, will you
get me such a man?'

" ' I s'pose I might. I'll look round, any way.'

" ' Between you and me,' said the editor, 'the chap
I'm going to assassinate is a poet—a fellow named
Markley. He has been sending poetry to this paper
every day for eight months. I never printed a line,
but he keeps stuffing it in as if he thought I was depos-
iting it in the bank and drawing interest on it. Well,
sir, it's got to be so bad that it annoys me terribly.
It keeps me awake at night. I'm losing flesh. That
man and his poetry haunt me. I'm getting gloomy
and morose. Life is beginning to pall upon me. I
seem to be under the influence of a perpetual night-
mare. I can't stand it much longer, Mr. Grady; my
reason will totter upon its throne. Here, only this

morning, he sent me a poem entitled "Lines to Hannah." Are you fond of poetry, Grady?'

" 'Oh, I dunno; I don't care so very much about it.'

" 'Well, I'll read you one verse of the "Lines to Hannah." He says—to Hannah, mind you—

> " The little birds sing sweetly
>   In the weeping willows green,
>   The village girls dress neatly—
>   Oh, tell me, do I dream ?"

Now, you see, Grady, that is what is unseating my mind. A man can't stand more than a certain amount of that kind of thing. What do the public care whether he is dreaming or whether he is drunk? What does Hannah care? Why, they don't care a cent. Now, do they?'

" 'Not a red cent.'

" 'Of course not. And yet Markley sends me another poem, entitled "Despondency," in which he exclaims,

> "Oh, bury me deep in the ocean blue,
>   Where the roaring billows laugh;
>   Oh, cast me away on the weltering sea,
>   Where the dolphins will bite me in half."

Now, Mr. Grady, if you can find a competent assassin, I wouldn't make it a point with him to oblige Mr. Markley. I don't care particularly to have the poet buried in the weltering sea. If he can't find a roaring billow, I'll be perfectly satisfied to have him

20

chucked into a creek. And I dare say that it'll make
no material difference whether the dolphins gobble
him or the catfish and eels nibble him up. It's all
the same in the long run. Mention this to your
murderer when you speak to him, will you? Now,
I'll show you why this thing takes all the heart out
of me. In his poem entitled "Longings" he uses
this language:

> "Oh, sing to me, darling, a sweet song to-night,
>   While I bask in the smile of thine eyes,
>   While I kiss those dear lips in the dark silent room,
>   And whisper my saddening good-byes."

Now, you see how it is yourself, Grady, don't you?
How is she going to sing to him while he kisses
those lips, and how is he going to whisper good-
bye? Isn't that awful slush? Now, isn't it? And
then, if the room is dark, what I want to know is
how he's going to tell whether her eyes are smiling
or not? Mr. Grady, either the man is insane or I
am; and if your butcher is going to stab Markley,
you'll oblige me by telling him that I want him to
jab him deep, and maybe fill him up with poison or
something to make it absolutely certain.

"'I know that when he sent me that poem about
"The Unknown" I parsed it, and examined it with a
microscope, and sent it around to a chemist's to be
analyzed, but hang me if I know yet what he's driv-
ing at when he says,

> "The uffish spectral gleaming of that wild resounding clang
>   Came hooting o'er the margin of the dusky moors that hang

Like palls of inky darkness where the hoarse, weird raven calls,
And the bhang-drunk Hindoo staggers on and on until he falls."

Isn't that— Well, now, isn't that just the most fearful
mess of stuff that was ever ground out of a lunatie
asylum ?'

" ' It's the awfullest I ever saw.'

" ' Well, then, I get eighteen of them a week, and
they madden me. They keep my brain in a frenzied
whirl. Grady, this man must die. Self-preservation
is the first law of nature. I have a wife and children ; I conduct a great paper ; I educate the public
mind. My life is valuable to my country. Destroy
this poet, and future generations will praise your
name. He must be wiped out, exterminated, ob-
literated from the face of the earth. Kill him dead
and bury him deep, and fix him in so's he will stay
down, and bring in the bill for the tombstone. I
leave the case to you. You need not tell me you
have done this job. When the poems cease to come
to me, I will know that he is dead. That will settle
it. Good-morning.' "

It is believed that the poet must have been
warned by Grady, for the supplies suddenly ceased ;
and Markley is saving up his effusions for some
other victim.

But the major has other persecutors. One of
them came into the editorial-room of the *Patriot*
during one of those very hot days in June. Major
Slott was perspiring in an effort to hammer out an

article on "The Necessity for Speedy Resumption."
The visitor seized a chair and nudged up close to the
major. Then he said,

"My name is Partridge. I called to show you a
little invention of mine."

"Haven't got time to look at it. I'm busy."

"I see you are. Won't keep you more'n a minute" (removing his hat). "Look at that hat and
tell me how it strikes you."

"Oh, don't bother me! I'm not interested in hats
just now."

"I know you ain't, and that's not a hat. That's
Partridge's Patent Atmospheric Refresher. Looks
exactly like a high hat, don't it? Now, what's the
thing you want most this kind of weather?"

"The thing I want most is to have you skip out
of here."

"What everybody wants is to keep cool, of course.
Now, how are you going to do it? Why, if you
know when you are well off, you will do it with this
hat. But how? I will explain. If you compress
air until it attains a considerable pressure, and then
suddenly release it, the rapid expansion causes the
air to absorb heat and to produce quite a marked
degree of cold. You know this, of course?"

"I wish you'd compress *your* air, and then expand
it in the ears of somebody besides me."

"Now, in my invention I have utilized this beautiful law of nature in a manner that is certain to confer an inestimable blessing upon the human race.

This hat is really made of light boiler iron covered with silk. The compressed air is contained in it. At the present moment it is subjected to a pressure of eighty-seven pounds to the square inch. If that hat should explode while I am sitting here, it would blow the roof off of this building."

"So it killed you I wouldn't care."

"Well, sir, the way I work this wonderful appliance is this: The air-pump is concealed in the small of my back, under my coat. A pipe connects it with the receiver in my hat, and there is a kind of crank running down my right trouser leg and fastened to my boot, so that the mere act of walking pumps the air into the receiver. But how do I effect the cooling process? Listen: Another pipe comes from the receiver and empties into a kind of a sheet-iron undershirt, perforated with holes, which I wear beneath my outside shirt—"

"If you'd wear something *over* that shirt, so as to hide the dirt, you'd be more agreeable."

"Now, s'posin' it's a warm day. I'm going along the street with the air-crank in operation. The receiver is full. I want to cool off. I pull the string which runs down my left sleeve; the air rushes from the receiver, suddenly expands about my body, and makes me feel so cold that I wish I had brought my overcoat with me."

"I wish to gracious you'd go home and get it now."

"You see, then, that this invention is of the utmost value and importance, and my idea in calling upon you was to give you a chance to mention and describe it in your paper, so that the public might know about it. You are the only editor I have revealed the secret to. I thought I'd give you the first chance to become a benefactor of your race."

" I'm the kind of benefactor that charges one dollar a line for such philanthropy."

" To assure yourself that the machine is perfect you must try it for yourself. Just stand up and take your coat off. Then I'll put the hat on your head, screw the pump into the small of your back and fix the other machinery down your legs."

" I'll see you hanged first."

" Well, then, I'll put it on myself and illustrate the theory for you. You see the rod here in my trousers? This is the air-pump here, just above my suspender buttons. The hat now contains about six atmospheres. Now I am ready to move. See? You observe how it works? The only noise you hear is a slight click of the valve in the pump. A couple more turns, and you put your hand on my shirt-collar and feel how near zero it is. I will get the pressure up to one hundred pounds before I—"

BANG!!!

As soon as the major began to realize the situation he crawled out from beneath his overturned desk, wiped the contents of the inkstand from his face and hair with the copy of that unfinished article upon " The Necessity for Speedy Resumption," and looked about him. Mr. Partridge was lying in the

BANG!!!

corner with a splintered table over his legs, his head in a spittoon, and fragments of ruined machinery bursting out through enormous rents in his trousers and his coat. His cast-iron undershirt protruded in jagged points from a dozen orifices in his waistcoat. As the major took him by the leg to haul him out of the *débris* Partridge opened his eyes wearily and said,

"Awful clap, wasn't it? You ought to've had lightning-rods on this building. Struck by lightning, wasn't I?"

"You intolerable ass!" exclaimed the major as the clerks and reporters came rushing in and began to place Partridge on his legs; "it wasn't lightning. It was that infernal machine that you wanted me to put on my head. If it had driven you under ground about forty feet, I'd have been glad, even if it had also demolished the building."

"What! the receiver exploded, did it? Too bad, ain't it? Blamed if I didn't think she was strong enough to bear twice that pressure. I must have made a mistake in my calculations, however," said Partridge, pinning up his clothes and holding his handkerchief to his bloody nose; "I'll have another one made, and come around to show you the invention to better advantage."

"If you do, I'll brain you with an inkstand," said the major.

Then Partridge limped out, and the major, abandoning the subject of resumption, began a fresh edi-

torial upon "The Extraordinary Prevalence of Idiots
at the Present Time."

The *Patriot* has shown a remarkable amount of
enterprise lately in obtaining, or professing to obtain, an interview with the Wandering Jew. The
reader can form his own estimate of the value of
the report, which appeared in the *Patriot* in the following fashion :

Reports were floating about the city yesterday to
the effect that the Wandering Jew had been seen
over in New Jersey. A reporter was sent over at
once to hunt him up, and to interview him if he should
be found. After a somewhat protracted search the
reporter discovered a promising-looking person sitting on the top rail of a fence just outside of Camden
engaged in eating some crackers and cheese. The
reporter approached him and addressed him at a
venture :

"Beautiful day, Cantaphilus !"

This familiarity seemed necessary ; because if the
Wandering Jew has any family name, the fact has
not been revealed to the public.

"Bless my soul, young man, how on earth did you
know me ?" exclaimed the Jew.

"Oh, I don't know ; something about your appearance told me who it was. I'm mighty glad to see
you, any way. When did you arrive ?"

"I came on here yesterday. Been down in Terra
del Fuego, where I heard about the Centennial, and

I thought I'd run up and have a look at it. Be a good thing, I reckon. Time flies, though, don't it? Seems to me only yesterday that a man over here in Siberia told me that you people were fighting your Revolutionary war."

He sat upon the fence as he talked; his feet, cased

in gum shoes, rested on the third rail from the bottom; his umbrella was under his arm; his face was deeply wrinkled, and his long white beard bobbed up and down as he ate his lunch voraciously, diving into his carpet-bag every now and then for more.

The reporter remarked that he feared that such a
liberal diet of cheese would disagree with the eater,
but the old man said,

"Why, my goodness, sonny, I've been hunting all
over the earth for seventeen centuries for something
to disagree with me. That's what I yearn for. If
I could only get dyspepsia once, I might hope to
wear myself out. But it's no use. I could lunch
on a pound of nails and feel as comfortable as a baby
after a bottle of milk. That's one of my peculiarities. You know nothing ever hurts me. Why,
I've been thrown out of volcanoes—lemme see: well,
dozens of times—and never been singed a bit. 'Most
always, in real cold weather, I step over to Italy and
roost around inside of Vesuvius; and then, maybe,
there's an eruption, and I'm heaved out a couple of
hundred miles or so, but always safe and sound.
What I don't know about volcanic eruptions, my
child, isn't worth knowing. I went sailing around
through the air when Pompeii was destroyed. Yes,
sir, I was there; saw the whole thing. Why, I could
tell you the most wonderful stories. You wouldn't
believe."

"How do you travel generally?"

"Oh, different ways. I have gone around some
in sleeping-cars, and had my baggage checked
through; but generally I prefer to walk. I'm never
in a hurry, and I like to take my own route. I'm a
mighty good walker. I did think of getting up some
kind of a pedestrian match with some of your cham-

pion walkers, but it's no use; it'd only create an excitement."

"How do people treat you usually?"

"Well, I can't complain. Snap me up for a tramp sometimes, or make disagreeable remarks about me. But generally I get along well enough. The under-takers are hardest on me. They say I exercise a depressing influence on their business by setting a bad example to other people; and one of 'em, over in Constantinople, he said a man who'd defrauded about fifty-four generations of undertakers ought to be ashamed to show his face in civilized society. But bless you, sonny, I don't mind them. Business, you know, is business. It's perfectly natural for them to feel that way about it; now, isn't it?"

"Will you have a cigar, after eating?"

"No; none for me. Raleigh wanted me to learn to smoke when he was in Virginia, but I didn't care for it. You remember him, of course? Oh no; I forgot how young you are. Pleasant man, but a little too chimerical. I liked Columbus better. Nero was a man who'd 've suited you newspaper people. 'Most always a murder every day. And then that fire in Rome when he fiddled; made a splendid report for the papers, wouldn't it? Poor sort of a man, though. The only time I ever saw him was when he was drowning his mother. Dropped the old lady over and let her drift off as if he didn't care a cent."

"Talking of newspapers, how would you like to

make an engagement as the traveling correspondent of the *Patriot?*"

"Well, I dunno. I wouldn't mind sending you a letter now and then, but I don't care to make any regular engagement. You see I haven't written a great deal for about eighteen hundred years, and a man kind of gets out of practice in that time. I write such an awful poor hand, too. No; I guess I won't contribute regularly. I have thought sometimes maybe I might do a little work as a book-agent, so's to pick up a few stray dollars. But I never had a fair chance offered to me, and I didn't care enough about it to hunt it up; and so nothing ever came of it. I could make a good book fairly hum around this globe, though, don't you think?"

"Were you ever married? Did you ever have a wife?"

"See here, my son, I never did you any harm, and what's the use of your bringing up such disagreeable reminiscences? The old lady died in Egypt in 73. They made her up into a mummy, and I reckon they put a pyramid on her to hold her down. That's enough; that satisfies me."

"Is your memory generally good?"

"Well, about fair; that's all. I know I used to get Petrarch mixed up in my mind with St. Peter, and I've several times alluded to Plutarch as the god of the infernal regions. I'm often hazy about people. The queerest thing! You know that once, in conversation with Benjamin Franklin, I confounded Mark

Antony with Saint Anthony, and actually alluded to
the saint's oration over the dead body of Cæsar.
Positive fact. I'll tell you how I often keep the run
of things: I say of a certain event, 'That happened
during the century that I was bilious,' or, 'It occurred in the century when I had rheumatism.' That's
the way I fix the time. I did commence to keep a
diary back in 134, but I ran up a stack of manuscript
three or four hundred feet high, and then I gave it
up. Couldn't lug it round with me, you know."

"I suppose you have known a great many celebrated people?"

"Plenty of 'em—plenty of 'em, sir. By the way,
did anybody ever tell you that you looked like Mo-
hammed? Well, sir, you do. Astonishing likeness!
Now, *there* was an old scalawag for you. A perfect
fraud! I lent that man a pair of boots in 598, and
he never returned them; said I'd get my reward
hereafter. I've regretted those boots for nearly
thirteen hundred years."

"Did it ever occur to you to lecture?"

"Oh yes; I've turned it over in my mind. But I
guess I won't. You see, my son, I'm so crammed
full of information that if I began a discourse I could
hardly stop under a couple of years; and that's too
long for a lecture, you know. Then they might
encore it; and so I hardly think I'd better go in.
No, I'll just trudge along in the old fashion."

"Have you any views about the questions of the
day? Are you in favor of soft money or hard?"

"Young man, the advice to you of a man who has studied the world for nearly two thousand years is to take any kind you can get. That's solid wisdom."

Then, as the old man babbled on, he descended from the fence, shouldered his umbrella, and together the two started for the ferry. He said he wanted to buy a new suit of clothes. That he had on he had bought in 1807 in Germany, and it was beginning to get threadbare. So the reporter led him over the river, put him in a horse-car, asked him to send his address to the office, and the aged pilgrim nudged up into a corner seat, put his valise on the floor and sailed serenely out of sight amid the reverberation of the oaths hurled by the driver at an Irish dray-man who occupied the track in front of the car.

CHAPTER XXVI.

THE ACHIEVEMENTS OF DR. PERKINS.

T might be hardly fair to say that Doctor Perkins, a former resident of the village, was a quack; he may be described in milder phrase as an irregular practitioner. He belonged to none of the accepted schools, but treated his patients in accordance with certain theories of his own. The doctor had a habit of relating remarkable stories of his own achievements, and the most wonderful of these was his account of an attempt that he once made to cure a man named Simpson of consumption by the process of transfusion of blood. The doctor, according to his own story, determined to inject healthy blood into Simpson's veins.

As no human being was willing to shed his blood for Simpson, the doctor bled Simpson's goat; and opening a vein in Simpson's arm, he injected about two quarts of the blood into the patient's system. Simpson immediately began to revive, but, singular to relate, no sooner had his strength returned than he jumped out of bed; and twitching his head about after the fashion of a goat, he made a savage attempt to butt the doctor. That medical gentleman, after having Simpson's head plunged against his stomach three or four times, took refuge in the closet; whereupon Simpson banged his head against the panel of the door a couple of times, and would probably have

broken it to splinters had not his mother-in-law entered at that moment and diverted his attention. One well-directed blow from Simpson floored her, and then, while she screamed for help, Simpson frolicked around over the floor, making assiduous efforts to nibble the green flowers in the ingrain carpet. When they called the hired man in and tied him down on the bed, an effort was made to interview him, but the only answer he could give to such questions as how he felt and when he wanted his medicine was a "ba-a" precisely like that of a goat, and then he would strain himself in an effort to butt a hole in the head-board. The condition of the patient was so alarm-ing, and Mrs. Simpson was so indignant, that Dr. Perkins determined to undo the evil if possible. So he first bled Simpson freely, and then, by heavily bribing Simpson's Irishman, he procured fresh blood from him, and injected Simpson the second time. Simpson recovered, but he shocked his old Republican friends by displaying an irresistible tendency to vote the Democratic ticket, and made his mother-in-law mad by speaking with a strong brogue. He gradu-ally gave up butting, and never indulged in it in a serious manner but once, and that was on a certain Sunday, when, one of the remaining corpuscles of goat's blood getting into his brain just as he was going into church, he butted the sexton halfway up the aisle, and only recovered himself sufficiently to apologize just as the enraged official was about to floor him with a hymn-book.

But the doctor did not succeed with private prac-tice in Millburg, and so one day he made up his mind to try to get out of poverty by inventing a patent medicine. After some reflection he concluded that the two most frequent and most unpopular forms of infirmity were baldness of head and torpidity of the liver, and he selected compounds recommended by the pharmacopœia as the remedies which he would sell to the public. One he called " Perkins' Hair Vigor," and the other " Perkins' Liver Regulator." Procuring a large number of fancy bottles and gaudy labels, he bottled the medicines and advertised them extensively, with certificates of imaginary cures, which were written out for him by a friend whose liver was active and whose hair was abundant.

It is not at all unlikely that Perkins would have achieved success with his enterprise but for one unfortunate circumstance: he was totally unfamiliar with the preparations, excepting in so far as the pharmacopœia instructed him; and as ill-luck would have it, in putting them up he got the labels of the liver regulator on the hair vigor bottles, and the labels of the latter on the bottles containing the former. Of course the results were appalling; and as Doctor Perkins had requested the afflicted to inform him of the benefits derived from applying the remedies, he had not sold more than a few hundred bottles before he began to hear from the purchasers.

One day, as he was coming out of his office, he observed a man sitting on the fire-plug with a shotgun in his hand and thunder upon his brow. The man was bare-headed, and his scalp was covered with a shiny substance of some kind. When he saw Perkins, he emptied one load of bird-shot into the inventor's legs, and he was about to give him

the contents of the other barrel, when Perkins hobbled into the office and shut the door. The man
pursued him and tried to break in the door with the
butt of the gun. He failed, and Perkins asked him
what he meant by such murderous conduct.

"You come out here, and I'll show you what I
mean, you scoundrel!" said the man. "You step
out here for a minute, and I'll blow the head off of
you for selling me hair vigor that has gummed my
head up so that I can't wear a hat and can't sleep
without sticking to the pillow-case. Turned my
scalp all green and pink, too. You put your head
out of that door, and I'll give you more vigor than
you want, you idiot! I expect that stuff'll soak in
and kill me."

Then the man took his seat again on the fire-plug,
and after reloading the barrel of his gun put on a
fresh cap and waited. Perkins remained inside and
sent a boy out the back way for the mail. The first
letter he opened was from a woman, who wrote:

"My husband took one dose of your liver regulator and immediately went into spasms. He has
had fits every hour for four days. As soon as he
dies I am coming on to kill the fiend who poisoned
him."

A clergyman in Delaware wrote to ask what were
the ingredients of the liver regulator. He feared
something was wrong, because his aunt had taken
the medicine only twice, when she began to roll over
on the floor and howl in the most alarming manner,

and she had been in a comatose condition for fifteen hours.

A man named Johnson dropped a line to say that after applying the hair vigor to his scalp he had leaned his head against the back of a chair, and it had now been in that position two days. He feared he would never be released unless he cut up the chair and wore the piece permanently on his head. He was coming to see Perkins in reference to the matter when he got loose, and he was going to bring his dog with him.

A Mr. Wilson said that his boy had put some of the vigor on his face in order to induce the growth of a moustache, and that at the present moment the boy's upper lip was glued fast to the tip of his nose and his countenance looked as if it had been coated with green varnish.

There were about forty other letters, giving the details of sundry other cases of awful suffering and breathing threatenings and slaughter against Mr. Perkins. Just as Mr. Perkins was finishing these epistles a friend of his came rushing in through the back door breathless, and exclaimed,

" By George, Aleck, you better get over the fence and leave 'town as quick as you can. There's thunder to pay about those patent medicines of yours. Old Mrs. Gridley's just gone up on that liver regulator, after being in convulsions for a week. Thompson's hired girl is lying at the last gasp, four of the Browns have got the awfulest-looking heads you ever saw from the hair vigor, and about a dozen other people are up at the sheriff's office taking out warrants for your arrest. The people are talking of mobbing you, and the crowd out here on the pavement are cheering a green-headed man with a gun who says he's going to bang the head off of you. Now, you take my advice and skip. It'll be sudden death to stay here. Leave! that's your only chance."

Then Doctor Perkins got over the fence and ran for the early train, and an hour later the mob gutted his office and smashed the entire stock of remedies. Perkins is in Canada now, working in a saw-mill. He is convinced that there is no money for him in the business of relieving human suffering.

CHAPTER XXVII.

GENERAL TRUMPS OF THE MILITIA.

THE principal warrior in our community is General Trumps, the commander of the militia of the district. The general has seen service in the South and West, and is a pretty good soldier. In these happy days of peace, however, he does not often have an opportunity to display his fighting qualities, but sometimes even now, when he is provoked to wrath, he becomes bloodthirsty and ferocious. Last summer the general went to Cape May. Previous to his arrival two young men, whom I will call Brown and Jones, occupied adjoining rooms at a certain hotel. One day Brown fixed a string to the covers on Jones' bed and ran the cord through the door into his own room. His purpose was to pull the covers off as soon as Jones got comfortably fixed for the night. But that afternoon General Trumps came down; and as the hotel was crowded, the landlord put Jones in the room with Brown and gave Jones' apartment to the general. Brown forgot about the string, and he and Jones went to bed. About midnight Jones' dog, while prowling around the room, got the string tangled about his leg, and in struggling to reach the window he slowly dragged the bed-clothes off of the soldier, next door. That gentleman awoke, and after scolding his wife for removing the blankets went to sleep again. Presently Jones' dog saw a rat and darted after it. Off came the covers again. Then the man of war was angry. He roused his wife and scolded her vigorously. She protested her innocence, and while she was speaking Jones' dog heard another dog outside, and hurried to the window to bark. The covers were again removed. Then the general fumbled about until he found the cord. Then he loaded up his revolver, drew his sword and dared Jones and Brown to open their door and come out into the entry. They peeped at him over the transom, observed his warlike preparations, glanced at the string and the dog, packed their carpet-bags, slid down the water-spout outside, and went home in the five-o'clock train. The manner in which that battle-scarred veteran roared around the hotel during the day was said to have been frightful; and when rumors came that Brown and Jones had gone to another place in the neighborhood, he spent the day hunting for them with a purpose to commit violence. He gradually became calmer, and as his anger subsided the humorous aspect of the matter appeared, and he felt rather glad that he had not encountered the two young men.

Several years ago the general was out upon the plains fighting the Indians. One of the men who

accompanied his command was a Major Bing.   It
happened that the major was captured by the savages,
and it devolved upon the general to bear the melancholy tidings to Mrs. Bing.   It appears that while the
general was on his way home Mrs. Bing moved into
another house; and when the general returned with
the sad intelligence, he did not know of the fact, but
went to the old house, which was now occupied by
Mrs. Wood.   He told the servant-girl to tell her
mistress to come into the parlor, and then he took a
seat on the sofa and thought how he could break the
news of the major's death to her so as not to give

her too violent a shock. When Mrs. Wood entered, the general greeted her mournfully; and when they had taken seats, the following conversation ensued:

"Madam, I have been the major's friend ever since our childhood. I played with him when we were boys together. I grew up to manhood with him; I watched with pride his noble and successful career; I rejoiced when he married the lovely woman before me; and I went to the West with him. Need I tell you that I loved him? I loved him only less than you did."

"I don't understand you, sir," said Mrs. Wood. "Whom are you referring to?"

"Why, to the major. I say that your love for him alone was greater than mine; and I am—"

"Your remarks are a mystery to me. I have no attachment of that kind."

"Call it what you will, madam. I know how strong the tie was between you—how deep the devotion which kept two loving souls in perfect unison. And knowing this, of course I feel deeply that to wound either heart by telling of misfortune to the other is a task from which a man like me might very properly shrink. But I have a duty to perform—a solemn duty. What would you say, my dear madam, if I should tell you that the major had lost a leg? What would you say to that?"

"I don't know. If I knew a major who had lost a leg, I should probably advise him to buy a wooden one."

"Light-hearted as ever," said the general. "Just as he told me you were. Poor woman! you will need your buoyant spirits yet. But, dear madam, suppose the major had lost not only one leg, but two; both gone; no legs at all; not a pin to stand on; now, how would that strike you?"

"Really, sir, this is getting to be absurd. I don't care whether your major has as many legs as a centipede or none at all. If you have any business with me, please transact it as quickly as possible."

"Madam, this is too serious a subject for jest. The major has lost not only his legs, but his arms. He is absolutely without limbs of any kind at this moment. That's as true as I'm sitting here. Now, don't scream, please."

"I haven't the slightest idea of screaming."

"Well, you take it mighty cool, I must say. But that's not the worst of it. All his ribs are gone, his nose has departed, and he only has one eye and a part of one shoulder-blade. I pledge you my word that's the truth. I hardly think he will recover."

"I shouldn't think he would, in that condition; but, upon my life, I cannot see that the fact interests me at all."

"Not interest you! Well, that is amazing! Not int— Why, my goodness, woman, that's not half of it. The major's scalp's all gone; he hasn't enough fuzz on his head to make a camel's-hair pencil; he has a stake through his body, and he's been burnt until he is all doubled up in a hard knot;

and, in my private opinion, it's mighty unlikely he'll ever be untied and straightened out again. If that doesn't fetch you, you must have a heart of stone."

" I don't care anything about it, sir. It's none of my business."

" Well, then, as long as you're so indifferent, let me tell you, plump and plain, that the major's dead as Julius Cæsar! The Indians killed him, burnt him and minced him up! Now, that's the solemn truth, and his last words to me were, ' Break the news gently to Maria.' You see the man loved you. He cared more for you than you seemed to do for him. He would have welcomed death if he had known you had ceased to love him."

" What did you say his last words were ?"

" Why, just before his soul took its eternal flight he whispered something in my ear. Then I made a sudden dash and escaped from the savages, to bring his message back to you. That message was : ' Break the news gently to Maria.' That's what the major said with his dying lips."

" Well, then, why don't you break the news to Maria ?"

" Madam, such levity is untimely. I have broken it—broken it gently. You have heard it all."

" Do you suppose I am Major Bing's wife ?"

" Certainly."

" Well, she moved around into Market street last December. Maybe you'd better hunt her up."

The general looked at Mrs. Wood solemnly for a

minute, and then he said he would. Then he bade
Mrs. Wood good-morning, bowed himself out and
walked around to look for the widow. When the real
widow heard the news, she was deeply affected, and
she sobbed in a most distressing manner. Subsequently she went into mourning. The life insurance
company paid her the money due upon the major's
policy. The major's lodge passed resolutions of
regret, his family divided up his property, and the
community settled down comfortably in the conviction that the major was finally and hopelessly
dead.

About a year afterward, however, Major Bing suddenly arrived in town without announcing his coming. He had been held as a prisoner by the Indians,
and had escaped. As he stepped from the cars a
policeman looked at him a minute, then seized him
by the collar and hurried him around to the coroner's
office. Before he could recover from his amazement
the coroner empaneled a jury, put the action of the
insurance company in evidence and promptly got
from the jury a verdict that "the said Bing came to
his death at the hands of the Indians."

Then the major went to his house and found his
widow sitting on the front porch talking to Myers,
the man to whom she was engaged to be married.
As he entered the gate his widow gave one little
start of surprise, and then, regaining her composure,
she said to Myers,

"Isn't this a new kind of an idea—dead people

coming around when common decency requires them to keep quiet?"

"It's altogether wrong," said Myers. "If I was dead, I'd lie still and quit wandering about over the face of the earth."

"Maria, don't you know me?" asked the major, indignantly.

"I used to know you when you were alive; but now that you're gone, I don't expect to recognize you until we meet in a better world."

"But, Maria, I am not dead. You certainly see that I am alive."

"Not dead! Didn't you send word to me that you were? Am I to refuse to believe my own husband? The life insurance company says you are deceased; the lodge says so; the coroner officially asserts the fact. What am I to do? The evidence is all one way."

"But you *shall* accept me as alive!" shouted the major, in a rage.

"Mr. Myers," said the widow, calmly, "hadn't we better send for the undertaker to come and bury these remains?"

"Look here!" said Myers. "I'm the last man to do a dead friend an injury, but I ain't going to have any departed spirit coming in here and giving this lady hysterics. You pack up and go back, and stay there, or I'll have you hustled into a tomb quicker'n lightning. Hurry up now; don't stop to think about it!"

"This beats the very old Harry!" said the major, in astonishment.

"No answering back, now," said Myers. "When I want communications from the other world, I'll hunt up a spiritualist medium and get my information out of knocks on a table. All you've got to do is to creep off into the tomb somewhere and behave."

"You're perfectly certain I'm dead, are you?" said the major, getting calmer.

"Why, of course."

"Can a dead man violate the laws?"

"Certainly not."

"Well, then, I'm going to hammer you with this club, and I reckon you'll find me the most energetic corpse in the county."

They say that the fight was terrific. First the major was on top, then Myers; and as they rolled over and over in the porch the widow sat by and surveyed the scene. Finally, Myers explained that upon the whole he believed he had enough; and when the major had given him a few supplementary thumps, he got up, and gazing at the prostrate Myers and at the widow, he said,

"Take her; take her, young man. You're welcome to her. I wouldn't have her if she was the only woman in the temperate zone. But let me tell you, before you get her, that when you are married to her you'll wish something'd happen to send you down to the bottom of the ocean and anchor you there."

Then the major slammed the gate and left; and
he started life afresh in New York. Myers has written to him since to say that the only grudge that he
has against him is that he didn't kill him in that fight
in the porch, for the widow has made death seem
blissful to him; and the major's answer was that the
reason why he spared his life was that he wanted to
make his revenge fiendish.

Of course I do not vouch for this part of the story

22

which tells of the major's return. General Trumps
is responsible for that; and I know that sometimes,
when his imagination is unduly warmed, he is prone to
exaggeration. The general's own domestic matters
are in the most charming condition. According to his
own story, he never had any unpleasant feeling in his
family but once. Several years ago he was in Williamsport attending to his business. While there he
had a strong premonition that something was the matter at home; so, in order to satisfy himself, he determined to run down to Philadelphia in the next train.
In the mean time, his mother-in-law sent him a despatch to this effect: "Another daughter has just arrived. Hannah is poorly; come home at once." The
lines were down, however, and the despatch was held
over; and meanwhile the general reached home, and
found his wife doing pretty well and the nurse walking around with an infant a day old. After staying
twenty-four hours, and finding that everybody was
tolerably comfortable, he returned to Williamsport
without anything having been said about the despatch, his mother-in-law supposing of course that
he had received it. The day after his arrival the
lines were fixed, and that night he received a despatch from the telegraph office dated that very day,
and conveying the following intelligence:

"Another daughter has just arrived. Hannah is
poorly; come home at once."

The general was amazed and bewildered. He
couldn't understand it. He walked the floor of his

room all night trying to get the hang of the thing; and the more he considered the subject, the more he became alarmed at the extraordinary occurrence. He took the early train for the city, and during the journey was in a condition of frantic bewilderment. When he arrived, he jumped in a cab, drove furiously to the house, and scared his mother-in-law into convulsions by rushing in in a frenzy and demanding what on earth had happened. He was greatly relieved to find that there was but one infant in the nursery, and to learn how the mistake occurred. But he felt as if he would like to see the telegraph operator who changed the date of that despatch. He wanted to remonstrate with him.

CHAPTER XXVIII.

THE MISDIRECTED ENERGIES OF MR. BRADLEY.

R. BRADLEY, our inventor, has had some experiences in addition to those already recorded which may perhaps be entertaining to the reader. One of the peculiarities of Bradley's contrivances is that when they are designed to do a specified work, that is conspicuously the work they cannot possibly be induced to do. There, for instance, was Bradley's famous steam-pump.

Some years ago Bradley invented a steam-pump for use on shipboard. He claimed for it that it would pump about three times as many gallons in a minute as any other pump, and he got some of his political friends in Congress to use their influence with the Navy Department to have it tried on one of the navy vessels. Finally he succeeded in having it introduced upon a small steamer, which we will call the Water Witch; and when everything was ready, the ship started upon a trial trip. Soon after she got to sea, Bradley, who was aboard, said he would like to try the pump upon the bilge-water to see how she worked.

The captain ordered the engineer to turn it on, and the machine operated apparently in the most beautiful manner. In about an hour one of the officers reported that the water was gaining rapidly in the hold, and the captain sent some men down to discover where the leak was. They came back and reported that they couldn't find the hole, but that the water was pouring in somewhere in frightful quantities.

Then some of the officers went down and spent half an hour in water up to their waists feeling around after that awful hole, but they couldn't ascertain where it was. The only thing that they were certain of was that the water was steadily gaining on them, and the ship was certain to sink unless something was done. All this time Mr. Bradley's pump was working away, and the captain continually enjoined the engineer to give it greater speed.

Then the captain himself went down and made an examination; and although he failed to find the leak, he was alarmed to discover a quantity of codfish and porpoises swimming about in the hold, because he knew that the hole in the hull must be very large indeed to admit the fish. And still the water rose steadily all the time, although Bradley's pump was jerking away at it in a terrific manner and all the other pumps were running at full speed.

At last the captain made up his mind that he should have to desert the ship, as she was certain to sink; and so the boats were made ready and packed with provisions and water and a few little comforts, and by this time the water in the bilge was nearly up to the furnace fires.

Just then Bradley's pump suddenly stopped; and then the captain turned pale as death and demanded to know who stopped that pump, while Bradley buckled a life-preserver around him, corked up a note to his wife in a bottle, and said that now that the pump had ceased he would give that steamer just four minutes to reach bottom.

While he was speaking the engineer came up and said,

"Mr. Bradley, what did you say was the capacity of your pump?"

"Six hundred gallons a minute."

"Six hundred. Well, Mr. Bradley, how many gallons do you estimate that there are in the Atlantic Ocean?"

"Blessed if I know. How in the mischief can I tell that?"

"Oh, it don't make any particular difference, only I thought you might have some kind of an indistinct idea how long it would take you to run the ocean through your pump."

"I dunno, I'm sure," said Bradley.

"Well, I merely wanted to say that, whatever your calculations respecting the number of gallons in the Atlantic, it is perfectly useless for you to try to load up that ocean in this vessel. She won't hold more'n half of it."

"What do you mean, sir?" demanded Bradley.

"Why, I mean that that diabolical pump of yours, instead of taking out the bilge, has been spurting water into this vessel for the past four hours, and that if you have a theory that you can strike dry land by that process it is ingenious, but it won't work, for it's going to sink this ship."

Then the captain swore till the air was blue. Then he put Bradley in irons, and ripped out his pump, and unpacked the boats, and pumped out the water, and picked up the codfish and porpoises, and set sail for home for the purpose of making a report on the subject of the new invention. The Bradley Improved Marine Steam-pump went right out of use at the end of the voyage.

Another invention of Bradley's was a scientific system of foretelling the weather. He had a lot of barometers, hygrometers and such things in his house, and he claimed that by reading these intelligently and watching the clouds, in accordance with his theory, a man could prophesy what kind of weather there would be three days ahead. They were getting up a Sunday-school picnic in town in May; and as Bradley ascertained that there would be no rain on a certain Thursday, they selected that day for the purpose. The sky looked gloomy when they started; but as Bradley declared that it absolutely *couldn't* rain on Thursday, everybody felt that it was safe to go. About two hours after the party reached the grounds, however, a shower came up, and it rained so hard that it ruined all the provisions, wet everybody to the skin and washed the cake into dough. On the following Monday the agricultural exhibition was to be held; but as Mr. Bradley foresaw that there would be a terrible north-east storm on that day, he suggested to the president of the society that it had better be postponed. So they put it off; and that was the only clear Monday we had during May. About the first of June, Mr. Bradley announced that there would not be any rain until the 15th; and consequently we had showers every day right along up to that time, with the exception of the 10th when there was a slight spit of snow. So on the 15th, Bradley foresaw that the rest of the month would be wet; and by an odd coincidence a drought set in and it only rained once during the two weeks, and that was the day on which Bradley informed the base-ball club that it could play a match, because it would be clear.

On toward the first of July he began to have some doubts if his improved weather-system was correct; he was convinced that it must work by contraries. So when Professor Jones asked him if it would be safe to attempt to have a display of fireworks on the night of the 5th, Bradley brought the improved system into play, and discovered that it promised rainy weather on that night. So then he was certain it would be clear; and he told Professor Jones to go ahead.

On the night of the 5th, just as the professor got

his Catherine-wheels and sky-rockets all in position, it began to rain; and that was the most awful storm we had that year: it raised the river nearly three feet. As soon as it began Bradley got the axe and went up stairs and smashed his hydrometers, hygrometers, barometers and thermometers. Then he cut down the pole that upheld the weathercock and burned the manuscript of the book which he was writing in explanation of his system. He leans on "Old Probs" now when he wants to ascertain the probable state of the weather.

When his first baby was born, Bradley invented a self-rocking cradle for it. He constructed the motive-power of the machine from some old clockwork which was operated by a huge steel ribbon spring strong enough to move a horse-car and long enough to run for a week without rewinding. When the cradle was completed, he put the baby in it upon a pillow and started the machinery. It worked beautifully, and after watching it for a while Bradley went to bed in a peaceful and happy frame of mind. Toward midnight he heard something go r-r-r-rip! Buzz-z-z-z! Crash! Bang! Then a pin or something of the kind in the clockwork gave way, and before Bradley could get out of bed the cradle containing the baby was making ninety revolutions a minute, and hopping around the room and slamming up against the furniture in a manner that was simply awful to look at.

How to get the child out was now the only consideration which presented itself to the mind of the
inventor.   A happy thought struck him.   He took
a slat out of the bedstead and held it under the cradle.   On the next down-stroke it stopped with a

jerk, and the baby was thrown, like a stone out of a
catapult, against the washstand, fortunately with the
pillow to break its fall.   But the machine kept whizzing round and round the room as soon as the slat
was withdrawn, and Bradley, in an ecstasy of rage,
flung it out the back window into the yard.   It con-

tinued to make such a clatter there that he had to
go down and pile up barrels and slop-buckets and
bricks and clothes-props and part of the grape-arbor
on it, so that all it could do was to lie there all night
buzzing with a kind of smothered hum and keeping
the next-door neighbors awake, so that they pelted
it with bootjacks, under the impression that it was
cats.

Mrs. Bradley expressed such decided views respecting cradles of that pattern that Mr. Bradley
turned his attention to other matters than those of
a domestic character. He resolved to revolutionize
navigation. It occurred to him that some kind of an
apparatus might be devised by which a man could
walk upon the surface of the water, and he went to
work at it. The result was that in a few weeks he
produced and patented Bradley's Water Perambulator. It consisted of a couple of shallow scows, each
about four feet long. These were to be fastened to
the feet; and Bradley informed his friends that with
a little practice a man could glide over the bosom of
a river with the ease and velocity with which a good
skater skims over the ice.

It looked like a splendid thing. Bradley said that
it would certainly produce a revolution in navigation,
and make men wholly independent of steamers and
other vessels when they desired to travel upon water
with rapidity. Bradley intimated that the day would
come when a man would mount a water perambulator and go drifting off to India, sliding over the

bounding billows of the dark blue sea as serenely as if he were walking along a turnpike.

And one day Bradley asked a select party to come down to the river to see him make a trial-trip. At the appointed time he appeared with something that looked like a small frigate under each arm; and when he had fastened them securely upon his feet, he prepared to lower himself over the edge of the wharf. He asked the spectators to designate a point upon the thither shore at which they wished him to land. It was immaterial to him, he said, whether he went one mile or ten, up stream or down, because he should glide around upon the surface of the stream with the ease and grace of a swallow. Then they fixed a point for him; and when he had dropped into the water, he steadied himself for a moment by holding to the pier while he fastened his eye upon his destination and prepared to start.

At last he said the experiment would begin; and he struck out with his left foot. As he did so the front end of that particular scow scuttled under water, and as he tried to save himself by bringing forward his right foot, that section of Bradley's Water Perambulator also dipped under, and Bradley fell.

A moment later he was hanging head downward in the river, with nothing visible to the anxious spectators but the bottoms of two four-foot frigates. The perambulator simply kept the body of Bradley under the water. Then a man went out in a skiff

and pulled the inventor in with a boat-hook. When
he came ashore, they unbuckled his scows, took off
his clothing and rolled him upon an oil-barrel. In
half an hour he revived, and with a deep groan he
said,

"Where am I?"

His friends explained his situation to him, and
then he asked,

"What drowned me?"

They told him sadly that he was injured during an attempt to revolutionize navigation and to prepare the way for a walk to India.

"How did I try to do it?" he inquired.

They wept as they reminded him that he had started to skim over the river like a swallow, with a scow upon each foot, and then he faintly said,

"Where in thunder are those machines?"

His friends produced the new motor with which Bradley intended to break up the steamship lines; and when he had looked at them for a moment, he fell back and whispered,

"It's no use. I can't do 'em justice. Eight men couldn't cuss 'em to satisfy me. But split 'em up! Have 'em mashed into kin'lin-wood before I get well, or the sight of 'em'll set me crazy."

Then he was carried home, and after being in bed about a fortnight he came out with a pallid cheek, a sorrowful heart and ideas for six or seven new machines.

CHAPTER XXIX.

THE TRIALS OF MR. KEYSER, GRANGER.

MR. KEYSER mentioned recently that he had employed a new hired girl, and that soon after her arrival Mrs. Keyser, before starting to spend the day with a friend, instructed the girl to whitewash the kitchen during her absence. Upon returning, Mrs. Keyser found the job completed in a very satisfactory manner. On Wednesday, Mrs. Keyser always churns, and on the following Wednesday, when she was ready, she went out; and finding that Mr. Keyser had already put the milk into the churn, she began to turn, the handle. This was at eight o'clock in the morning, and she turned until ten without any signs of butter appearing. Then she called in the hired man, and he turned until dinner-time, when he knocked off with some very offensive language, addressed to the butter, which had not yet come. After dinner the hired girl took hold of the crank and turned it energetically until two o'clock, when she let go with a remark which conveyed the impression that she believed the churn to be haunted. Then Mr. Keyser came out and said he wanted to

know what was the matter with that churn. It was
a good enough churn if people only knew enough to
use it. Mr. Keyser then worked the crank until half-
past three, when, as the butter had not come, he surrendered it again to the hired man because he had
an engagement in the village. The man ground the
machine to an accompaniment of frightful impreca-
tions. Then the Keyser children each took a turn for
half an hour, then Mrs. Keyser tried her hand; and
when she was exhausted, she again enlisted the hired
girl, who said her prayers while she turned. But
the butter didn't come.

When Keyser came home and found the churn
still in action, he felt angry; and seizing the handle,
he said he'd make the butter come if he stirred up an
earthquake in doing it. Mr. Keyser effected about
two hundred revolutions of the crank a minute—
enough to have made any ordinary butter come from
the ends of the earth; and when the perspiration began to stream from him, and still the butter didn't
come, he uttered one wild yell of rage and disappoint-
ment and kicked the churn over the fence. When
Mrs. Keyser went to pick it up, she put her nose
down close to the buttermilk and took a sniff. Then
she understood how it was. The girl had mixed the
whitewash in the churn and left it there. A good,
honest and intelligent servant who knows how to
churn could have found a situation at Keyser's the
next day. There was a vacancy.

Mr. Keyser during the summer made a very nar-

row escape from a melancholy ending. He dreamed
one night that he would die on the 14th of September. So strongly was he assured of the fact that the
vision would prove true that he began at once to
make preparations for his departure. He got mea-
sured for a burial-suit, he drew up his will, he picked
out a nice lot in the cemetery and had it fenced in,
he joined the church and selected six of the deacons as his pall-bearers; he also requested the choir
to sing at the funeral, and he got them to run over
a favorite hymn of his to see how it would sound.
Then he got Toombs, the undertaker, to knock together a burial-casket with silver-plated handles, and
cushions inside, and he instructed the undertaker to
use his best hearse, and to buy sixty pairs of black
gloves, to be distributed among the mourners. He
had some trouble deciding upon a tombstone. The
man at the marble-yard, however, at last sold him a
beautiful one with an angel weeping over a kind
of a flower-pot, with the legend, "Not lost, but
gone before."

Then he got the village newspaper to put a good
obituary notice of him in type, and he told his wife
that he would be gratified if she would come out in
the spring and plant violets upon his grave. He
said it was hard to leave her and the children, but
she must try and bear up under it. These afflictions
are for our good, and when he was an angel he would
come and watch over her and keep his eye on her.
He said she might marry again if she wanted to; for

although the mere thought of it nearly broke his
heart, he wished her, above all, to be happy, and to
have some one to love her and protect her from the
storms of the rude world. Then he and Mrs. Keyser and the children cried, and Keyser, as a closing
word of counsel, advised her not to plough for corn
earlier than the middle of March.

On the night of the 13th of September there was
a flood in the creek, and Keyser got up at four
o'clock in the morning of the 14th and worked until night, trying to save his buildings and his wood-
pile. He was so busy that he forgot all about its
being the day of his death; and as he was very tired,
he went to bed early and slept soundly all night.

About six o'clock on the morning of the 15th
there was a ring at the door-bell. Keyser jumped
out of bed, threw up the front window and exclaimed,

" Who's there ?"

" It's me—Toombs," said the undertaker.

"What do you want at this time of the morning?"
demanded Keyser.

" Want ?" said Toombs, not recognizing Keyser.
" Why, I've brought around the ice to pack Keyser
in, so's he'll keep until the funeral. The corpse'd
spoil this kind of weather if we didn't."

Then Keyser remembered, and it made him feel
angry when he thought how the day had passed and
left him still alive, and how he had made a fool of
himself. So he said,

"Well, you can just skeet around home agin with that ice; the corpse is not yet dead. You're a little too anxious, it strikes me. You're not goin' to inter me yet, if you have got everything ready. So you can haul off and unload."

About half-past ten that morning the deacons came around, with crape on their hats and gloom in their faces, to carry the body to the grave; and while they were on the front steps the marble-yard man drove up with the flower-pot tombstone and a shovel, and stepped in to ask the widow how deep she wanted the grave dug. Just then the choir arrived with the minister, and the company was assembled in the parlor, when Keyser came in from the stable, where he had been dosing a horse with patent medicine and warm "mash" for the glanders. He was surprised, but he proceeded to explain that there had been a little mistake, somehow. He was also pained to find that everybody seemed to be a good deal disappointed, particularly the tombstone-man, who went away mad, declaring that such an old fraud ought to be buried, anyhow, dead or alive. Just as the deacons left in a huff the tailor's boy arrived with the burial-suit, and before Keyser could kick him off the steps the paper-carrier flung into the door the *Patriot*, in which that obituary notice occupied a prominent place.

Anybody who wants a good reliable tombstone that has a flower-pot and an angel on it, with an affecting inscription, can buy one of that kind, at a

sacrifice for cash, from Keyser.   He thinks the bad
dream must have been caused by eating too much at
supper.

After he felt assured that he should have to remain
a little longer in this troublous world, Mr. Keyser
determined to effect some improvements of his farm
that he had thought of.   He greatly needed a constant supply of water, and he resolved to bore an
artesian well in the barn-yard.   The boring was done
with a two-inch auger fixed in the end of an iron
rod, which was twisted around by a wheel worked
by two men.   One day, after they had gone down a
good many feet, they tried to pull the rod out, but it
would not come.   They were afraid to use much
force lest the auger should come off and stay in the
hole, and so, as the boring went along well enough,
they concluded to keep on turning, and to trust to the
force of the water, when they struck it, to drive the
loose dirt up from the hole.   When they had gone
down about three hundred and fifty feet, they began
to think it queer that there were no signs of water,
but they bored a hundred feet farther ; and one day,
just as they were beginning on another hundred,
something odd happened.

On the day in question Keyser's boy came running into the house and told him to come into the
garden quick, for there was some kind of an extraordinary animal with a sharp nose burrowing out of the
ground.   Keyser concluded that it must be either a
potato-bug or a grasshopper that had been hatched

in the spring, and he took out a bottle of poison to drop on it when it came up. When Keyser reached the spot, a couple of hundred yards from where they were boring the well, there certainly was some kind of a creature slowly pushing its way up through the sod. Its nose seemed to resemble a sharp point like steel. Keyser dropped some poison on it; but it didn't appear to mind the stuff, but kept slowly creeping up from the ground. Then Keyser felt it, and was astonished to find that it felt exactly like the end of a fork-prong. He sent the boy over to call

Perkins and the rest of the neighbors. Pretty soon a large crowd collected, and by this time the animal had emerged to the extent of a couple of inches.

Everybody was amazed to see that it looked exactly like the end of a large auger; and two or three timid men were so scared at the idea of such a thing actually growing out of the earth that they suddenly got over the fence and left. Perkins couldn't account for it; but he suggested that maybe somebody might have planted a gimlet there, and it had taken root and blossomed out into an auger; but he admitted that he had never heard of such a thing before.

The excitement increased so that the men who were boring the artesian well knocked off and came over to see the phenomenon. It was noticed that as soon as they stopped work the auger ceased to grow; and when they arrived, they looked at it for a minute, and one of them said,

"Bill, do you recognize that auger?"

"I think I do," said Bill.

"Well, Bill, you go and unhitch that wheel from the other end of the rod."

Bill did so; and then the other man asked the crowd to take hold of the auger and pull. They did; and out came four hundred and fifty feet of iron rod. The auger had slid off to the side, turned upward and come to the surface in Keyser's garden. Then the artesian well was abandoned, and Keyser bought a steam-pump and began to get water from the river.

Another remarkable boring experience that occurred in our neighborhood deserves to be related here. When Butterwick bought his present place, the former owner offered, as one of the inducements to purchase, the fact that there was a superb sugar-maple tree in the garden. It was a noble tree, and Butterwick made up his mind that he would tap it some day and manufacture some sugar. However, he never did so until last year. Then he concluded to draw the sap and to have "a sugar-boiling."

Mr. Butterwick's wife's uncle was staying with him, and after inviting some friends to come and eat the sugar they got to work. They took a huge wash-kettle down into the yard and piled some wood beneath it, and then they brought out a couple of buckets to catch the sap, and the auger with which to bore a hole in the tree.

Butterwick's wife's uncle said that the bucket ought to be set about three feet from the tree, as the sap would spurt right out with a good deal of force, and it would be a pity to waste any of it.

Then he lighted the fire, while Butterwick bored the hole about four inches deep. When he took the auger out, the sap did not follow, but Butterwick's wife's uncle said what it wanted was a little time, and so, while the folks waited, he put a fresh armful of wood on the fire. They waited half an hour; and as the sap didn't come, Butterwick concluded that the hole was not deep enough, so he began boring again, but he bored too far, for the auger went clear

through the tree and penetrated the back of his
wife's uncle, who was leaning up against the trunk
trying to light his pipe. He jumped nearly forty
feet, and they had to mend him up with court-plaster.

Then he said he thought the reason the sap didn't
come was that there ought to be a kind of spigot in
the hole, so as to let it run off easily. They got the
wooden spigot from the vinegar-barrel in the cellar
and inserted it. Then, as the sap did not come,
Butterwick's wife's uncle said he thought the spigot
must be jammed in so tight that it choked the flow;
and while Butterwick tried to push it out, his wife's
uncle fed the fire with some kindling-wood. As the
spigot could not be budged with a hammer, Butterwick concluded to bore it out with the auger; and
meanwhile his wife's uncle stirred the fire. Then
the auger broke off short in the hole, and Butterwick
had to go half a mile to the hardware-store to get
another one.

Then Butterwick bored a fresh hole; and although
the sap would not come, the company did; and they
examined with much interest the kettle, which was
now red-hot, and which Butterwick's wife's uncle was
trying to lift off the fire with the hay-fork. As the
sap still refused to come, Butterwick went over for
Keyser to ask him how to make the exasperating
tree disgorge. When he arrived, he looked at the
hole, then at the spigot, then at the kettle and then
at the tree. Then, turning to Butterwick with a
mournful face, he said,

TOO MUCH OF A BORE.

"Butterwick, you have had a good deal of trouble in your life, an' it's done you good; it's made a man of you. This world is full of sorrow, but we must bear it without grumbling. You know that, of course. Consequently, now that I've some bad news to break to you, I feel 'sif the shock won't knock you end-ways, but'll be received with patient resignation. I say I hope you won't break down an' give away to your feelin's when I tell you that there tree is no sugar-maple at all. Grashus! why, that's a black hickory. It is, indeed; and you might as well bore for maple-sugar in the side of a telegraph-pole."

Then the company went home, and Butterwick's wife's uncle said he had an engagement with a man in Hatboro' which he must keep right off. But-terwick took the kettle up to the house; but as it was burned out, he sold it next day for fifteen cents for old iron and bought a new one for twelve dollars. He thinks now maybe it's better to buy your maple sugar.

CHAPTER XXX.

MR. BANGER'S AUNT.

THERE are two families of Bangers in our neighborhood, the heads of which have the same name — Henry Banger. The Henry who married the widow, heretofore mentioned, is a lawyer in the village, while the other, having no relationship to the former, is a "professor," and he lives on the opposite side of the river, in a hamlet that has grown up there. One day Henry Banger, the lawyer, received a telegram saying that his aunt had died suddenly in Elmira, New York, and that the body would be sent on at once by express. Mr. Banger made preparations for the funeral, and upon the day that the remains were due he went down to the express office to receive them.

They did not come, however; and when the agent telegraphed to ask about them, he ascertained that Mr. Banger's aunt had been carried through to Baltimore by mistake. Orders were sent at once to reship the body with all possible speed; and accordingly, it was placed upon the cars of the Northern Central Railroad. As the train was proceeding north a collision occurred. The train was wrecked, and Mr. Banger's aunt was tossed rudely out upon the roadside.

The people who were attending to things supposed that she was one of the victims of the accident, and so the coroner held an inquest; and as nobody knew who she was, she was sent back to Baltimore and interred by the authorities. As she did not reach Mr. Banger, he induced the express company to hunt her up; and when her resting-place was discovered, they took her up, placed her in a casket and shipped her again.

During that trip some thieves got into the express car and threw out the iron money-chest and Mr. Banger's aunt, supposing that the casket contained treasure. On the following morning a farmer discovered Mr. Banger's aunt in the casket leaning up against a tree in the woods. He sent for the coroner; and when another inquest had been held, they were about to bury the remains, and would have done so had not a telegram come from the express company instructing the authorities to ship Mr. Banger's aunt back to Baltimore.

Mr. Banger, meantime, endured the most agonizing suspense, and began to talk about suing the express company for damages. At last, however, he received information that the departed one had been sent on upon the Philadelphia, Wilmington and Baltimore Railroad. So she had. But as the train was crossing Gunpowder River the express car gave a lurch, and the next moment Mr. Banger's aunt shot through the door into the water. She sailed around in the bay for several days, apparently uncertain whether to seek the ocean and move straight across for Europe, or to go up into the interior. She chose the latter course, and a week afterward she drifted ashore in the Lower Susquehanna.

As soon as she was discovered the coroner held an inquest, and then put her on the cars again. This time she came directly to Millburg, and Mr. Banger was at the dépôt waiting for her with the funeral. By some mistake, however, she was carried past and put out at the next town above, and the agent said that the best thing he could do would be to have her brought down in the morning. In the morning she came, and Mr. Banger was there with the friends of the family to receive her.

When they reached the cemetery, Rev. Dr. Dox delivered a most affecting discourse; and when all was over, and Mr. and Mrs. Banger had wiped away their tears, they went slowly home, sorrowful, of course, but somewhat glad that the long suspense was ended.

As Mr. Banger entered his sitting-room he saw a lady reposing in front of the fire, with her back toward him, toasting her toes. Before he had time to speak she looked around, and he was amazed to perceive that it was his dead-and-buried aunt. He was a little frightened at first, but in a moment he summoned up courage enough to ask,

"Why, how did you get here?"

"I came on the train, of course."

"Yes, I know; but how did you get out of the cemetery?"

"Cemetery? What cemetery? I haven't been in any cemetery!"

"Not been in the cemetery! Why, either I buried you an hour ago, or I am the worst mistaken man on earth."

"Mr. Banger, what do you mean? This is a curious sort of a jest."

Then Banger explained the situation to her; and as she solemnly protested that she had not been in Elmira, Banger was about to conclude that he had been the victim of a joke, when it suddenly occurred to him that maybe it was the aunt of Professor Banger. He sent out to investigate the matter, and found that the conjecture was correct. And when Professor Banger heard about it, he became very angry, and he entered suit against the lawyer Banger for embezzling his aunt. Then Lawyer Banger sued the professor for the express charges and the funeral expenses, and for a time it looked as if that eccentric and roving old lady would be the cause of infinite trouble; but the difficulty was finally compromised by the lawyer Banger accepting half the amount of his expenses.

Professor Banger was originally a telegraph-operator, but some years ago he saved up a small sum of money, with which he constructed a balloon.

Then he tacked "professor" to his name, and began to devote himself to science and the show business. His account of one of his recent excursions is not only entertaining, but it proves that he is an ardent student of natural phenomena. He said to me,

"We went up at Easton, Pennsylvania; Conly, Jones and myself, and it was the finest trip I ever took. Perfectly splendid! We got the balloon full about twelve o'clock, and the crowd held her down until we were ready. Then I gave the word and they let go, and we went a-humming into the air. One man got caught in a twist of the rope as she gave her first spurt upward, and it slammed him up against a fence as if he'd been shot out of a gun. Smashed in three or four of his ribs, I believe, and cracked his leg.

"But we went up beautifully about fifteen hundred feet, and while we were looking at the charming scenery we ran into a cloud, and I told Conly to throw out some ballast. He heaved over a couple of sand-bags, and one of them accidentally fell on Major Wiggins' hired girl, who was hanging clothes in the garden, and the other went into his chimney and choked it up. He was mad as fury about it when we came down. No enthusiasm for science. Some men don't care a cent whether the world progresses or not.

"Well, sir, we shot up about a thousand feet more, and then Jones dropped the lunch-basket overboard by accident, and we went up nearly four miles.

Conly got blue in the face, Jones fainted, and I came near going under myself. A minute more we'd all've been dead men; but I gave the valve a jerk, and we came down like a rocket-stick. When the boys came to, Jones said he wanted to get out; and as we were only a little distance from the ground, I threw out the grapnel.

"That minute a breeze struck her, and she went along at about ninety miles an hour over some man's

24

garden, and the grapnel caught his grape-arbor, snatched it up, and pretty soon got it tangled with the weathercock on the Presbyterian church-steeple. I cut the rope and left it there, and I understand that the deacons sued the owner because he wouldn't take it down. Raised an awful fuss and sent the sheriff after me. Trying to make scientific investigation seem like a crime, and I working all the time like a horse to unfold the phenomena of nature! If they had loved knowledge, they wouldn't 've cared if I'd 've ripped off their old steeple and dropped it down like an extinguisher on top of some factory chimney.

"So, when we left the grape-arbor, we went up again, and Jones got sicker and said he must get out. So I rigged up another grapnel and threw it over. We were just passing a farm near the river; and as the wind was high, the grapnel tore through two fences and pulled the roof off of a smoke-house, and then, as nothing would hold her, we swooped into the woods, when we ran against a tree. The branches skinned Conly's face and nearly put out my right eye, and knocked four teeth out of Jones' mouth. It was the most exciting and interesting voyage I ever made in my life; and I was just beginning to get some satisfaction from it—just getting warmed up and preparing to take some meteorological observations—when Jones became so very anxious to quit that I didn't like to refuse, although it went fearfully against the grain for the reason that

I hated to give up and abandon my scientific in-
vestigations.

"So I threw out my coat and boots, and made the
other fellows do the same, and we rose above the
trees and sailed along splendidly until we struck the
river. Then she suddenly dodged down, and the
edge of the car caught in the water; so the wind
took her, and we went scudding along like lightning,
nearly drowned. Conly was washed overboard, and
that lightened her, so she went up again. I was for
staying up, but Jones said he'd die if he didn't get
out soon; and besides, he thought we ought to look
after Conly. But I said Conly was probably drowned,
anyhow, so it was hardly worth while to sacrifice
our experiments on that account; and I told Jones
that a man of his intelligence ought to be willing to
endure something for the sake of scientific truth.
And Jones said, 'Hang scientific truth!'—actually
made that remark; and he said that if I didn't let
him out he'd jump out. He was sick, you know.
The man was not himself, or he would never have
talked in that way about a voyage that was so full
of interest and so likely to reveal important secrets
of nature.

"But to oblige him I at last got her down on the
other side of the river, and a farmer ran out and
seized the rope. While we were talking to him I
was just telling him that, as the gas was running out
of the neck of the balloon, maybe he'd better put
out his cigar, when all of a sudden there was a ter-

rific bang. The gas exploded and wrapped us in a
sheet of flame, and the next minute some of the
neighbors picked up me and Jones. Jones was
roasted nearly to a crisp. Exciting, wasn't it?

"And they took him over to the farmhouse,
where we found that they had fished out Conly and
were bringing him to. When he revived, they sent
the invalid corps back to town in a wagon, Jones
groaning all the way and I arguing with him to show
that science requires her votaries to give up a little
of their personal comfort for the benefit it does the
human race, and Conly saying he wished he was
well enough to go out and bang the inventor of balloons with a gun.

"As soon as we got back to Easton a constable
arrested me for chucking that ignorant opponent of
scientific inquiry up against the fence and wrecking
him. When I was let off on bail, I began to build a
new balloon. She's nearly done now, and I'm going
to make an ascension early next month in search of
the ozone belt. Won't you go up with me? The
day is going to come when everybody will travel
that way. It's the most exhilarating motion in the
world. Come on up and help me make scientific
observations on the ozone belt."

But the invitation was declined. The *Patriot*, however, will have a good obituary notice of the professor
all ready, in type.

CHAPTER XXXI.

VARIOUS THINGS.

T is a notorious fact that itinerant circus companies pay very poorly, and that the man who does not get his money from them in advance is not very likely to get it at all. Major Slott of *The Patriot* has suffered a good deal from these concerns; and when "The Great European Circus and Metropolitan Caravan" tried to slip off the other day without settling its advertising bill, he called upon the sheriff and got him to attach the Bengal tiger for the debt. The tiger was brought in its cage and placed in the composing-room, where it consumed fifteen dollars' worth of meat in two days—the major's bill was only twelve dollars—and scratched one trouser leg off of the reporter, who was standing in front of the cage stirring up the animal with a broom. On the third day the bottom fell out of the cage; and as the tiger seemed to want to roam around and inquire into things, the whole force of compositors all at once felt as if they ought to go suddenly down stairs and give the animal a chance. With that mysterious instinct which distinguishes dumb animals, and which goes far to prove that they have

souls, the tiger went at once for the door of the
major's sanctum, and it broke in just as Slott was
in the middle of a tearing editorial upon " Our Tend-
encies toward Cæsarism."   The major, however, did
not hesitate to knock off.   He stopped at once, and
emerged with a fine, airy grace through the window,
bringing the sash with him; and then he climbed up
the water-spout to the roof, where he sat until a hook-
and-ladder company came and took him off.   *The
Patriot* did not issue for a week; for although the
major bombarded the tiger with shot-guns pointed
through the windows, and although the fire-engine

squirted hot water at him, the brute got along very comfortably until Saturday night, when he tried to swallow a composing-stick and choked to death. When they entered the room, they found that the animal had upset all the type and had soaked himself in ink and then rolled over nearly every square inch of the floor, while the major's leader on "Cæsarism" was saturated with water and perforated with shot-holes. After this circus advertisements in *The Patriot* will be paid for in advance.

In one of the issues of his paper, just after the trouble with the tiger, the major offered some reflections upon the general subject of "Tigers," in which he gave evidence that he had recovered his good-humor to some extent. He said,

"We have read with very deep interest a description of how Van Amburgh used to obtain control over tigers and other wild beasts. All he did was to mesmerize them two or three times, and they soon recognized his power and obeyed him. The thing seems simple and easy enough, now that we understand it, and we have a mysterious impression that we could walk out into a jungle and subdue the first tiger we met by making a few passes at him with our hands. But we are not anxious to do this—for one reason, because the Indian jungles are so far away, and for

another, because we do not want to hurt an innocent
tiger.　If we have to meddle with such animals, we
always prefer to operate with those that are stuffed.
Show us a tiger with sawdust bowels, and we will
stand in front of him and make mesmeric motions
for a week without the quiver of a nerve.　Not that
we are timid when the tiger is alive, but simply because a fur-store is more convenient than a jungle,
and there is less danger of wetting our feet.　If we
happened to be in India and we wanted a tiger, we
should unhesitatingly go out and stand boldly in
front of the very first one we saw—tied to a tree—
and we should bring him home instantly if we could
find a man willing to lead him with a string.　But
this kind of courage is born in some men.　It cannot be acquired; and timid persons who intend to
practice Van Amburgh's method will find it more
judicious to begin the mesmerizing operation by
soothing the animal with a howitzer."

The lightning-rod man haunts our county as he
does the rest of the civilized portion of the country;
and although occasionally he secures a victim, sometimes it happens that he gets worsted in his attempts
to beguile his fellow-men.　Such was his fate upon a
recent occasion in our village.

The other day a lightning-rod man drove up in
front of a handsome edifice standing in the midst of
trees and shrubs in Millburg, and spoke to Mr.
Potts, who was sitting on the steps in front.　He

accosted Potts as the owner of the residence, and said,

"I see you have no lightning-rods on this house."

"No," said Potts.

"Are you going to put any on?"

"Well, I hadn't thought of it," replied Potts.

"You ought to. A tall building like this is very much exposed. I'd like to run you up one of my rods; twisted steel, glass fenders, nickel-plated tips— everything complete. May I put one up to show you? I'll do the job cheap."

"Certainly you may, if you want to. I haven't the slightest objection," said Potts.

During the next half hour the man had his ladders up and his assistants at work, and at the end of that time the job was done. He called Potts out into the yard to admire it. He said to Potts,

"Now, that is all well enough; but if it was *my* house, I'd have another rod put on the other side. There's nothing like being protected thoroughly."

"That's true," said Potts; "it would be better."

"I'll put up another, shall I?" asked the man.

"Why, of course, if you think it's best," said Potts.

Accordingly, the man went to work again, and soon had the rod in its place.

"That's a first-rate job," he said to Potts as they both stood eyeing it. "I like such a man as you are. Big-hearted, liberal, not afraid to put a dollar down for a good thing. There's some pleasure in dealin' with you. I like you so much that I'd put a couple more rods on that house, one on the north end and one on the south, for almost nothin'."

"It would make things safer, I suppose," said Potts.

"Certainly it would. I'd better do it, hadn't I, hey?"

"Just as you think proper," said Potts.

So the man ran up two more rods, and then he came down and said to Potts, "There! that's done. Now let's settle up."

"Do what?"

"Why, the job's finished, and now I'll take my money."

"You don't expect me to pay you, I hope?"

"Of course I do. Didn't you tell me to put those rods on your house?"

"My house!" shouted Potts. "Thunder and lightning! I never ordered you to put those rods up. It would have been ridiculous. Why, man, this is the court-house, and I'm here waiting for the court to assemble. I'm on the jury. You seemed to be anxious to rush out your rods; and as it was none of my business, I let you go on. Pay for it! Come, now, that's pretty good."

The people who were present say that the manner in which that lightning-rod man tore around and swore was fearful. But when he got his rods off of the court-house, he left permanently. He don't fancy the place.

Keyser had lightning-rods placed upon his barn three or four years ago; but during last summer the building was struck by lightning and burned. When he got the new barn done, a man came around with a red wagon and wanted to sell him a set of Bolt & Burnam's patent lightning-rods.

" I believe not," said Keyser; " I had rods on the barn at the time of the—"

" I know," exclaimed the agent—" I know you had; and very likely that's the reason you were struck. Nothin's more likely to attract lightnin' than worthless rods."

" How do you know they were worthless ?"

" Why, I was drivin' by yer in the spring, and I seen them rods, and I says to myself, ' That barn'll be struck some time, but there's no use in tryin' to convince Mr. Keyser;' so I didn't call. I knowed it, because they had iron tips. A rod with iron tips is no better'n a clothes-prop to ward off lightnin'."

" The man who sold them to me said they had platinum tips," remarked Keyser.

" Ah! this is a wicked world, Mr. Keyser. You can't be too cautious. Some of these yer agents lie like a gas-meter. It's awful, sir. They are wholly untrustworthy. Them rods was the most ridicklus sham I ever see—a regular gouge. They wa'n't worth the labor it took to put 'em up. They wa'n't, now. That's the honest truth."

" What kind do you offer ?"

" Well, sir, I've got the only genuine lightnin'-rod

that's made. It's constructed on scientific principles. Professor Henry says it's sure to run off the electric fluid every time—twisted charcoal iron, glass insulators, eight points on each rod, warranted solid platinum. We give a written guarantee with each rod. Never had a house struck since we began to offer this rod to the public. Positive fact. The lightnin'll play all around a house with one of 'em and never touch it. A thunder-storm that'd tear the bowels out of the American continent would leave your house as safe as a polar bear in the middle of an iceberg. Shall I run you one up?"

" I don't know," said Keyser, musingly.

" I'll put you up one cheap, and then you'll have somethin' reliable—somethin' there's no discount on."

" You say the old rod was a fraud?"

" The deadliest fraud you ever heard of. It hadn't an ounce of platinum within a mile of it. The man that sold it ought to be prosecuted, and the fellow that put it up without insulators should be shot. It's too bad the farmers should be gouged in this sort of way."

" And Bolt & Burnam's rod is not a fraud?"

" A fraud? Why, really, my dear sir, just cast your eye over Professor Henry's letter and these certificates, and remember that we give a *written guarantee*—a positive protection, of course."

" Just cast *your* eye over that," said Keyser, handing him a piece of paper.

"Well, upon my word! This is indeed some-what—that is to say it is, as it were—it looks—it looks a little like one of our own certificates."

"Just so," said Keyser. "That old rod was one of Bolt & Burnam's. You sold it to my son-in-law; you gave this certificate; you swore the points were platinum, and your man put it up."

"Then I suppose we can't trade?"

"Well, I should think not," said Keyser. Where-upon the man mounted the red wagon and moved on.

When Benjamin P. Gunn, the life insurance agent, called upon Mr. Butterwick, the following conversa-tion ensued:

Gunn. "Mr. Butterwick, you have no insurance on your life, I believe? I dropped in to see if I can't get you to go into our company. We offer unparalleled inducements, and—"

Butterwick. "I don't want to insure."

Gunn. "The cost is just nothing worth speaking of; a mere trifle. And then we pay enormous divi-dends, so that you have so much security at such a little outlay that you can be perfectly comfortable and happy."

Butterwick. "But I don't want to be comfortable and happy. I'm trying to be miserable."

Gunn. "Now, look at this thing in a practical light. You've got to die some time or other. That is a dreadful certainty to which we must all look for-ward. It is fearful enough in any event, but how

much more so when a man knows that he leaves
nothing behind him! We all shrink from death, we
all hate to think of it; the contemplation of it fills
us with awful dread; but reflect, what must be the
feelings of the man who enters the dark valley with
the assurance that in a pecuniary sense his life has
been an utter failure? Think how—"

Butterwick. "Don't scare me a bit. I want to die;
been wanting to die for years. Rather die than live
any time."

Gunn. "I say, think how wretched will be the
condition of those dear ones whom you leave behind
you! Will not the tears of your heartbroken widow
be made more bitter by the poverty in which she is
suddenly plunged, and by the reflection that she is
left to the charity of a cold and heartless world.
Will not—"

Butterwick. "I wouldn't leave her a cent if I had
millions. It'll do the old woman good to skirmish
around for her living. Then she'll appreciate me."

Gunn. "Your poor little children, too. Father-
less, orphaned, they will have no one to fill their
famished mouths with bread, no one to protect them
from harm. You die uninsured, and they enter a life of
suffering from the keen pangs of poverty. You insure in our company, and they begin life with enough
to feed and clothe them, and to raise them above the
reach of want."

Butterwick. "I don't want to raise them above
the reach of want. I want them to want. Best

thing they can do is to tucker down to work as I did."

Gunn. "Oh, Mr. Butterwick, try to take a higher view of the matter. When you are an angel and you come back to revisit the scenes of earth, will it not fill you with sadness to see your dear ones exposed to the storm and the blast, to hunger and cold?"

Butterwick. "I'm not going to be an angel; and if I was, I wouldn't come back."

Gunn. "You are a poor man now. How do you know that your family will have enough when you are gone to pay your funeral expenses, to bury you decently?"

Butterwick. "I don't want to be buried."

Gunn. "Perhaps Mrs. Butterwick will be so indignant at your neglect that she will not mourn for you, that she will not shed a tear over your bier."

Butterwick. "I don't want a bier, and I'd rather she wouldn't cry any."

Gunn. "Well, then, s'posin' you go in on the endowment plan and take a policy for five thousand dollars, to be paid you when you reach the age of fifty?"

Butterwick. "I don't want five thousand dollars when I'm fifty. I wouldn't take it if you were to fling it at me and pay me to take it."

Gunn. "I'm afraid, then, I'll have to say good-morning."

Butterwick. "I don't want you to say good-morning; you can go without saying it."

Gunn. "I'll quit."

Butterwick. "Aha! now you've hit it! I *do* want you to quit, and as suddenly as you can."

Then Mr. Gunn left. He thinks he will hardly insure Butterwick.

FINIS

www.ingramcontent.com/pod-product-compliance
Lightning Source LLC
Chambersburg PA
CBHW030903270326
41929CB00008B/552